Exploring Professional Communication

Routledge Introductions to Applied Linguistics is a series of introductory level textbooks covering the core topics in Applied Linguistics, primarily designed for those entering postgraduate studies, or taking an introductory MA course as well as advanced undergraduates. Titles in the series are also ideal for language professionals returning to academic study.

The books take an innovative 'practice to theory' approach, with a 'back-to-front' structure. This leads the reader from real-world problems and issues, through a discussion of intervention and how to engage with these concerns, before finally relating these practical issues to theoretical foundations. Additional features include tasks with commentaries, a glossary of key terms, and an annotated further reading section.

Exploring Professional Communication addresses the nature of professional communication and why it should be studied, as well as outlining the fundamental topics relevant for an understanding of the area, from an applied linguistics approach.

The book is divided into eight chapters, each dealing with a specific area of professional communication, such as identity in the workplace, and the issues of gender, leadership and workplace culture. Throughout, Stephanie Schnurr takes an interactive approach that is reflected in the numerous examples of authentic discourse data, from a variety of written and spoken contexts.

Exploring Professional Communication is critical reading for postgraduate and upper undergraduate students of applied linguistics and communication studies.

Stephanie Schnurr is Associate Professor at the University of Warwick. She is the author of *Leadership Discourse at Work* (2008).

Routledge Introductions to Applied Linguistics

Series editors:

Ronald Carter, *Professor of Modern English Language,*
University of Nottingham, UK

Guy Cook, *Chair of Language in Education*
King's College London, UK

Routledge Introductions to Applied Linguistics is a series of introductory level textbooks covering the core topics in Applied Linguistics, primarily designed for those beginning postgraduate studies, or taking an introductory MA course as well as advanced undergraduates. Titles in the series are also ideal for language professionals returning to academic study.

The books take an innovative 'practice to theory' approach, with a 'back-to-front' structure. This leads the reader from real-world problems and issues, through a discussion of intervention and how to engage with these concerns, before finally relating these practical issues to theoretical foundations. Additional features include tasks with commentaries, a glossary of key terms, and an annotated further reading section.

Exploring English Language Teaching
Language in Action
Graham Hall

Exploring Classroom Discourse
Language in Action
Steve Walsh

Exploring Corpus Linguistics
Language in Action
Winnie Cheng

Exploring World Englishes
Language in a Global Context
Philip Seargeant

Exploring Health Communication
Language in Action
Kevin Harvey and Nelya Koteyko

Exploring Professional Communication
Language in Action
Stephanie Schnurr

'The innovative approach devised by the series editors will make this series very attractive to students, teacher educators, and even to a general readership, wanting to explore and understand the field of applied linguistics. The volumes in this series take as their starting point the everyday professional problems and issues that applied linguists seek to illuminate. The volumes are authoritatively written, using an engaging 'back-to-front' structure that moves from practical interests to the conceptual bases and theories that underpin applications of practice.'
Anne Burns, *Aston University, UK,*
University of New South Wales, Australia

Exploring Professional Communication

Language in Action

Stephanie Schnurr

Routledge
Taylor & Francis Group

LONDON AND NEW YORK

First published 2013
by Routledge
2 Park Square, Milton Park, Abingdon, Oxon OX14 4RN

Simultaneously published in the USA and Canada
by Routledge
711 Third Avenue, New York, NY 10017

Routledge is an imprint of the Taylor & Francis Group, an informa business

British Library Cataloguing in Publication Data
A catalogue record for this book is available from the British Library

Library of Congress Cataloging in Publication Data
Schnurr, Stephanie, 1975–
Exploring professional communication : language in action / Stephanie Schnurr.
p. cm.
Includes bibliographical references and index.
1. Interpersonal communication. 2. Oral communication. 3. Business communication.
4. Communication in organizations. I. Title.
P94.7.S36 2012
302.2--dc23
2012011359

ISBN: 978-0-415-58481-4 (hbk)
ISBN: 978-0-415-58483-8 (pbk)
ISBN: 978-0-203-09532-4 (ebk)

Typeset in Sabon
by Saxon Graphics Ltd, Derby

MIX
Paper from
responsible sources
FSC
www.fsc.org   FSC® C004839

Printed and bound in Great Britain by the MPG Books Group

To Jonah, Sophie and Nico

Contents

Figures and tables

Figures

Tables

Series editors' introduction

The *Introductions to Applied Linguistics* series

This series provides clear, authoritative, up-to-date overviews of the major areas of applied linguistics. The books are designed particularly for students embarking on master's-level or teacher education courses, as well as students in the closing stages of undergraduate study. The practical focus will make the books particularly useful and relevant to those returning to academic study after a period of professional practice, and also to those about to leave the academic world for the challenges of language-related work. For students who have not previously studied applied linguistics, including those who are unfamiliar with current academic study in English speaking universities, the books can act as one-step introductions. For those with more academic experience, they can also provide a way of surveying, updating and organising existing knowledge.

The view of applied linguistics in this series follows a famous definition of the field by Christopher Brumfit as

> The theoretical and empirical investigation of real-world problems in which language is a central issue.
>
> (Brumfit 1995: 27)

In keeping with this broad problem-oriented view, the series will cover a range of topics of relevance to a variety of language-related professions. While language teaching and learning rightly remain prominent and will be the central preoccupation of many readers, our conception of the discipline is by no means limited to these areas. Our view is that while each reader of the series will have their own needs, specialities and interests, there is also much to be gained from a broader view of the discipline as a whole. We believe there is much in common between all enquiries into language related problems in the real world, and much to be gained from a comparison of the insights from one area of applied linguistics with another. Our hope therefore is that readers and course designers will not choose only those volumes relating to their own particular interests, but use this series to construct a wider knowledge and understanding of the field, and the many cross-overs and resonances between its various areas. Thus the topics to be covered are wide in range, embracing an exciting mixture of established and new areas of applied linguistic enquiry.

The perspective on applied linguistics in this series

In line with this problem-oriented definition of the field, and to address the concerns of readers who are interested in how academic study can inform their own professional practice, each book follows a structure in marked contrast to the usual movement *from* theory *to* practice. In this series, this usual progression is presented back to front. The argument moves *from* Problems, *through* Intervention, and *only* finally to Theory. Thus each topic begins with a survey of everyday professional problems in the area under consideration, ones which the reader is likely to have encountered. From there it proceeds to a discussion of intervention and engagement with these problems. Only in a final section (either of the chapter or the book as a whole) does the author reflect upon the implications of this engagement for a general understanding of language, drawing out the theoretical implications. We believe this to be a truly *applied* linguistics perspective, in line with definition given above, and one in which engagement with real-world problems is the distinctive feature, and in which professional practice can both inform and draw upon academic understanding.

Support to the reader

Although it is not the intention that the text should be in any way activity-driven, the pedagogic process is supported by measured guidance to the reader in the form of suggested activities and tasks that raise questions, prompt reflection and seek to integrate theory and practice. Each book also contains a helpful glossary of key terms.

The series complements and reflects the *Routledge Handbook of Applied Linguistics* edited by James Simpson, which conceives and categorises the scope of applied linguistics in a broadly similar way.

Ronald Carter
Guy Cook

Acknowledgements

I don't think I would have embarked on this project (let alone been able to ever complete it!) if it hadn't been for the encouragement and support of a number of people. Above all, I would like to thank Ronald Carter for asking me to write this book and for providing endless support and enthusiasm throughout the various stages of this project, and Meredith Marra and Francesca Bargiela-Chiappini who have provided very useful comments on the whole manuscript. Another big thank you goes to Janet Holmes, Helen Spencer-Oatey and Keith Richards who all encouraged me to take on this project and who provided very useful feedback at the various stages. And to Andi, of course, for always being there and cheering me up when I needed it.

In writing this book I have learned a lot, not only by reading and engaging with the various topics of professional communication but also through discussions with colleagues, friends and students. I am particularly grateful to the following people for generously sharing their time with me and for providing detailed feedback on the various chapters: Olga Zayts, Sue Wharton, Angela Chan, Keith Richards, Dorien van de Mieroop, Louise Mullany, Janet Holmes, Helen-Spencer-Oatey and Malcolm MacDonald. Their comments have helped improve the chapters tremendously. I have also benefited immensely from discussions with other colleagues and friends who are not mentioned here but who have also contributed to shaping the contents and discussions of the various chapters. I would also like to thank Julia deBres, Gudrun Ziegler, Bernie Mak and Hans-Georg Wolf for generously sharing some of their examples with me, and to several of my colleagues and friends who will remain anonymous but who have agreed to let me include examples of their own professional communication.

A very big thank you also to Sophie Reissner-Roubicek for proofreading the manuscript in a rather short time, and for designing the cover image; and to my students in ET917 and other classes who have acted as guinea pigs for the various exercises and who have provided valuable suggestions for improvements. All remaining infelicities are, of course, entirely my own.

The publishers would like to thank the following for permission to reprint their material:

KPMG, for the extract from the KPMG 'Code of Conduct' document. DILBERT © 2001 Scott Adams. Used By permission of UNIVERSAL UCLICK. All rights reserved.
www.cartoonstock.com for the images in Chapter 3 (© Harley Schwadron) and Chapter 6 (© Fran), reproduced with permission.

Every effort has been made to seek permission to reproduce copyright material before the book went to press. If any proper acknowledgement has not been made, we would invite the copyright holders to inform us of the oversight.

Stephanie Schnurr

1 What is professional communication?

This book aims to provide a comprehensive approach to some of the topics that are captured under the broad umbrella of professional communication, and to discuss some of the current trends in this important field of academic enquiry.

Communication plays a central role in most (if not all) workplaces, and many of the tasks people typically perform in their everyday workplace lives are in one way or another related to communication. This crucial role of communication is particularly obvious in those professional contexts where doing work means doing communication and where tasks are accomplished in and through communicating with clients, colleagues and other professionals. In these professions, which include for example, healthcare, service professions, social work, and many white collar professions, communication is the main tool for getting work done; and telephone calls, faxes, meetings, emails, conference calls, PowerPoint presentations, memos, and the like constitute essential means through which goals are met and work is accomplished. However, even in work settings that are characterised by manual labour, such as the factory floor and many pink-collar professions, communication plays an important role – perhaps less in terms of getting things done but, possibly equally important, in terms of maintaining good relationships with colleagues and clients.

The chapters in this book draw on various authentic examples of communication that occurred in a wide range of workplace contexts, and employ numerous conceptual models developed in different disciplines to illustrate and discuss how some of the complexities of professional communication may be captured and explored in meaningful ways. In approaching the various topics of professional communication, the book mainly takes the perspective of applied linguistics, which is supplemented with theoretical and empirical insights gained in several other disciplines, including communication studies, sociology, anthropology, business and management, organisational sciences and leadership studies.

This first introductory chapter approaches the crucial question of what professional communication is. In line with the three-part structure that characterises this series – starting with problems and practices, then moving towards interventions and engagements with the problems, to a final theory section – this chapter and all those following are divided into three parts. Section A looks at some examples of communication that occurred in various workplace contexts, and asks whether all these different kinds of communicative exchanges that take place in such a context should be described as professional communication. Section B takes this discussion to the next level by comparing and critically assessing some conceptualisations of professional communication (and related terms). The last section outlines some of the advantages of approaching professional communication from the perspective of applied linguistics, and provides a brief outline of the remaining chapters in the book.

Section A: Examples of professional communication

Example 1.1[1]

1.	Clara:	okay well we might just start without Seth
2.		he can come in and can review the minutes from last
3.		week
4.	Renee:	are you taking the minutes this week
5.	Clara:	no I'm just trying to chair the meeting
6.		who would like to take the minutes this week
7.	Renee:	who hasn't taken the minutes yet
8.	Benny:	I haven't yet I will
9.	Clara:	thank you //Benny\
10.	Renee:	/oh Benny\\ takes beautiful minutes too
11.	Benny:	don't tell them they'll want me doing it every week

[general laughter]

12.	Clara:	it's a bit of a secret
13.		okay shall we kick off and just go round the room
14.		um doing an
15.		update and then when Seth comes in with the minutes
16.		we need to check on any action items from our
17.		planning
18.		over to you Marlene

Source: Holmes and Stubbe (2003b: 57).

Most people would probably agree that this extract is an example of professional communication: it occurred during the early stages of a meeting in a large commercial organisation. All interlocutors are professionals (that is, they work for this organisation and they get paid for their work), and the topic of their interaction is mostly transactional (work-related) and focuses on establishing who will chair the meeting and take the minutes (since the usual chair is absent). However, participants also engage in relational talk (that is, in talk that aims at enhancing interpersonal relationships): for example the humour around Benny's minute-taking skills (lines 10–11). The concepts of transactional and relational talk are explained in more detail in Section B. Moreover, there seems to be a power imbalance, with Clara being in a more powerful position (which is, for example, reflected in the observation that she does most of the talking and she is the one to open the meeting (line 13)).

Another relatively typical instance of professional communication is shown in Example 1.2, which is taken from a service encounter at a self-service petrol station. It is a brief interaction between a customer (C) and a shopkeeper (SK). Just before this exchange takes place the customer has served herself some petrol and is now paying at the till.

Example 1.2

1. SK: morning
[the price comes up on the till]
2. SK: that's twenty-two
[C hands over the money]
3. SK: thanks good bye
4. C: Goodbye

Source: Kerbrat-Orecchioni (2006: 81).[2]

This brief exchange is another good example of professional communication: like in Example 1.1, the interaction takes place at a workplace (a petrol station), and involves not only a professional (the shopkeeper) but also a non-professional (the customer). As Kerbrat-Orecchioni (2006: 81) notes, exchanges like this can be characterised as 'specific work interactions' because only one of the interlocutors (the shopkeeper) is 'at work' while the other is not. There are thus apparently different types of professional communication, including inter-professional interactions, such as those between two professionals as displayed in Example 1.1 and professional–lay interactions, such as the one shown in Example 1.2. These differences are further explored in Section B and in the subsequent chapters.

The overall encounter between the professional and the non-professional in Example 1.2 is rather short, and the topic of the interaction is clearly transactional and includes both verbal and non-verbal elements: it focuses almost exclusively on the exchange of money for the petrol the customer has purchased. The shopkeeper does most of the talking and the customer's only verbal contribution is 'goodbye' in line 4. In this sense, the shopkeeper controls the 'script' or the development of the interaction (see also Kerbrat-Orecchioni 2006). Moreover, both interlocutors seem to have specific roles: the shopkeeper sells a product while the customer pays for it. Because of these characteristics, it would have probably been possible to guess that this interaction is part of a sales encounter even if no contextual information had been provided (although without any contextual clues it might have been hard to guess that it took place at a petrol station).

> ### Exercise 1.1
>
> Read Example 1.3a and discuss whether you would classify it as professional communication, and why.

Example 1.3

Subject: Coffee?

I am for coffee (and sandwiches!) outside in the sun in about 30 minutes or so – anybody want to join?
Anna

This email has been included here to illustrate that not all workplace interaction is necessarily transactionally focused and strictly outcome-oriented. Rather, more relational aspects may be equally important in some interactions that take place in professional contexts. Thus, unlike in Examples 1.1 and 1.2, in this email exchange transactional objectives do not take centre stage but rather the main aim of the exchange is relationally oriented: that is, to do collegiality and to maintain good relationships among colleagues.

The examples of professional communication discussed so far have come from a range of different workplaces, including a commercial organisation, a petrol station, and an educational institution. Yet, in spite of this diversity of context, there are some good reasons for describing all of these instances as professional communication, as we have seen. The next example is taken from yet another type of workplace: a hospital. The exchange occurred during a prenatal genetic counselling session between a pregnant woman (P) and a medical provider (MP) at a public hospital in Hong Kong. Both, the patient[3] and the medical provider are non-native speakers of English.

Example 1.4

1.	MP:	Now, so today we invite you to come to see if you
2.		want to have a test for Down Syndrome
3.		and after you've watched the video erm do you have

4.		any idea of Down Syndrome
5.	P:	what– what's the– Down Syndrome?
6.	MP:	you don't know what it is
7.	P:	mm hm it I – do you think I need to (do it)?
8.	MP:	OK now it's up to you //some people doesn't\
9.	P:	/I want to know\\ huh
10.	MP:	some people prefer to know whether the baby's
11.		Down Syndrome beforehand
12.		so they go for tests
13.		but some people doesn't want to know

Source: Zayts and Schnurr (2011: 14).

This is another relatively obvious example of professional communication: the exchange takes place in a workplace context (a public hospital) and involves a professional (the medical provider) and a client (the pregnant woman). The main purpose of the talk is to ensure the patient has enough information about Down Syndrome in order to make an informed decision about which (if any) tests the client wants to undergo. Communication thus plays a crucial role in the professional activities which the medical provider is engaged in. In this way, communication is central to what the medical provider actually does, and it crucially contributes to creating and shaping a certain image of the profession of medical providers. This aspect is discussed in more detail in Chapter 5.

Examples 1.1 to 1.4 have illustrated that professional communication may take different forms and may perform a wide range of different (more or less transactionally and relationally oriented) functions. However, all these examples are taken from interactions (both spoken and written) between two or more participants. So what about instances of one-way communication? What about those communicative events that do not require a response (verbally or in written form) but that primarily aim at providing information? Examples 1.5 and 1.6 are examples of such one-way communication in professional contexts.

Example 1.5 displays some of the values of an IT company. These values, which were displayed in a framed document in the entrance hall to the company's office and on their internet site, are mainly targeted at staff (to remind them of the values of the company, which is an important aspect of its culture, as will be elaborated in more detail in Chapter 3), but also at clients (who may read them, for example, while they are waiting in the entrance hall) and at potential new employees (who may encounter them while searching the company's online profile).

Example 1.5

> *Commitment*: Solving problems, overcoming obstacles and
> delivering on our promises and obligations to our customers and
> to each other.
> *Teamwork*: A willingness to share information, accepting and
> soliciting input from others and promoting win/win situations.
> *Quality of Life*: Making sure it is all worthwhile. Fostering good
> relationships internally and externally, celebrating success and
> giving back whenever we can.

An organisation's values, like the ones described above, are said to be
at the heart of what makes an organisation what it is (Hatch 1997).
However, in reality, the values of different companies working in the
same domain often resemble each other to some extent. Hence, values
like 'commitment' and 'teamwork' are almost generic and are typically
included, in one form or another, in a company's list of values (see also
Example 1.6). Nevertheless, an organisation's values constitute
important aspects of professional communication as they construct a
certain image of a workplace both internally (among employees) and
externally (for the wider public). These aspects are discussed in more
detail in Chapters 3 and 5.

A relatively similar type of professional communication is shown in
the next example, which is taken from a company's internal document:
it is a paragraph from the code of conduct (here, a glossy brochure
targeted at partners and employees) in the China branch of a large
international consulting company.

Example 1.6

> The fundamental importance of ethics and integrity is reflected in
> KPMG's vision of being a great place for advancing the careers of
> all our people in a rewarding and fulfilling environment. For our
> partners and all our employees, that means a strong sense of
> inclusion, mutual respect, open and honest communication,
> fairness, teamwork, and pride in being associated with each other
> and being part of KPMG. Our unshakeable commitment to
> integrity and to our vision of being an Employer of Choice is
> closely interconnected with the values that guide our actions.

According to the company's own definition the code of conduct is
designed to outline ethical standards at the company. It is targeted
specifically at people who work at the company and it is intended to
provide some kind of guideline for them of what is considered to be
acceptable and expected (or in the company's terms 'ethical')

behaviour. While there is a lot to say about this excerpt, I would like to draw attention here to the ways in which the company portrays itself, namely as 'a great place' and 'a rewarding and fulfilling environment'. The company describes itself as being characterised by 'a strong sense of inclusion, mutual respect, open and honest communication, fairness, teamwork, and pride'. These values together with the company's vision are viewed as guiding members' actions.

Due to the background knowledge they provide, these kinds of documents are important windows through which outsiders may gain interesting insights into an organisation's self-perception. They provide good starting points, for example, to explore what aspects are considered important for a particular organisation. And these documents often show whether an organisation is rather competitive and achievement oriented or whether it puts considerable effort into maintaining a healthy work–life balance for its employees. However, as mentioned above, insights gained from organisational documents need to be treated with some caution as they do not necessarily capture the everyday realities employees are experiencing but rather describe how the organisation views and presents itself (this aspect is further elaborated in Chapter 3).

Exercise 1.2

(TC)

Look again at the examples of professional communication displayed above and make a list of some of the features they have in common. You may want to consider, for example, interlocutors' role relationships (such as whether they have a symmetrical or asymmetrical relationship with each other, what their roles are in the interaction, and how these issues are reflected in what they say), the topics of the exchanges, lexical choices and overall organisation of the communication excerpts.

This section has begun to explore the question of what professional communication is by looking at a range of different kinds of communicative instances which occur in different kinds of workplace contexts. Despite some differences between these exchanges they also shared several similarities, which leads to the question of how we can usefully conceptualise professional communication in terms that are broad enough to capture the different kinds of exchanges displayed above. Section B approaches this issue and tries to find some more answers to the question of what professional communication is.

Section B: Conceptualising professional communication

In approaching the question of how to conceptualise professional communication, we could perhaps start by saying that at the most basic level, as the instances in Section A have shown, professional communication takes place in work contexts: that is, in places where at least one of the participants is engaged in some kind of (usually paid) work. We have also seen that professional communication may take place between professionals and customers (as in the sales encounter at the petrol station), among professionals (such as the email among colleagues), and among the organisation and the wider public (in the case of the organisation's values). And while these possible constellations are by no means exhaustive, they provide a useful starting point for exploring the context in which professional communication takes place. A useful way of conceptualising these different contexts is suggested by Goffman (1969), who distinguishes between so-called front and back regions.

Frontstage and backstage encounters

In describing ways of studying social life in general, Goffman (1969) uses the dramaturgical metaphors *frontstage* and *backstage*. Thus, he identifies 'the place where the performance is given' (Goffman 1969: 93) as 'front regions', and as 'back regions' those areas where 'the impression fostered by the performance is knowingly contradicted as a matter of course' (Goffman 1969: 97). According to this metaphor, then, frontstage performances include an audience (for whom a 'show' of 'best behaviour' is put on) whereas backstage interactions are not usually accessible for an audience and may even contradict the frontstage performance.

This notion has also been applied to workplace contexts (e.g. Sarangi and Roberts 1999; Koester 2010) where frontstage encounters usually include interactions between professionals and lay people, such as between doctors and patients, lawyers and clients, and typical service encounters (such as in Examples 1.2 and 1.4). Backstage encounters, by contrast, refer to those interactions that take place between co-workers and colleagues, such as a meeting of a group of colleagues working on the same project or an email exchange (such as Examples 1.1 and 1.3).

However, as Goffman himself points out, there is not always a clear distinction between frontstage and backstage. Rather, there is some overlap in the actual behaviours displayed in both regions and in the activities associated with each (see also Sarangi and Roberts 1999). For example, in their everyday workplace realities, professionals may regularly move between front region and back region: healthcare professionals, for example, may attend so-called case conferences (backstage) to discuss the future treatment of their patients after and before seeing the patients (frontstage); they may also routinely interact with other health professionals (including doctors, nurses and lab technicians) as well as administrative staff at the hospital (backstage). And while a lot of attention has been paid to frontstage encounters (in particular in medical contexts), activities performed in both regions crucially contribute to the work of a health professional. It is thus clearly important to explore both areas in any attempt to capture the complexities of professional communication.

The distinction between frontstage and backstage is not only based on the presence of an audience, but is also reflected in specific activities and in distinctive communicative behaviours typically displayed in encounters in each region. As Goffman (1969: 111) summarises:

> [t]he backstage language consists of reciprocal first-naming, co-operative decision-making, profanity, open sexual remarks, elaborate griping, smoking, rough informal dress, 'sloppy' sitting and standing posture, use of dialect or substandard speech, mumbling and shouting, playful aggressivity and 'kidding', inconsiderateness for the other in minor but potentially symbolic acts, minor physical self-involvements such as humming, whistling, chewing, nibbling, belching, and flatulence. The frontstage behaviour language can be taken as the absence (and in some sense the opposite) of this.

As the examples in this and the other chapters illustrate, the specific context in which an interaction takes place (and whether it is frontstage or backstage) has a considerable impact on the communicative practices participants employ.

Another feature that the instances of professional communication in Section A have in common is an orientation to transactional objectives or work-related outcomes while at the same time considering relational aspects. However, the extent to which individual examples orient (more or less) towards transactional or relational aspects differs dramatically.

Transactional and relational aspects

The distinction between transactional and relational aspects is useful for understanding professional communication. As was shown in the examples in Section A, transactional aspects of an encounter refer to those behaviours that (more or less explicitly) aim at getting things done and achieving outcomes, while relationally oriented aspects describe behaviours that aim at enhancing interpersonal relationships and creating a positive working atmosphere.

Although both transactional and relational aspects are clearly important, in many workplace interactions transactional goals seem to be participants' main concern (Koester 2006: 26). This is also reflected in the examples in Section A: in the medical encounter (Example 1.4), the medical provider's aim is to ensure the patient has sufficient information to reach an informed decision, and in Example 1.5 the organisational values of the IT company are aimed at creating a certain image of the company and to attract future clients. However, as we have seen in the examples, in addition to these overall transactional objectives, relational aspects are also of some importance. And it would probably be quite hard, if not entirely impossible, to act exclusively transactionally in a professional context. A hypothetical scenario where interlocutors might concentrate exclusively on transactional objectives is ticket-selling at a tourist destination, where the seller is occupied with serving long queues of impatiently waiting tourists, selling literally hundreds of tickets which may leave no time for relationally oriented talk. However, this is only a hypothetical situation, and as we have seen in Section A, even predominantly transactional exchanges (such as the one at the petrol station) may include some relational aspects (such as the greeting and friendly closing).

And although participating in relational behaviours may not seem strictly relevant for professional communication, doing collegiality and establishing or maintaining good relationships with colleagues, clients, superiors and subordinates is a crucial aspect of communication at work. After all, the nature of people's relationships may eventually impact on doing business: for example, getting along with each other and being on friendly terms may facilitate negotiations with clients and may improve the effectiveness of teamwork. A typical example of these relationally oriented aspects of professional communication is small talk which is often regarded as dispensable, superfluous and trivial although it may perform a wide range of useful functions in a workplace context (for a more detailed discussion see for example the contributions in Coupland 2000, Holmes and Stubbe 2003b ch. 5, and Koester 2010 ch. 5).

Moreover, as Koester (2010: 97) maintains, 'it is not possible to neatly separate talk that is purely instrumental from talk that has a relational or social purpose'. Rather, in their everyday work-communication, people typically combine transactional and relational elements, as the next example illustrates.

Example 1.7

Context: Email exchange between two academics.

Dear Rebecca,
Thanks so much for your prompt reply and for agreeing to review one of the papers!

And congratulations on the new baby!! [...] Is it a little boy/girl??
A while back, I sent you a Facebook friend request, not sure
whether you received it or whether you use FB at all, but if you
do, I would love to see some pics of the children... I attended
[name of conference], but did not go to [name of city1]. I do hope
to get to [name of city2] next year though. I am also organizing a
conference in [name of city3], for [topic]. I will be sending info out
in the next month or so .... I know it is a long way to travel, but
it'd be great if you could come. ...

I have attached the paper and the evaluation form. Great to hear
that mid September works for you. As I mentioned, the special
issue focuses on [topic].
Thanks again!
All best wishes,
Nina

This email contains both transactional and relational aspects: Nina
uses some small talk (for instance when enquiring about Rebecca's
children) before she moves on to the more work-related reason for this
email, namely to send a paper to her colleague for peer review. What
is particularly interesting in this email is the ways in which relational
and transactional topics follow each other closely and how they are
interwoven with each other.

Exercise 1.3 ⓉⒸ

In the email in Example 1.7 identify the transactional and relational
aspects, and describe how they are intertwined with each other.

The examples of professional communication displayed in Section A
have provided just a glimpse of the communicative exchanges that can
be described as professional. They have shown that professional
communication may employ different media (such as emails, face-to-
face interactions and internet sites), it may involve different participants
(including professionals and lay people), it may occur in a range of
very different places where people work, and it may perform various
(more or less transactional and relational) functions. This diversity is
also reflected in the range of different labels that are used by scholars
and practitioners to refer to and describe communication in workplace
settings: institutional talk, professional discourse, organisational
communication, workplace discourse, business communication and
many more. On the one hand, this plethora of terms indicates a
growing interest in what this book refers to as professional

communication, but on the other hand, the use of these different terms also suggests that there are differences (as well as overlaps) between the various phenomena. Five of these terms are briefly introduced below.

Institutional talk

Much of the early work on the language used in workplaces has used the term institutional talk (e.g. Drew and Heritage 1992), which is still frequently used in more recent research (e.g. Thornborrow 2002). Institutional talk is often described as 'talk between an expert representing some authority and a layman' (Gunnarsson, Linell and Nordberg 1997: 7). In their influential collection of essays *Talk at Work*, Drew and Heritage (1992: 3) conceptualise institutional talk as 'the principal means through which lay persons pursue various practical goals and the central medium through which the daily working activities of many professionals and organisational representatives are conducted'. Drew and Heritage (1992: 22) outline the three following features of institutional talk:

- orientation by at least one of the participants to some core goal, task or identity (or set of them) conventionally associated with the institution in question
- special and particular constraints on what one or both of the participants will treat as allowable contributions to the business at hand
- inferential frameworks and procedures that are particular to specific institutional contexts.

Participants' goal orientation is, for example, reflected in the overall organisation and structure of the various phases in institutional encounters (such as the various stages in a medical consultation, a job interview or a meeting). The second point (that is, the constraints on what kinds of contributions interlocutors are allowed to make) refers to the observation that different interlocutors may have different rights and obligations in terms of their contributions. In Example 1.1, for instance, Clara dominates the talking time and makes some decisions (for instance, that she does not take the minutes) and assigns tasks to others (such as when she decides that Seth 'can review the minutes from last week' when he comes in later). A good illustration of the specific constraints on allowable contributions is shown in the next example.

Example 1.8

Context: During the expert witness testimony in court.

1. Counsel: Based on your observations of the Bronco
2.   the times you've looked at it
3.   can you see those two circled areas if the door is
4.   closed?
5. Witness: Let me comment on about this photograph first if
6.   I may, because I can't –
7. The Court: No You have to answer the question
8. Witness: Okay

Source: Cotterill (2003: 164).

This brief exchange between Counsel, the Court and a witness nicely demonstrates that interlocutors may have very different speaking rights and obligations and that deviations from them may be rebuked (as the Court does in line 7 after the witness attempts to comment rather than to answer the question by Counsel).

The third point made by Drew and Heritage refers to the observation that professional encounters tend to be characterised by different conversational 'rules' from those of ordinary conversations. For example, in courtroom settings, medical examinations and police interviews the professionals (such as a legal counsel, judge, nurse, midwife or police officer) are generally required to withhold expressions of their emotions (such as empathy or agreement). And while such behaviours would be interpreted as unusual, uncooperative and perhaps even rude in ordinary conversations, in the professional contexts they constitute normal and appropriate practice.

Drew and Heritage (1992: 3–4) further note that 'the institutionality of an interaction is not determined by its setting. Rather, an interaction is institutional insofar as participants' institutional or professional identities are somehow made relevant to the work activities in which they are engaged.' In other words, an encounter cannot automatically be classified as institutional simply because it takes place in an institutional setting. For example, a chat between two friends in a hospital where one is a patient and the other works as a doctor does not necessarily have to be considered institutional as presumably none of the characteristics described above are met. However, if in the course of their encounter, participants switch into their institutional roles (and portray themselves as patient and doctor rather than friends) the nature of their interaction changes and becomes institutional (see also Chapter 5; Schegloff 1987).

Another term that is frequently used to capture communicative practices in professional contexts is professional discourse.

Professional discourse

In her book *Professional Discourse*, Gunnarsson (2009: 5) defines professional discourse as 'cover[ing] text and talk – and the intertwinement of these modalities – in professional contexts and for professional purposes'. This definition is rather broad, and includes different types or modes of communication produced by professionals. A professional is defined by her as somebody who is paid for their work (whether skilled or unskilled). And although such a definition may pose potential problems (for example, it does not capture the work done by volunteers in non-profit organisations), it is nevertheless useful since it captures a wider range of interactions than the definition of institutional discourse.

According to Gunnarsson, the following features distinguish professional discourse from other types of discourse:

1 Professions are typically characterised by specific discourses which distinguish them from other professions. These discourse and profession-specific ways of using language create, reflect and reinforce those activities, knowledge and skills that characterise a specific profession. Newcomers need to lean these aspects of professional discourse as part of their professional or vocational training.

2 Professional discourse is often explicitly goal-oriented and situated. In other words, the goals of professional discourse are typically specified in written documents (such as mission statements, contracts, etc.) and they are often linked to specific actions with concrete results (such as examining patients and prescribing treatments in order to cure them). Most workplaces have specific expectations and norms about what is considered appropriate communication, specifically in terms of who communicates with whom, how and when.

3 The discourses of professions are often conventionalised, in particular, where they reflect specific practices which are characteristic for that profession (e.g. conventionalised patterns of doctor-patient interactions or courtroom interactions).

4 Professional discourse often reflects and reinforces the activities and practices that characterise a workplace unit or group within an organisation. These groups exist on various levels within a workplace, including small local working groups (e.g. a team on the factory floor), a specific workplace, and even an entire organisation.

5 Professional discourse depends on four societal frameworks: the legal political-framework, the technical framework, the socio-cultural framework, and the linguistic framework. These frameworks relate to important aspects of professional communication, such as issues

of multiculturalism at work (socio-cultural framework) and language policy (linguistic framework).

6 Professional discourses are not stable entities but change over time, for example due to technological advancements and political changes (such as internationalisation and globalisation). Some of these dynamic changes are outlined in more detail below and in the next chapter.

(Gunnarsson 2009: 8–10, 25–6)

Exercise 1.4

Drawing on the information provided above, describe the differences between institutional and professional discourse in your own words.

Answer Exercise 1.4 before reading on.

In discussing the differences between institutional and professional discourse, Sarangi and Roberts (1999: 13–19) outline some of the characterising features of each. They start by emphasising differences in the ways in which the terms 'profession' and 'institution' and their adjectives are used in everyday language, and they argue that an institution is the larger entity in which various professions are located. They provide the example of universities (as institutions), where different kinds of professionals interact with each other and with their clients (that is, students); in this sense some of the professions that can be found in universities include lecturers, technicians, cleaners and administrative staff. Based on these differences, Sarangi and Roberts (1999: 15, emphasis in original) propose that 'what the professionals routinely do as a way of accomplishing their duties and responsibilities can be called *professional discourse*' while '[i]nstitutional discourse would then comprise those features which are attributed to institutional practice, either manifestly or covertly, by professionals (and clients)'. In other words, how professionals communicate during the medical examination (as described in Section A) is an example of professional discourse, while institutional discourse refers to those communicative practices that are sanctioned by the institution and which, in turn, may be reflected in the ways in which medical examinations are routinely conducted.

Another example to illustrate this distinction is provided by Sarangi and Roberts (1999), who note that when communicating with each other and their clients, professionals perform institutional practices (such as record keeping in medical and educational settings) while the specific ways in which these practices are accomplished reflect aspects of professional discourse in the sense that different professions may have different views about what is considered good record keeping. However, the distinction between professional and institutional discourse is not always straightforward, and in accomplishing their everyday work professionals routinely draw on both institutional and professional discourses (Roberts 2010: 183). As a consequence, the terms 'professional discourse' and 'institutional discourse' are often used interchangeably (Koester 2010: 5; Sarangi and Roberts 1999).

Two more terms that are also regularly often used to describe some of the phenomena displayed in the examples in Section A will be briefly introduced here, namely workplace discourse and business discourse.

Workplace discourse and business discourse

According to Koester (2010: 7), 'workplace discourse' is almost like an umbrella term for institutional, professional and business discourse, as it may be used to encompass all of these terms. In her book *Workplace Discourse* she defines workplace discourse as 'spoken and written interaction occurring in a workplace setting' (Koester 2010: 3). This term is rather general and includes all sorts of occupational contexts, such as white-collar and blue-collar workplaces, hospitals, courtrooms, as well as corporate and non-profit organisations, and many more. In this definition the term workplace discourse may be used to refer to communication between different companies (such as a contract about future collaboration) and it also includes communication between professionals and lay people (such as the prenatal genetic counselling session or the brief encounter at the petrol station discussed in Section A). However, the term workplace discourse also captures company internal communication, such as the email exchanges between the colleagues at the educational institution, and the organisational values from the IT company provided in Section A.

'Business discourse', by contrast, has a more restricted meaning, and refers to those interactions that occur specifically in commercial organisations. In their book *Business Discourse* Bargiela-Chiappini, Nickerson and Planken (2007: 3) define business discourse as being 'all about how people communicate using talk or writing in commercial organizations in order to get their work done'. Being conceptualised as 'social action in business contexts', their definition of business discourse explicitly focuses on spoken talk and written texts produced in business settings, thereby not including other types of workplaces or professional settings, such as factories, hospitals and courtrooms. Thus, due to its specific focus on the commercial sector, business discourse is often viewed as one type of workplace discourse.

The brief overview of the various communication phenomena that occur in workplace contexts has shown that there are some differences but also considerable overlaps in what phenomena the various traditions or research strands look at, and how they approach and conceptualise them. In this book I will use the term 'professional communication' to avoid some of the limitations and possible confusions over conceptual overlaps and differences. Moreover, using a relatively broad definition of professional communication (as outlined below) it will be possible to take language use in professional contexts a little beyond discourse boundaries into broader parameters of communication – for example by also considering multimedia and multimodal instances of professional communication, including videoconferencing, websites and associated images, logos and non-verbal communication.

Professional communication

The term 'professional communication' will be used to describe the phenomena shown in the examples in Section A. In particular, professional communication is conceptualised very broadly as interactions which may take various forms and which take place in a context that is broadly related to work, and involve at least one participant who is engaged in some work-related activity.

Such a definition of professional communication is broad enough to explore different types of encounters in the variety of workplaces described in Section A, including interactions between professionals and lay people (such as the encounter at the petrol station), exchanges among professionals (such as the email exchange between the colleagues at an educational institution), as well as one-way communication between an organisation and its members and clients (such as the code of conduct). In this way, then, professional communication is used as an umbrella term for communicative encounters that take place in a workplace context in the widest sense.

The main focus throughout the book will be on the various aspects of verbal communication, but non-verbal aspects are discussed where relevant (most notably in Chapters 3 and 4). In exploring the multiple aspects of professional communication, the subsequent chapters draw on examples of authentic professional communication collected in a wide range of workplaces including white-collar and blue-collar workplaces, corporate and non-profit environments, as well as medical, classroom and legal settings. Although as Sarangi and Candlin (2011: 1) argue, 'it will be an overstatement to claim that language is the only modality in which professional practice is manifest', the main focus of this book is on the language used in professional contexts. However, other components of communication, in particular multimodal features such as textual, rhetorical, visual and audible features that have also been found to be relevant for an understanding of (professional) communication, are mentioned and referred to where useful.

Before exploring specific aspects of professional communication in more detail in the subsequent chapters, I will briefly outline some of the changes that have affected professional communication in a variety of ways and which are crucial for an understanding of how communication is done in any workplace.

Changes in professional communication

In the past few decades organisations have undergone considerable structural changes which also impact professional communication. These changes, as Gunnarsson (2009: 10) notes, are reflected in various aspects of professional communication, including 'purpose, content and language, as well as ... linguistic form and patterns'. Three of these changes are briefly outlined here, namely the internationalisation and globalisation of the economy, technological advances, and what has been described as the 'new work order'.

It is widely acknowledged that the worldwide internationalisation and globalisation of the economy is contributing to an increasing number of multicultural and multilingual workplaces. More and more corporations are opening offices around the globe and operating in a range of different countries, and the workforce is becoming increasingly mobile. These social and economic changes impact on professional communication in a variety of ways, including the use of English and other languages as lingua franca in intercultural encounters (see e.g. Koester 2010 ch. 6). These trends also pose several concrete challenges for employees, such as the need to be proficient in several languages to communicate with colleagues, clients and stakeholders across different countries (see also Chapter 4).

A second change is related to technological advances that have taken place over the last couple of decades and that have considerably contributed to changing the image of professional communication. It has even been noted that '[e]very strand of workplace communication has, in one way or the other, been transformed by technology' (Gunnarsson 2009: 249). Fax, email, the World Wide Web and mobile phones play a crucial part in what has been called 'a new era of mobile computing' (Blundel 2004: 152) that allows employees to work at remote locations while still being able to access corporate intranets. The various developments in new communication technology have created new, and often more complex, forms of professional interaction which may combine (and sometimes replace) several traditional forms of communication, such as videoconferencing (see also Chapter 2).

A last change discussed here refers to changes in professional ideology, often referred to as the 'new work order' (see Geis, Brown and Wolfe 1990), which are increasingly being adopted by organisations. These ideological changes are reflected in and affect several aspects of organisational reality. For example, they have led to transitions in workplace culture, which in turn are often reflected in a restructuring of organisational hierarchies where flatter structures with fewer levels of management are increasingly becoming the norm (see also Chapters 5 and 7). These changes have also affected communication and have been referred to as the 'democratisation' of discourse (Fairclough 1992: 201). This democratisation is reflected on the level of discourse practices: for example, in the elimination of overt power markers and a tendency towards more informal language. In this respect, then, the discourse of organisations (similar to other types of public discourse) is becoming increasingly more informal, and more and more resembles discourse that occurs in the private domain. In fact, it has been noted that 'conversational discourse practices which traditionally belong in the private sphere are being systematically simulated within organizations' (Fairclough 1992: 8). These tendencies have been referred to as the 'conversationalisation' of discourse (Fairclough 1992). As a consequence of these trends, workplace communication tends to occur in a more informal, conversational manner.

The new work order, in turn, has also led to changes in divisions of labour and management approaches which put increasing emphasis on empowering employees: rather than telling them what to do 'they are made responsible for motivating, disciplining and directing themselves' (Cameron 2000: 14; this aspect is elaborated in Chapter 5 where the effects on professional identities are discussed in more detail). As a consequence, working together and collaborating with colleagues from other teams and departments is becoming increasingly important, and certain organisational practices, such as problem solving and standardising procedures, are reconceptualised as teamwork and are not the responsibilities of individuals anymore (Iedema and Scheeres 2003: 318).

These changes also have profound effects on the professional identities of employees: that is, the ways in which they perceive themselves and their role and responsibilities in the wider context of their workplace (see also Fairclough 1992). In a study of a gaming-machine factory and a teaching hospital, for instance, Iedema and Scheeres (2003) observed how structural changes in these workplaces have affected staff members. These restructuring processes include increased worker knowledge of and responsibility for productivity targets (in the factory) and the introduction of a new management structure which increases, for example, doctors' accountability for their activities to management and colleagues (at the hospital). As a consequence of these changes, the factory workers and the clinical staff were facing specific challenges in constructing their professional identities:

> [j]ust as it is becoming harder for factory workers to deny responsibility for their work and for their role in that work, and to ignore the workings of the organization as a whole, doctors can no longer presume status and privilege, and act on the basis of a professional autonomy that is not accountable in some way to colleagues, the rest of the organization, management, or the public.
>
> (Iedema and Scheeres 2003: 332)

The study showed that the ways in which the factory workers and the hospital staff perceived themselves, the work they do and their roles in their specific workplaces have undergone dramatic changes.

In addition to the changes outlined here, there are, of course, other changes which affect professional communication in one way or another and which may pose a challenge to more traditional forms of communication. Some of these challenges dealt with in the literature include, for example, blurred organisational boundaries (for example in joint ventures between organisations) and increasing involvement of stakeholders (e.g. Blundel 2004).

The next section briefly discusses the relevance of communication for an understanding of what is going on in workplaces, and addresses the question of why professional communication should be studied from an applied linguistics perspective.

Section C: Approaching professional communication from the perspective of applied linguistics

Sections A and B have established that the role of communication cannot be overemphasised for an understanding of workplace realities. Many of the activities that characterise, and to a certain extent form and create, workplaces and professional practices are related to communication. In a similar vein, Gunnarsson et al. (1997: 1) maintain that:

> language has become one of the most important tools of many new professions where oral and written contact with the general public forms the core of professional work. Telephone calls, meetings, negotiations and conferences have become the cornerstones of professional contacts. Many experts – business people, lawyers, health care personnel, street-level bureaucrats – spend a lot of their working hours in talk with clients, colleagues and other professionals.

However, although the crucial role of language and communication for organisational practices is now widely accepted, this was not always the case. It was only a few decades ago when organisational studies took a 'discursive turn' and began to acknowledge the usefulness of conceptualising 'issues of power, hegemony and ideology' no longer as purely historical or psychological issues but as being dynamically and constantly created, reflected, reinforced, and challenged in 'social and linguistic practices' (Iedema and Wodak 1999: 7). As a consequence of this shift in attention towards linguistic and communicative practices, researchers were no longer primarily interested in the interplay between the perceptions, practices, behaviours and motivations of organisational members in relation to organisational macro-structures, but began to pay closer attention to the linguistic and communicative practices through which organisations are actually formed and performed (Iedema and Wodak 1999: 7). In line with this trend, communication in its various forms was and still is perceived as being at the heart of what is going on in many workplaces.

This crucial role of communication in workplace contexts is also increasingly recognised by practitioners and is, for example, reflected in an increasing demand for professional training (including workshops and conferences) targeted at improving professional communication, both internally and externally. Issues of particular interest to practitioners are, for example, how to improve internal communication (in particular top-down communication), how to communicate changes (such as restructuring plans), how to facilitate company mergers, how to improve external communication (for example by involving shareholders more systematically), and how to improve or change a company's public image. The list seems endless, and demonstrates the wide applicability of issues of professional communication in the 'real world'.

Perhaps not surprisingly, professional communication has received a lot of attention from researchers in different disciplines, including sociology, anthropology, psychology, sociolinguistics and applied linguistics.[4] These diverse disciplines bring with them not only different epistemological stances but also different ways of approaching professional communication. The multidisciplinary nature of research on professional communication is further reflected in the diversity of paradigms, research methods and theoretical frameworks that are at play when members of different disciplines analyse the ways in which people communicate at work. However, if we follow Candlin and Sarangi, who 'see applied linguistics as a many centred and interdisciplinary endeavour whose coherence is achieved in purposeful, mediated action by its practitioners' (2004: 2), it becomes clear why applied linguistics provides a particularly valuable perspective through which professional communication may be approached. One of the main tenets of applied linguistics, as Candlin and Sarangi (2004) go on to argue, is to combine and manage potential tensions between 'reflexivity and relevance' (Sarangi and Candlin 2003): that is, between the potentially opposing demands of adhering to and furthering the theoretical principles and practices that characterise the field of applied linguistics on the one hand, and producing research outcomes that are of practical relevance for participants and collaborators from other disciplines on the other hand. In achieving these aims, research conducted within applied linguistics often usefully engages in 'crossdisciplinary dialogue' (Bargiela-Chiappini et al. 2007: 66) and draws on theoretical constructs and methodologies from other disciplines. Such an approach is particularly fruitful for capturing the theoretical complexities of professional communication as well as their practical implications and applications.

This multidisciplinarity of research on professional communication is also to some extent reflected in the various chapters, which provide insights into some of the diverse ways in which the complexities of professional communication may be approached. In doing this, I draw on research conducted in different disciplines, using different research methods and different analytical frameworks when approaching specific issues of professional communication. Such an emphasis on diversity, I hope, will illustrate some of the advantages that these different angles and perspectives may bring to an analysis of professional communication. Combining their strengths, I believe, can only be beneficial for an understanding of the complexities of professional communication.

Some of the research methods and analytical frameworks frequently used to approach professional communication within applied linguistics include ethnography, conversation analysis (CA), genre analysis, interactional sociolinguistics, and critical discourse analysis (CDA) (Koester 2010: 9; Iedema and Wodak 1999). Most of them are introduced in more detail in the subsequent chapters, where it is demonstrated how these different approaches and research methods provide useful starting points to approach the various topics of professional communication. A particular emphasis throughout this book is on discourse-analytic approaches to professional communication. As Iedema and Wodak (1999: 12) note, discourse analytic approaches have the advantage of 'being able to highlight the dynamic social construction of institutional relations and structures (Woolard, 1985)'. They thus enable analysts to identify and observe the specific micro-level practices which contribute to creating the very structures and realities that characterise particular workplaces, while also considering wider organisational processes and phenomena on a macro level. Thus, although applied linguistics is often perceived as being primarily concerned with a wide range of pedagogical issues relating to language use and acquisition, research on professional communication within this discipline predominantly explores how people in a workplace setting communicate with each other and with their clients, stakeholders and the wider public (see also Bargiela-Chiappini et al. 2007: 5).

Brief outline of the book

The subsequent chapters introduce a variety of different topics of professional communication, including genres, workplace culture, culture and politeness at work, professional identities, gender, and leadership. In choosing these topics I have tried to combine more traditional subjects (such as genres) with more non-traditional and perhaps unconventional ones (such as leadership and gender). While I am aware that such a choice almost inevitably means that some other (equally relevant and interesting) topics have to be excluded, I believe that the various chapters nicely illustrate some of the everyday problems and practices that are typical for communication in many professional contexts. I thus hope that the subsequent chapters will contribute towards reaching an understanding of some of the issues and complexities that characterise professional communication.

Chapter 2 follows up on some of the issues raised in this introductory chapter. Its particular focus is on further exploring how the various different kinds of professional communication outlined in this chapter can be grouped together in meaningful ways. In approaching this issue, Chapter 2 focuses on genres of professional communication, and explores what the notion of genre has to offer in terms of accounting for potential differences and similarities between different kinds of professional communication. Genre analysis is introduced as an approach to systematically describing the specific features and functions of different kinds of professional communication.

After this chapter has provided a general picture of professional communication and some of the genres that fall under this term, Chapter 3 begins to further explore some of the differences in communicative behaviour displayed by members in different workplaces. In doing so, it looks for reasons underlying these differences in communication habits that typically characterise different workplaces. These differences are not only reflected in the form and function of communication but are also made visible in other aspects of workplaces, such as dress code, organisational hierarchies and office layout. The notion of workplace culture is introduced to help conceptualise some of these observable (as well as invisible) differences, and its crucial relevance for professional communication is discussed. Three approaches to workplace culture, namely models by Edgar Schein and Geert Hofstede and the concept of community of practice, provide useful starting points for gaining insights into the complexities of the culture(s) of a workplace.

Chapter 4 stays with the topic of culture, and explores the role of national culture in professional encounters, with a particular focus on the complex relationship between culture and politeness. Due to the increasing globalisation and mobility of the workforce, multicultural (and often multilingual) workplaces have become the norm. The chapter thus approaches the question of whether culture is an issue at work and what role politeness plays in these contexts. In line with recent research developments, this chapter challenges essentialist assumptions that tend to treat culture as the default explanation for a wide range of phenomena. Rather than assuming that (national) culture is an issue in any kind of intercultural encounter, the examples in this chapter demonstrate that culture is often just an unremarkable aspect of workplace realities. However, in those instances where miscommunication occurs, culture (and in particular, cultural stereotypes) tend to be perceived as the source of these mismatches by lay people. And in many instances of miscommunication, participants' face needs are often particularly vulnerable and issues of politeness become relevant. However, in analysing intercultural (and cross-cultural) communication, it is crucial to take a critical stance towards culture and to move beyond stereo-typical assumptions and consider other factors when explaining specific communicative events. Two frameworks that may help understand the role of face and politeness in intercultural and cross-cultural contexts are politeness theory and rapport management. They both explore how specific ways of perceiving and enacting face needs and politeness may help making sense of those instances where a misunderstanding might occur – in particular in intercultural encounters.

Chapter 5 focuses on the complex notion of identity, and explores some of the ways in which the notion of 'who we are' is particularly relevant in a professional context. The chapter takes as a starting point the observation that issues of identity are omnipresent in professional (and other) contexts which are reflected in various aspects of professional communication. In interacting with each other, people at work constantly set up subject positions for themselves and each other and orient towards who they are (to each other) in the specific context of the encounter as well as in the wider context of their workplace. Participants thereby create, negotiate and sometimes challenge their own and each other's identities and roles, which are always to some extent related to issues of power. The crucial role of language in the various processes involved in identity construction is accounted for by social constructionism. One specific framework for analysing identity construction (proposed by Mary Bucholtz and Kira Hall) is outlined and its five principles of identity construction are applied to examples of professional communication.

Chapter 6 illustrates some of the ways in which gender is an important aspect of workplace realities, and how it interacts with professional communication in myriad ways. Not only does the existence of gender stereotypes about how men and women supposedly talk and act sometimes surface in people's discourse these stereotypical expectations may also have implications for the often discriminatory perception and treatment of women in specific workplaces and professions. Some of the disadvantages that women are faced with are the double-bind and the glass ceiling. Although gender is always potentially relevant in any (professional and other) encounter, its impact may become particularly obvious in the use and perception of gendered speech styles and the existence of gendered discourses. Through these avenues gender is enacted and reinforced (or sometimes challenged) in professional communication. One of the approaches frequently used to identify and expose some of the discriminatory practices (and the ways in which they are reinforced in and through discourse) is critical discourse analysis, which aims at changing social inequalities by making people aware of the (often communicative) mechanisms that contribute to their existence.

The topic of Chapter 7 is leadership. This chapter approaches the question of what leadership is by focusing on discourse. It explores how leadership is accomplished through communication. Examples from various workplaces illustrate that in addition to traditional hierarchical and often asymmetrical relationships, there are various alternative leadership constellations where power and responsibilities are more equally shared among participants. Various factors have an impact on how leadership is performed, including the working teams of the leaders, the cultures of their workplaces, the wider sociocultural context in which they interact, gender, and the medium or channel of communication. Discursive leadership, a tradition established in leadership research, acknowledges the central role of communication in leadership processes and provides a useful framework for approaching the complexities of leadership discourse, especially when combined with discourse analytical approaches, such as conversation analysis or interactional sociolinguistics. These approaches offer valuable tools for analysing leadership discourse and for exploring how leadership is actually done on the micro level.

Chapter 8 provides a brief conclusion by bringing together some of the arguments provided in the previous chapters, and by outlining some avenues for future research in professional communication, in particular for student projects.

Summary

This chapter has explored the question of what professional communication is. Several examples of authentic communication have illustrated the vast diversity of communicative events that fall under the umbrella of professional communication, and similarities as well as differences between these examples have been discussed. In particular, most instances of professional communication are characterised by an overall orientation towards outcomes (transactional aspects) while still considering relational aspects.

This diversity is also reflected in the various labels that have been proposed to describe interactions in workplace contexts, including institutional talk, professional discourse, workplace discourse and business discourse. Professional communication is conceptualised here rather broadly as any interaction that takes place in a workplace context (in the wider sense) and that involves at least one professional. This definition captures various forms of communication that take place in both the front region and the back region of any workplace.

Professional communication has also undergone crucial changes over the last few decades, which are mainly related to the internationalisation and globalisation of the economy, technological advances, and ideological changes (as reflected in, for example, the new work order). These social tendencies and developments have had (and still have) an impact on how people communicate at work.

Clearly, professional communication is of multidisciplinary interest. However, this book mainly takes an applied linguistics perspective, in particular by drawing on insights gained from discourse-analytical approaches, some of which are outlined in the chapters to come. And while this chapter has established the crucial role of communication in most (if not all) workplaces, the next chapter further explores some of the multiple forms or genres of professional communication and how they can be conceptualised in meaningful ways.

2 Genres of professional communication

After discussing what professional communication means and what kinds of interactions this term incorporates, this chapter addresses the issue of how we can categorise the various (often very different) communicative instances that fall under the broad umbrella of professional communication. What does the language spoken in business meetings have in common with the language used on the factory floor? Are there similarities between courtroom discourse and classroom interactions? Are promotional letters and job applications really that different? This chapter aims to address these questions by exploring how we can capture potential similarities while at the same time accounting for the diversity of different types of professional communication.

Section A: Exploring genres of professional communication

In Chapter 1 several very different examples of professional communication were listed, including a sales encounter, an email exchange between colleagues, the opening of a business meeting, a prenatal genetic screening consultation, the values of an organisation, and an excerpt from the code of conduct of a corporate company. According to the broad definition of professional communication introduced in Chapter 1 all these (spoken and written) exchanges fall under the umbrella of professional communication: all of them take place in work-related contexts and involve at least one professional. While there are certain advantages in such a broad definition, it still leaves us with the question of what these apparently different instances of professional communication have in common and how they can be grouped together in meaningful ways.

Examples 2.1 and 2.2 show two types of professional communication – a promotional letter and a job application – which may at first look rather different. However, upon closer scrutiny, it becomes clear that they have several features in common.

Example 2.1

Excerpt from sales promotion letter.

Dear Sir,

We are expertly aware that international financial managers need to be able to ask the right questions and work in the market place with confidence.

Corporate Treasury Services, Standard Bank, now provides a week-long Treasury Training programme designed to develop awareness and confidence in managers. We explain the mechanics of foreign exchange and money markets. We discuss risk from an overall standpoint and practical hedging techniques to manage foreign exchange risks. We also discuss treasury management information systems, taxation and the latest treasury techniques.

We will be holding our next Treasury Training Programme from 24–28 February 1987, inclusive. The fee for the Training Programme will be US$1,500 per person to include all luncheons and a dinner as indicated in the schedule as well as all course materials.

The programme is both rigorous and flexible. It can be tailored to fit the needs of a whole corporation or just a few levels within the company.

We are pleased to inform you that if your company sponsors 6 or more staff on the course, we will offer you a discount of US$100 per person.

For your convenience, I enclose a reservation form which should be completed and returned directly to me. If you have any questions or would like to discuss the programme in more detail, please do not hesitate to contact me (Telephone No. 532 6488 / telex No. 29052).

As the number of participants at each training programme is limited, we would urge you to finalize as soon as possible your plans to participate.

Thank you very much for your kind consideration.

Yours faithfully

Mr. G. Huff

Source: Bhatia (1993: 47).

According to Bhatia (1993: 45), a sales promotion letter is 'an unsolicited letter addressed to a selected group of prospective customers ... in order to persuade them to buy a product or service'. The letter above is a good example of such a document as it is used by a member of Standard Bank to offer the bank's services (i.e. a 'Treasury Training Programme') to an individual (who is representing another company). However, since sales promotion letters are generally unsolicited, their writers are faced with the difficult task of capturing the addressees' attention and convincing them of the benefits of the offered services so that they will respond to the letter (Bhatia 1993: 45). Some of these functions are also performed by job applications, as the next example shows.

Example 2.2

A cover letter accompanying a job application.

Dear Mr Peters
Supply Chain Transformation – Assistant Director (ref: DUR002KL)
I have been referred to the above role with [company name] by May Petrol, and was very interested to read the job description. As someone who is committed to managing and leading productive teams, and striving towards excellence in customer and supplier relationships, I believe I can contribute strongly to the work of [company] in Supply Chain transformation.
    I have vast experience of supply chain and change management. At [other company] I managed the end-to-end international supply chain across Asia and Europe, managing the supplier relationships and making sure their service was delivered with the most cost efficient way. Additionally, I have extensive experience of transforming supply chains: I have implemented two WMS systems, fully integrated with the demand planning and forecasting IT system; restructured the whole supply chain moving from in-house operations to out-sourcing the manufacturing, packing and distribution; and moved from a hardcopy list-picking system to a fully automated scanner-picking and pick-to-light system in the distribution centre, achieving cost and time efficiencies.
    I believe that my experience is a great match with the requirements of this role, which I see as needing someone with a combination of supply chain and retail management skills, together with excellent communication and team working skills and the vision to enable change. I would be very grateful for the chance to discuss my contribution further with you.
Yours sincerely,
Paul Summers

At a first glance job applications and sales promotion letters may not necessarily be perceived as having many commonalities. For example, the former tries to persuade the address to purchase a particular good or service while the purpose of the latter is to get the writer invited for a job interview. Moreover, job applications are usually sent in response to job advertisements while sales promotion letters are mainly unsolicited. However, in spite of these differences, a closer look reveals indeed a range of similarities. Most importantly perhaps, both types of texts have a similar communicative purpose, namely to promote something: the applicant in the job application and a service or good in the case of the sales promotion letter. In comparing the two, Bhatia thus notes that a 'job application letter is closely related to a sales promotion letter not simply because both of them are persuasive in nature and both of them share the same communicative purpose ... but also use the same medium, and exploit the same form' (1993: 59).

Both types of documents perform persuasive functions, they focus only on the most relevant aspects (of the applicant's experience and the product's features), and they both aim at engaging the addressees in future correspondence with the aim of establishing a business or working relationship (Bhatia 1993: 60). These similarities in function are also reflected in the overall structure of the letters: both start by establishing credentials before introducing the candidature/offer; and both typically refer to enclosed documents (a CV in the job application letter and further information material in the sales promotion letter) and aim to solicit a response from the addressee before ending politely (for more details see Bhatia 1993 ch. 2). Although there is clearly some variation in the ways in which job applications and sales promotion letters are composed (for example in different socio-cultural contexts), they display a number of important similarities in terms of medium, participants' role relationships and overall communicative purpose.

Examples like these thus demonstrate that the question of how to conceptualise professional communication and how to bring some order into this diverse mix of spoken and written exchanges may sometimes require neglecting the labels that are assigned to specific communicative instances and to focus on their form and function when deciding how to categorise them and where to draw the boundaries of a genre. As we will see in later sections of this chapter, there are different approaches to genre analysis which to a certain extent influence these discussions about genre categorisation. The next three examples provide further illustration of this. Examples 2.3 to 2.5 are taken from very different professional contexts, including a courtroom, a GP surgery and a classroom, and yet they share some remarkable similarities (as well as differences).

Exercise 2.1

Read through Examples 2.3 to 2.5 and identify similarities and differences between the exchanges. You may want to consider the context, participants (for instance, their roles and status), the overall purpose of the exchanges, and discursive features (such as turn-taking rights and obligations of participants).

Example 2.3

Extract from official court transcripts.
Context: At a jury trial during an interrogation of a witness.
Q = Counsel, A = witness

1. Q: Thank you very much I am going to ask you about an
2.   incident which occurred on
3.   Saturday 4th April of this year round about midday
4.   Where were you at that time?
5. A: We'd just taken the horses on to the beach
6.   We were riding along a small narrow road on the way home
7.   Ginger Walters is my friend
8.   She was riding her horse
9. Q: Ginger Walters was riding her horse and you were
10.   riding your horse?
11. A: Yes
12. Q: You had the horses on the beach
13. A: We went on at the place which is known as The Mound
14.   I believe
15.   We'd ridden all the way up to Heathsway and come
16.   back again
17.   We'd come off the beach on the way home

Source: Heffer (2005: 115).

This extract is a fairly typical instance of courtroom discourse. It is taken from an interrogation of a witness (A) by a Counsel (Q). A similar question–answer sequence is shown in the next exchange, which occurred between a patient and a general practitioner (GP) during a physical examination of the patient.

Example 2.4

Context: During a physical examination in a GP consultation.
Dr = Doctor (GP), P = patient.

1. Dr: Smoking?
(1.2)
2. Dr: //How\ many?
3. P.   /oh yes\\ but I have CUT down a lot
(1.8)
4. Dr: To?
(0.6)
5. Dr: From? (0.2) To?
6. P.   //Well\ I use to smoke about twenty a day but
7. Dr: /hhh\\

8. P.   //I have\ cut them down
9. Dr: /erm\\

Source: Heffer (2005: 115).

The last question–answer sequence shown here is taken from yet another professional context, namely from a classroom interaction.

Example 2.5

Context: Classroom interaction between teacher and multilingual group of students. T = teacher; L = student.

1. T: right yes where was Sabina? (4) in unit ten where was she?
2. L: er go out
3. T: she went out yes
4.   so first she was in the
5. L: kitchen
6. T: kitchen good and then what did she take with her?
7. L: Er drug
8. T: good she took the memory drug and she ran OUT

Source: Walsh (2011: 13; slightly shortened).

Based on the differences and similarities between these instances of professional communication (as described in the task commentaries in the appendix), the question is whether they should be classified as similar types or categories of interaction or whether they are different enough, in spite of obvious similarities, to warrant individual consideration and treatment. This issue is discussed in more detail in Section B.

The examples discussed so far have shown that grouping together instances of professional communication in meaningful ways is not a straightforward undertaking. These difficulties are also reflected in the wide diversity of communicative events that lay people tend to summarise under the same heading. Meetings are a good example of this: although most people usually have a good idea about what a meeting is – in particular when they are attending one – matters are more complicated from an analytic perspective. Examples 2.6 and 2.7 are instances of regular staff meetings which occurred at different workplaces. Both examples are taken from the opening sequences.

Example 2.6

Context: Fortnightly meeting of management team in white-collar workplace.

1. Tricia: it'll be a quick meeting //[laughs]\

2.   we're just waiting for Carol now
3.   do you want to just give her a ring
[several minutes of chat among participants during which Carol arrives]
4. Tricia: okay well Tracey's not here and Isabelle's laid up +
5.   so there's only [voc]

Source: Marra, Schnurr and Holmes
(2006: 249; shortened version of longer extract).

This brief excerpt looks like a typical opening sequence in a meeting in a white-collar workplace: Tricia (the chair) indicates that they are about to start with 'a quick meeting' (line 1). And after the missing participant (Carol) has arrived, she opens the meeting by giving apologies for those who are not present (line 4). In a lot of ways this meeting is a typical example of what most people associate with this type of professional communication: people come together for a particular purpose (which often involves some discussion), there is a chair who leads through the meeting, and often there is an agenda with items that need to be discussed during the meeting. However, as the next example illustrates, not all meetings adhere to this format.

Example 2.7

Context: Regular 6 am briefing meeting of a factory team. Team members are gradually drifting in during Ginette's speech (which is delivered in an ironic tone of voice).

1. Ginette: good morning everybody
2.   it's lovely to see you all this morning +
3.   just can't imagine my life coming into work not
4.   seeing you every day +
5.   nice to see you all well
[general laughter and some indecipherable responses with tone of good-humoured riposte]
6. Ginette: one one three +++
7.   nice to see everybody's here on time +++

Source: Holmes and Stubbe (2003b: 129).

In this short extract Ginette, the leader of a factory team, greets her staff members for their daily briefing meeting before they begin their day shifts. Like in the example above, Ginette also has to deal with latecomers, which she uses as the source for some humour (line 7). Using an ironic tone, she comments on their lateness as they drift in. Other similarities between the two meetings include the chairing role of Tricia and Ginette (although members in Ginette's team may not refer to her as the chair) and a relatively similar communicative purpose of updating staff on developments and discussing issues. However, although there are some similarities between this meeting and the one in Example 2.6, the meetings differ remarkably from each other in the formality and the tone in which they are delivered: the staff meeting in the white-collar workplace is relatively formal (reflected in the fact that there is an agenda, for example) and the overall tone is serious albeit friendly but with a clear orientation towards transactional goals. The briefing meeting in the factory, on the other hand, appears more informal and Ginette's style is often 'extremely direct and critical, using explicit imperatives, often reinforced by strong expletives' and a high amount of banter and humour (Holmes and Stubbe 2003b: 128) (these aspects are illustrated further in Chapter 3 where the linguistic repertoire of this group is described in more detail).

Although Examples 2.6 and 2.7 occurred during what participants themselves would describe as a meeting, as we have seen there are differences as well as similarities between the two exchanges. These differences in the ways in which people do meetings are discussed in more detail in Section B, where I address the question of what a meeting is.

In dealing with some of the issues outlined in this section with regards to difficulties in capturing and conceptualising differences and similarities among instances of professional communication, the concept of genre may be 'useful in trying to make sense of this diversity' as it 'provides a systematic approach to describing workplace discourse' (Koester 2010: 18). The next section discusses the notion of genre in more detail.

Section B: Engaging with genres of professional communication

What is genre?

Although genre has been (and continues to be) the focus of many research studies across disciplines (including literary studies, rhetoric, and linguistics), the concept of genre itself remains relatively slippery (Swales 1990). Moreover, different approaches to genre analysis exist which take different stances towards defining and analysing genres. These issues are discussed in more detail in Section C. However, among the various definitions of genre that have been provided within (applied) linguistics, Bargiela-Chiappini and Nickerson's (1999) is one of the most comprehensive. They define genres as 'relatively stable forms of communication which develop in the course of production and reproduction of communicative practices, and which are recognized by the members of that community' (1999: 8). In other words, genres evolve as a response to a 'recurrent situation': they form established and approved ways of dealing with 'established practices, social relations, and communication media within organizations' (Yates and Orlikowski 1992: 301).

In contrast to earlier conceptualisations of genre which typically tended to view genre as 'a more or less standardized communicative event with a goal or a set of goals mutually understood by the participants in that event' (Swales 1981: 19), this recent definition is more dynamic, and moves away from classifying genres on the basis of a 'seemingly straightforward correspondence between form and function' (Yeung 2007: 158). Rather than strictly focusing on the communicative purpose of a text and on the rhetorical features that characterise it, more recent definitions of genre acknowledge the importance of the sociocultural context in which genres emerge, and they propose that in identifying genres it is crucial to look beyond 'typical communicative practice' and to also consider 'typical participants and their stock of knowledge of how to deal with typical situations in their typical social community' (Yeung 2007: 158; see also Askehave and Swales 2001).

According to this conceptualisation of genre, which acknowledges the role of the sociocultural context in which a genre is enacted, the sales promotion letter and the job application letter described in Section A would probably not be categorised as belonging to the same genre since they emerged in different sociocultural contexts. However, Bhatia (1993) argues that they both belong to what he calls the 'promotional genre'. He argues that there are different levels of genre; while promotional is the overarching genre category under which both examples fall, these two letters can be usefully conceptualised as subgenres of the promotional genre. However, distinguishing these different 'levels of abstraction' (Yates and Orlikowski 1992: 303) within a genre is not always straightforward, and as Bhatia (1993: 13–14) acknowledges, it may not always 'be possible to draw a fine line between genres and sub-genres'.

Exercise 2.2

Would you classify Examples 2.3 to 2.5 (in Section A) as instances of the same genre? Why (or why not)? Are there any problems in making this decision?

(TC)

Genres of professional communication

Genres of professional communication have attracted the interest of many researchers, and numerous studies on this topic have been conducted. Most of these studies explore written genres, such as business reports (Yeung 2007), business letters (van Nus 1999; dos Santos 2002), tax computation letters (Flowerdew and Wan 2006), as well as faxes (Louhiala-Salminen 1997; Akar and Louhiala-Salminen 1999) and email (Mulholland 1999; Gimenez 2002; Jensen 2009). But there are also some studies that have looked at spoken genres of professional communication, most notably meetings (e.g. Handford 2010; Angouri and Marra 2010). Most of these studies have identified several moves and linguistic features that characterise these specific genres of professional communication.

In a study of written genres, dos Santos (2002) analysed the shared communicative purposes and rhetorical features of 117 commercial letters in English faxed between members of a Brazilian and two European companies. Based on a range of distinctive common features of the letters, she identified the generic structure of business negotiation letters (BLN). Three different types of BNL were found in the corpus, which all follow a relatively similar pattern of (obligatory) rhetorical moves and (optional) steps. This way of analysing genres by identifying and describing specific moves is characteristic of a particular school of genre analysis (ESP) which is elaborated in more detail in Section C. These moves, in turn, were characterised by specific lexical choices including the use of informal I, the use of formal expressions (such as modals and hypothetical expressions), and 'indirect questions with hypothetical expressions, interrogatives to request services, and minimized imperatives to request either services or information' (dos Santos 2002: 187). Through these lexical choices 'an atmosphere of cordiality and respect' was created among members of the different companies (dos Santos 2002: 186–7).

In another study of business reports collected in Hong Kong, Singapore, Malaysia and the United Kingdom, Yeung (2007) identified specific textual features that are typical for this genre. She observed certain 'regularities in structure, rhetorical moves, and lexico-grammatical choices' which she interpreted as a 'reflection of the conventions which members of the business community evoke when they use business reports as a mode of communication' (Yeung 2007: 160). More specifically, the features of the business reports that Yeung (2007) analysed on different levels resembled each other in terms of their overall pragmatic goal of facilitating decision making and providing recommendations, as well as in terms of their funnel shaped structure, topical organisation, and an emphasis on recommendations. These aspects, in turn, are reflected in the lexico-grammatical choices that were characteristic of the business reports, such as the use of modals, nominalisation, impersonality and evaluative lexis.

However, in spite of this abundance of research on genres of professional communication, categorising genres and perhaps even devising taxonomies are not straightforward undertakings. It is thus perhaps not surprising that there are not many taxonomies of professional genres. One exception is Koester (2006), who identifies three different 'macro-genres' of professional communication in her corpus of American and British office talk (ABOT): unidirectional genres, collaborative genres and non-transactional genres.

In identifying these genres, Koester first distinguishes between transactional and non-transactional discourse (see also Chapter 1). The category of transactional discourse is further divided between unidirectional and collaborative talk. Unidirectional genres refer to those instances of communication where one interlocutor plays a more dominant role 'in so far as s/he imparts information the other participant does not possess, instructs/directs the other participant in some action to be taken, or requests some action from the interlocutor' (Koester 2006: 32). Instances of unidirectional genres in the ABOT corpus include among others service encounters, reporting and requesting. Collaborative genres, on the other hand, refer to those encounters where 'both (all) participants contribute more or less equally towards accomplishing the goal of the encounter (although there may still be some asymmetry in both the institutional and the discursive roles)' (Koester 2006: 32). Examples of collaborative genre in the ABOT corpus are making arrangements, decision making, and discussing and evaluating. Non-transactional discourse, then, includes the two specific genres of small talk and office gossip. The genre that occurs most frequently in the ABOT corpus is decision making, which accounts for 26 per cent of the interactions in the corpus.

Exercise 2.3

Using the taxonomy of different workplace genres proposed by Koester (2006), how would you classify the exchange in Example 2.8.? Are there any problems with this classification?

Example 2.8

Context: Two young women at work.

1.	I:	so how are things (amongst) your um +
2.		your holiday how was your holiday
3.	M:	oh it was really funny the holiday was like really really
4.		awesome
5.	I:	right
6.	M:	and then my first day back I was just like kicking back
7.		+ in my desk just
8.		just still really relaxed and I
9.	I:	trying to get back into it [laughs]

10.	M:	yeah and a girl from (my–) a woman from my section
11.		came up and
12.		said oh [inhales] do you want to do this horrible
13.		speech that I have to give
14.		in front of students for work day
15.		they had career work day thing and the students have
16.		to come in to the
17.		building and I said
18.	I:	yeah
19.	M:	yeah yeah sure I'll do it and she goes
20.		[surprised tone] really
21.		I thought I'd have to get down on my knees and BEG
22.		and I was going oh no no it's cool
23.		and I'm sure it was because I was just you know still in
24.		holiday mode
25.		'cause I don't normally like speaking in front of anyone
26.		[laughs] but
27.	I:	yeah
28.	M:	yeah I agreed (to) and it was fine
29.	I:	so you might have um taken er a while
30.	M:	so [laughs]
31.	I:	longer t-to come to the decision (would you) [laughs]
32.	M:	yeah oh yeah I would have gone no no go away
33.		but yeah it was really good
34.	I:	it was a good trip oh (okay)
35.	M:	yeah but now back into it again
36.	I:	yeah things are pretty full on here
37.	M:	yeah I can imagine
38.	I:	mm sort of working I just did my first submission +
39.		for the minister

Source: Holmes (2000a: 44–5).

As this example illustrates, the boundaries between different genres are often fuzzy, and it is not always easy to decide how to classify a particular exchange. Koester (2006) acknowledges this herself in her discussion of some instances of advice giving which display elements of both unidirectional and collaborative genres. In dealing with these instances, she suggests that '[t]he distinction between collaborative and unidirectional discourse is not always a sharp one, but should be seen as a cline along which some interactions are more collaborative or unidirectional than others' (Koester 2006: 50). The same could be said to apply to the distinction between transactionally oriented and non-transactional genres where the boundaries are equally fuzzy (see also Chapter 1). Another difficulty in identifying genres relates to the question of whether certain communicative events, such as decision making, constitute genres in their own right or whether they should be more productively viewed as subgenres. As we have seen, sometimes communicative events that share the same name may differ remarkably from each other, such as the various events that fall under the broad umbrella of meetings.

What is a meeting?

'[M]eetings are the very stuff of "work"' (Holmes and Stubbe 2003b: 56). They are a typical aspect of many workplaces. As was shown in some of the examples in Section A, meetings come in different forms and sizes: in addition to the relatively formal staff meetings and the rather informal briefing meetings mentioned above, there are also other types of meetings, such as external meetings with clients or potential partners from another company and public meetings, for example of some government committees. Meetings usually have various purposes, including reporting, updating, decision making, exploring and problem solving. And they may take place in different locations as Pan, Scollon and Scollon (2002) explain:

> [r]eal business meetings take place in conference rooms, of course, but also in corridors, at the water cooler and office coffee machines, on the metro or subway on the way to or from offices, in airport lounges, at lunches, or in coffee shops.

Given this diversity in form and purpose of what people tend to refer to as meetings, it is perhaps not surprising that the question 'what is a meeting?' is rather complex and continues to capture researchers' interest (e.g. Boden 1994; Handford 2010; Holmes and Stubbe 2003b; Bargiela-Chiappini and Harris 1997b). And while a lot could be said about this question (for example, in terms of the underlying essentialist assumptions of such a question), what is of interest to us here is whether meetings constitute a genre. Perhaps not surprisingly, given such a diversity of interactions that fall under the umbrella of the category meeting, there is no agreement among researchers on this issue. Koester (2010: 28), for example, does not classify meetings as a genre because of the different purposes these events may have. Rather, she proposes to view meetings as a secondary genre 'with a recognized cultural identity in the workplace'. She thereby contrasts meetings with primary genres (such as decision making) which may also occur in other contexts outside the workplace. Others, including Bargiela-Chiappini and Harris (1997b), Angouri and Marra (2010) and Handford (2010), do treat meetings as a genre, based on a range of similarities in terms of structural features and certain practices and strategies that are shared by all meetings.

For example, based on an analysis of informal meetings in different sociocultural contexts, Angouri and Marra (2010) argue that the activity of chairing crucially contributes to the idea of meetings as a genre. And Handford (2010: 69) maintains that '[b]usiness meetings lend themselves to genre categorization, because they tend to have relatively clear beginnings and endings' which, in turn, 'may involve highly conventionalized practices and give rise to formulaic language'. Based on an analysis of spoken data from 26 companies of different types and sizes mostly located in the UK (but also in other European countries and in Japan) he proposes the meeting structure summarised in Figure 2.1.

Stage pre-2 is an optional stage during which work is done that might potentially be relevant for the subsequent meeting, such as distributing the agenda and making relevant decisions before the meeting. Stage pre-1 also takes place before the meeting is officially opened; it may include a discussion of the meeting topic, other work-related issues as well as small talk. Stage 1 is a necessary stage at which the meeting 'begins when a quorum of participants is present and then the issues to be discussed are highlighted' (Handford 2010: 72). The chair or most senior person in the meeting usually plays a crucial role in this stage. Stage 2 is the heart of many (but not all) meetings, and typically consists of several phases often around the discussion of the agenda. Such discussions can be either linear or spiral/cyclical, and some meetings display elements of both. For example, based on data collected in fourteen different workplaces in New Zealand, Holmes and Stubbe (2003b: 68) observed that in their Language in the Workplace corpus 'linear sections of meetings tended to follow an explicit or implicit agenda relatively closely, while spiral sections were more exploratory'. During the next stage, Stage 3, the meeting as such is closed, while Stage 4 'concerns the effects and repercussions of the meeting, such as another meeting at a later date, a change (not) implemented following the meeting, or a nullification of the relationship between two companies' (Handford 2010: 75). Including pre-meeting and post-meeting stages in such a meeting structure is very useful and accounts for the observation that in some workplaces important negotiations take place and decisions are reached before the actual meeting (e.g. Pan et al. 2002).

The different stages of meetings are characterised by specific recurring discursive practices, such as summarising (for instance, progress or information) and bringing discussions on track, which may, of course, differ across meetings. These practices, in turn, are realised by certain lexico-grammatical features (see also Holmes and Stubbe 2003b). All these aspects contribute to shaping the meeting genre. However, Handford (2010: 89) cautions that although '[c]ertain lexico-grammatical features and various practices are commonly found in business meetings, ... it should not be deduced from this that they will always be found in that particular type of meeting'. There is thus clearly no one-to-one relation between the occurrence of certain features and practices and specific genres.

Stage pre-2:	Meeting preparation
Stage pre-1:	Pre-meeting
Transition move	
Stage 1:	Opening of meeting
Transition move	
Stage 2:	Discussion of agenda
Transition move	
Stage 3:	Closing of meeting
Stage 4:	Post-meeting effects

Figure 2.1 Structural aspects of business meetings
Source: based on Handford (2010: 69).

Changing old and developing new genres

In the previous chapter it was argued that the dramatic changes in organisational reality have also affected the image and actual enactment of professional communication. These changes are particularly apparent with regard to genres of professional communication because as was outlined in Chapter 1, the work domain has undergone (and is still undergoing) considerable structural changes which include, for example, technological advances. These changes, in turn, have led to the introduction of a range of new media, as Louhiala-Salminen (2002: 213) observes:

> [i]n the last few years, faxes and email have replaced letters and telexes (Louhiala-Salminen, 1995, 1996, 1998). Mobile phones and voice mail have freed people from sitting in the office. Now the use of the Internet is spreading into the corporate world and will soon shake business practices and traditions, strengthening, for example, the position of email as a communication channel.

As this quotation indicates, one of the changes in organisational reality that has had particular wide-reaching implications for the existence and use of genres at work is the emergence of computer-mediated communication (Gimenez 2006; Flowerdew and Wan 2006; Akar and Louhiala-Salminen 1999). More specifically, the various new technological advancements and new technological practices that come with them have not only affected some of the old genres of professional communication, but the emergence of new modes has influenced changes in register, which in turn have given rise to some new genres. Email, for example, is becoming more and more important in professional communication – although some authors (such as Flowerdew and Wang 2006: 136) maintain that other genres such as 'faxes, and indeed posted letters, still play a very important role in certain forms of business communication'. However, while these old genres of communication remain important means to achieve specific communicative purposes, they too are affected by technological advancements and new business practices (Akar and Louhiala-Salminen 1999: 221).

These changes often result in new conventions and norms of doing business. And (changes in) communicative conventions of one genre or medium may also have an impact on other genres. For example, in comparing the language used in electronic and written business communication, Gimenez (2000: 249) found that 'the spoken nature of emails has started to affect the discursive practices in the context of interpersonal communication, making it more informal and personalized in many respects'.

With the increasing importance of computer-mediated communication in professional contexts, the use of email has also dramatically increased so that 'e-mail has almost replaced ordinary business letters in most contexts' (Jensen 2009: 16). Some people even wonder whether email may have become the most important means of professional communication (e.g. Koester 2010: 34). It is thus perhaps not surprising that a substantial amount of research has focused on email at work (e.g. Gimenez 2000; Nickerson 1999; Mulholland 1999; Jensen 2009). Yet, in spite of the popularity of email (both among users at work and among researchers as the subject of their studies), there seems to be an ongoing debate among researchers as to whether email should be classified as a genre in its own right or whether it should be viewed more productively as a medium through which a range of different genres may be enacted.

In an early study when email communication in the professional context was still (relatively speaking) in its infancy, Yates and Orlikowski (1992) explained how the memo genre has influenced email and other computer-mediated genres of professional communication. They argued that in spite of some similarities between the two (for instance, both are used for internal record-keeping and documentation purposes), there are also remarkable differences: for example, 'electronic mail differs from paper in its capabilities, creating new options and new constraints affecting the invocation of the memo genre' (1992: 317). Based on these observations, Yates and Orlikowski (1992) describe email as a medium rather than a genre (see also Jensen 2009).

One of the proponents of classifying emails as a genre is Nickerson (1999), who researched the use of English in the emails of a Dutch manager who works in a large multinational corporation. Her findings indicate that 'the use of English in electronic communication is embedded in the organizational practices of the corporation' (1999: 52). More specifically, the emails that Nickerson looked at displayed remarkable similarities with regards to their use of corporate communication patterns, communicative purpose, layout and lexical choice. She argues that, based on these similarities, it would be justified to describe these business emails as a genre. However, in a study comparing the email replies of American and Dutch companies to customer enquiries, van Mulken and van der Meer (2005: 106) came to the conclusion that 'there is no necessity to distinguish the electronic company replies from their paper-based counterparts' since there was little stylistic variation between company replies in email as opposed to paper format. Thus, rather than claiming the existence of different genres or subgenres, the authors argue that the observed differences are primarily related to the choice of medium, which has consequences for the register. And in a study of administrative emails at a university in Australia, Mulholland (1999: 58, 66–7) describes emails as a 'companion genre' which is always 'ancillary to other genres' in that, in her data, emails were hardly every used to perform 'major institutional communications'. These more formal communications (such as notices of appointments or meeting agendas) were typically presented in paper format. Some of these disagreements on whether email constitutes a distinct genre seem to be related to substantial differences in the use and functions of emails in different workplaces.

Another consequence of the increasing importance of computer-mediated communication and the general digitisation of many aspects of the work domain is the increasing importance of multimodal forms and genres of communication. As Bargiela-Chiappini et al. (2007: 49) maintain, 'the digitization age has been responsible for a shift from monomodality, expressed in static generic types such as the traditional, printed business letter, to increasingly complex and dynamic examples of "multimodality" (e.g. online commercial websites)'. In analysing these new, often web-based, media and genres, researchers often employ multimodal analyses in order to capture not only the meaning of text but also that of 'nonverbal, visual and sound components of the interaction' including images, captions, colours, as well as sound files and many more (Bargiela-Chiappini et al. 2007: 57). In order to account for and capture the increasing complexity and multimodality of social practices in professional contexts, it is becoming increasingly relevant for researchers to conduct multimodal analyses. Such an analysis could, for example, look at the use of images and characteristics of the layout in a particular text, including the use of colour, angles between items, different sizes of captions, texts and pictures and so on (see e.g. Kress and van Leeuwen 2001, 2006; Koller 2007; Marsh and White 2003). It could moreover explore what meanings are created through the interplay of the text and the other multimodal components.

> ### Exercise 2.4
>
> Collect five information brochures from similar kinds of companies and explore the ways in which meaning is created through the various modalities, including textual, rhetorical and visual features. You could, for example, focus on banks, leisure parks, car rentals or beauty spas. In approaching this task you may want to consider, for example, the interplay between text and images, as well as specific characteristics of the layout, the brochures' length, and the context in which the brochures are used to what purposes, and so on.

Using genres at work

Different workplaces, as well as different groups within the same workplace are often characterised by the use of different genres. More specifically (as will be elaborated in more detail in Chapter 3), the nature, structure and culture of a workplace all have a crucial impact on the kinds of genres that are used by members and on the specific ways in which these genres are put into practice. For example, Gunnarsson (1997: 41) notes that:

> [w]riting in an organization is not only a matter of knowing how to write a certain document for a specific audience but also a matter of knowing how to fit into the organizational structure and how to adapt to the organizational subculture and its norms, attitudes and values.
>
> (Gunnarsson 1997: 41; in dos Santos 2002: 168)

Thus, the genres that are regularly used by the members of a particular community at the same time characterise that particular group (Yates and Orlikowski 1992: 300). However, equally importantly, genres do not only constitute the means for specific professional individuals or groups to accomplish their ends but also tell their users what ends they may have. As Miller puts it, this includes learning 'that we may eulogize, apologize, recommend one person to another, instruct customers on behalf of a manufacturer, take on an official role, account for progress in achieving goals' (1984: 165) and so on. In this way, not only is the use of genres in a particular workplace influenced by its culture, but the genres that are regularly employed by members of a workplace or profession also have an impact on shaping and defining the nature and structure of work, which in turn influences the culture of this workplace (see also Chapter 3).

This also means that by looking at the genres that are typically used by members of a particular community, valuable insights may be gained about 'the way in which that community operates as a social group' (Bargiela-Chiappini and Nickerson 1999: 9). For example, in an analysis of the genres used by members of a specific discourse community, namely tax accountants in Hong Kong, Flowerdew and Wan (2006: 134) found that through the group's specific ways of communicating via the use of distinctive genres 'the accounting community at the same time is contributing to the discursive construction of the reality of the activity known as "accounting"'.

However, 'members of a community rarely depend on a single genre for their communication' but typically 'use multiple, different, and interacting genres over time' (Orlikowski and Yates 1994: 542 in Bargiela-Chiappini and Nickerson 1999: 12). And rather than relying exclusively on spoken or written genres, most professional groups use both – sometimes even simultaneously. This simultaneous use of genres is also reflected in a mixing of modes of communication, as Louhiala-Salminen (2002: 217) found when she observed a middle manager of a multinational corporation for a whole day:

> spoken and written communication were totally intertwined, there was hardly any activity in either mode where the other would not be present as well; many of the phone calls were to confirm an issue in an email message, email messages referred to phone calls, and they were constantly discussed in face to face communication with colleagues.

The observation that genres do not stand alone but tend to interact with other genres has been described with reference to intertextuality and interdiscursivity. These terms refer to links between different genres of texts or interactions. As Loos (1999: 315) notes, 'actors communicating with each other construct an intertextual network which is based on sequence of actions and which consists of both written and oral texts'. For example, in their face-to-face or videoconference meetings, professionals may refer to written documents (such as contracts), they may use PowerPoint and other visual aids, and they may make links to previous or subsequent spoken interactions (such as previous meetings or telephone conversations).

Figure 2.2 Mixed modes of communication

Similarly, written texts may also contain reference to previous or subsequent spoken interactions or written texts. According to Bakhtin (as cited in Akar and Louhiala-Salminen 1999: 216), '[a]ll utterances (or texts) are linked to prior texts they respond to, as well as future texts that they anticipate'. This link is particularly obvious in what are called 'embedded emails' (Gimenez 2006), where individual emails build on each other and where previous emails are included in the current one. The following two examples are taken from embedded emails: that is, they follow previous email exchanges which are included below these messages (but which have not been included in the excerpts below because of limitations of space).

Example 2.9

Context: Internal email between two colleagues at a non-profit organisation.

Betty
I have reviewed and updated this. Please remove yellow bits and email to Martina.
If she is happy, prepare for Sabitha's signature so that we give to Martina on Monday.
Thanks
Faye

The meaning of 'this' in the first sentence can only be deduced if the message is understood in the context of the other parts of the embedded email that precede this particular message between Betty and Faye on the same matter. In this case, 'this' refers to a contract that was saved under an electronic link that Betty had sent Fay in a previous email. The use of 'this' thus provides a link not only between this and previous emails but also between the email and the contract in both electronic as well as paper version. Other ways in which intertextuality is typically displayed include conventionalised ways of referring to other texts or communicative events, and highly contextualised language (Akar and Louhiala-Salminen 1999: 219).

Example 2.10

Context: Email written to an external client (Annalie) at same workplace as example above.

Dear Annalie
Thank you for your registration. Breakfast will be served. If you wish to have vegetarian food, please let me know.

The launch of [name of document] will take place on 23 October (8:30 – 10:30am) at [name of location]. Registration starts at 8:00am. We look forward to seeing you.

Please find the attached invoice for payment.

Do not hesitate to contact me if you need further information.

Best regards,

Betty

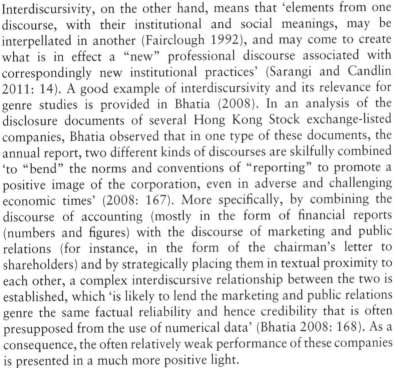

Exercise 2.5

Identify the intertextual links in the email in Example 2.10.

Interdiscursivity, on the other hand, means that 'elements from one discourse, with their institutional and social meanings, may be interpellated in another (Fairclough 1992), and may come to create what is in effect a "new" professional discourse associated with correspondingly new institutional practices' (Sarangi and Candlin 2011: 14). A good example of interdiscursivity and its relevance for genre studies is provided in Bhatia (2008). In an analysis of the disclosure documents of several Hong Kong Stock exchange-listed companies, Bhatia observed that in one type of these documents, the annual report, two different kinds of discourses are skilfully combined 'to "bend" the norms and conventions of "reporting" to promote a positive image of the corporation, even in adverse and challenging economic times' (2008: 167). More specifically, by combining the discourse of accounting (mostly in the form of financial reports (numbers and figures) with the discourse of marketing and public relations (for instance, in the form of the chairman's letter to shareholders) and by strategically placing them in textual proximity to each other, a complex interdiscursive relationship between the two is established, which 'is likely to lend the marketing and public relations genre the same factual reliability and hence credibility that is often presupposed from the use of numerical data' (Bhatia 2008: 168). As a consequence, the often relatively weak performance of these companies is presented in a much more positive light.

Now that we have explored the notion of genre and described some of the ways in which the various genres are used in professional contexts, the next section looks at how genres can be analysed and how specific features that characterise professional genres can be identified and described.

Section C: Analysing different genres of professional communication

Different ways of doing genre analysis

There are at least three different traditions of genre analysis: the New Rhetoric, the Sydney school and English for Specific Purposes (Hyon 1996; Swales 2009; Hyland 2003). The New Rhetoric school conceptualises genre as social action (Miller 1984), and research carried out in this tradition tends not to conduct close textual analysis but rather explores the context in which specific genres develop and the impact of institutional, cultural and other factors on the use of genres (e.g. Devitt 1991, 2004). According to this tradition, genre is conceptualised as 'social action' which acknowledges that 'a rhetorically sound definition of genre must be centred not on the substance or the form of discourse but on the action it is used to accomplish' (Miller 1984: 151; Yates and Orlikowski 1992). A particular focus of research carried out in this tradition is on 'the special purposes, or actions, that these genres fulfil within these situations' (Hyon 1996: 696; Hyland 2003). Thus in analysing genres, researchers in the New Rhetoric school often employ ethnographically oriented methodologies such as observation or interviews.

The Sydney school, on the other hand, builds on the work by Halliday (e.g. 1994) and views genres as 'staged goal-oriented social processes' (Martin 1997: 13). This approach to genre focuses on the functions or purposes that genres perform in a particular social context. Researchers in this tradition tend to have a pedagogical agenda, often linked to literacy teaching and 'empowering students with linguistic resources for social success' (Hyon 1996: 701), and typically conduct detailed analyses of how the various stages of a genre are realised linguistically. Thus, rather than considering the context in which specific genres emerge, they are primarily interested in text-internal, linguistic features that are characteristic of a particular genre.

Drawing on some of the methodologies used by the New Rhetoric and some of the analytic models proposed by the Sydney school, English for Specific Purposes (ESP) is a third tradition in genre analysis. Genre analysis within ESP is mainly based on the work of Swales (e.g. 1990) and Bhatia, who in his earlier work defined genres as 'recognizable communicative events, characterized by a set of communicative purpose(s) identified and mutually understood by members of the professional or academic community in which it regularly occurs' (Bhatia 1993: 13). Thus, ESP researchers tend to view communicative purpose as a crucial criterion in defining what constitutes a genre, paying less attention to the social context in which it appears. Like the Sydney school, research in the ESP tradition is also often characterised by a pedagogical agenda, and aims 'to offer an approach to the teaching of academic and research English', often to non-native speakers (Swales 1990: 1). However, as we have seen in Section B, more recent research has moved towards more dynamic views of genre which rely less heavily on communicative purpose as the distinguishing criterion of a genre, and which also acknowledge the role of the context (Askehave and Swales 2001; Swales 2009). As a consequence, the boundaries between the different traditions of genre analysis 'have become much less sharp – although by no means disappeared', as Askehave and Swales (2001: 147) maintain.

As the examples and research studies described in Sections A and B have shown, there are different ways of approaching genres in professional contexts. Depending on the tradition of genre analysis they subscribe to, some researchers are interested in looking at apparently similar communicative events across workplaces to see whether they can be usefully seen as belonging to the same genre (for instance, the discussion about whether email is a genre), while others focus on the ways that context influences genre (such as how meetings are done in different workplaces) and explore the use of various genres within a specific workplace or professional group (e.g. Devitt 1991; Louhiala-Salminen 2002; see also Koester 2010). And while all of these approaches promise to provide interesting insights into professional genres, the question remains – how to do genre analysis?

Methods of genre analysis

Considering the different schools or traditions outlined above, there are clearly multiple ways of approaching and analysing genres. Askehave and Swales (2001), for example, make a broad distinction between text-driven and context-driven procedures of analysing genres. A text-driven procedure may be particularly useful for looking at a particular genre in a specific context (or even comparing the same genre across contexts), whereas context-driven approaches may be more appropriate for an analysis of the various genres that occur in a particular context or that are used by a particular community. However, in spite of these different starting points and different foci of interest, both approaches tend to include (albeit to different degrees and at different stages of the analysis) an identification and description of genre-specific features as well as a consideration of the context in which they occur. Thus, as Koester (2006: 23) maintains, '[a] central concern in all descriptions of genre is how to account for both stability and variation in genre'. In other words, the question is how we can analyse and describe what constitutes a genre while considering both stability and hence predictability of a genre, as well as variation within a genre. The discussion around whether email is or is not a genre (as briefly summarised in Section B) is a good illustration of how important such an account is. In what follows, I will briefly outline just one of the many possible approaches to genre analysis which is often pursued by researchers within ESP.

In analysing texts (or talk), ESP researchers usually identify certain categories, so-called rhetorical moves, that tend to recur (often even in the same order) and that reflect the communicative purpose of the text or interaction. These moves can be obligatory or optional in the realisation of a particular genre. Once these moves have been identified, the next step is to describe and analyse the ways in which they are typically realised linguistically (Flowerdew and Wan 2006: 134). Bhatia (1993) outlines three levels on which genres may be analysed linguistically, that is, where the distinctive linguistic features of a particular genre are captured:

Level 1:   Analysis of lexico-grammatical features.
Level 2:   Analysis of text-patterning or textualization.
Level 3:   Structural interpretation of the text-genre.

An analysis of the lexico-grammatical features that characterise a particular genre often includes the quantitative (as well as qualitative) analysis of specific linguistic features that characterise a representative sample of a particular genre. This level of analysis may, for example, involve a statistical analysis of a corpus. An example of this can be found in Yeung (2007), who observed that the business reports she collected in different cultural contexts displayed similarities in their lexico-grammatical features, such as the use of modals, nominalisation, impersonality and evaluative lexis. While such an analysis may confirm (or challenge) initial hypotheses about the frequency of specific lexical or grammatical features in a text or genre, it does not explain how these features contribute to establishing the overall communicative purpose of that particular genre. An analysis of text-patterning (Level 2), on the other hand, explores 'the way members of a particular speech community assign restricted values to various aspects of language use' (Bhatia 1993: 26). This level of analysis explores, for example, the specific functions certain recurring syntactic structures may have on meaning creation. An example of this level of analysis is provided by Gimenez (2000: 241), who identified 'simple, straightforward syntactic structures, showing preference for co-ordinated rather than subordinated ideas' as being characteristic for the email messages that he studied. An analysis on Level 3, then, aims at identifying 'preferred ways of communicating intention' in a particular genre (Bhatia 1993: 29). Such an analysis often revolves around the identification and description of specific moves of the genre under investigation.

An example of this level of analysis are the four obligatory moves that characterise the business letters of negotiation that dos Santos (2002: 176) looked at:

Move 1:   Establishing the negotiation chain.
Move 2:   Providing information/answers.
Move 3:   Requesting information/favours.
Move 4:   Ending.

However, rather than viewing the various levels of analysis as distinctive and 'atomistic' steps, they should be viewed in a more holistic manner (Bhatia 1993: 40), and rather than prescribing a strictly linear and chronological approach (from Levels 1 to 3), it is up to the researcher to decide which level of analysis might be the most convenient to start with. As Bhatia maintains, 'analysis at any level helps the investigator to understand the structuring at other levels' (1993: 40–1) .

Exercise 2.6

In the business fax shown as Example 2.11, identify the rhetorical moves used by the writer and describe their communicative functions.

Example 2.11

Context: Business fax from a Finnish export company to a Korean customer.

1996-03-26

Sang San Industrial Co. Ltd
12-34 Young dang
Young dang
Korea

Fax.123-456-789-123

Attn. Director John Chang

Re. Your fax of 26th march

Dear Mr. John Chang,
Thank you for your telefax regarding the Fair in march.

We were glad to hear that the Fair was a success for you. Hope that you can get orders from ABC products.

If you need more leaflets, catalogues or information, please don't hesitate contacting us again.

We look forward to hearing from you soon.

Yours sincerely

For Vuorio and Co.
ABC-products

[signature]

Teija Tainio
P.O.Box 12   Tel. +385-12-12121212
FIN-12345 Vuorio   Fax +385-12-13131313

PS. Have sent you today Heliseam leaflets and price list.
Source: Louhiala-Salminen (1997: 325).

In addition to analysing the linguistic features of a particular genre, it is also crucial, as Bhatia (2008: 169) acknowledges, to consider text-external information and 'to integrate the analysis of professional genres with professional practices and cultures'. As a consequence of these more encompassing approaches to genre, more recent genre analyses do not exclusively focus on analysing 'the language used in isolated written texts or speech events' but rather explore 'contextualised communicative genres, emphasising the organisational and/or cultural factors' that have an impact on how specific communicative events are performed, as Nickerson (2005: 369) observes. Most instances of genre analysis within the ESP tradition thus include (some of) the following aspects: identification of recurring rhetorical moves, analysis of how these moves are realised linguistically, investigating of intertextual and interdiscursive links to other communicative events, and consideration of text-external information (including the context in which a communicative event takes place).

As some of the examples in this chapter have shown, genre analysis seems to be particularly useful when it is applied to written texts which progress through various moves (sometimes in a linear fashion). And although applying genre analysis to spoken interactions tends to be more difficult and complex – in particular in highly interactional sequences (Koester 2006) – as was established in Section B, genre analysis may provide a useful framework to analyse more ritualistic types of spoken professional interactions, such as meetings. Thus, as Koester (2010: 43) maintains, '[w]hile the notion of genre remains difficult to pin down, it nevertheless provides a useful lens through which to view workplace discourse'.

Summary

This chapter has explored some ways of conceptualising the diversity of professional communication in terms of genre. In particular, several instances of spoken and written professional communication were analysed in terms of similarities and differences in form and function. Similarities between differently named texts (a sales promotion and job application letter), as well as differences in interactions which share the same name (meetings) led to the conclusion that the labels assigned to specific communicative events may be misleading, and that a focus on form and function may often be more productive.

The notion of genre was introduced as a systematic way of describing the diversity of professional discourse. Although genres of professional communication have been the topic of many research studies, the boundaries between different genres are not always clear-cut but often remain fuzzy, and there is some variation in the ways in which specific genres may be realised. Genres do not constitute stable entities but are dynamic and regularly undergo changes. It is thus perhaps not surprising that as a result of the dramatic changes in organisational reality over past decades, genres of professional discourse have also changed and new modes have emerged (for example email and fax) which have led to the emergence of new genres. However, the kinds of genres that are typically used to perform specific functions, as well as the ways in which particular genres are realised, may vary considerably across workplaces and sometimes even across departments or working groups within the same workplace.

Most research on genres falls within the realm of one of the three major traditions of genre analysis: the New Rhetoric, the Sydney school, and ESP. Research carried out in these traditions has looked at a variety of different professional genres and has described the specific communicative function, as well as structural and linguistic features of these genres. In analysing genres of professional communication, researchers tend to employ a variety of methodologies, including quantitative and qualitative linguistically and ethnographically informed analyses.

The next chapter follows up on the observation that workplaces may differ significantly from each other in terms of the genres members use to perform particular functions. These differences are not only reflected in the use of genre but also in various other aspects of professional communication, and they are often linked to the specific culture of a workplace.

3   Workplace culture

This chapter explores how and why people in different workplaces tend to communicate differently. For example, while the employees of a particular workplace usually engage in a lot of small talk including personal topics, at another workplace people may hardly use any small talk, and if they do, this could involve relatively impersonal topics like sport and the weather. Equally, when it comes to decision making, the staff at one workplace may stick very closely to rules, regulations and approved practices while at other workplaces people tend to approach each problem individually, making up the rules as they solve the problems. These distinct ways of doing and saying things are particularly obvious to newcomers or outsiders when they enter a new workplace. People who are new to a work environment often notice how people communicate, dress or behave. For example, they might find the frequent use of expletives inappropriate, and they might be surprised to see that some people are not wearing shoes in the office. An important part of understanding what is going on in a workplace and of becoming a fully integrated member of that workplace involves identifying and learning some of these practices that characterise a particular workplace and that distinguish it from others.

Section A: Communicating differently in different workplaces

Swearing – taboo or acceptable behaviour?

Perhaps because of its multiple meanings, swearing is one of the linguistic practices that vary dramatically across workplaces, as Examples 3.1 to 3.3 show.

Example 3.1

Context: Ginette, a team coordinator, is talking to one of her subordinates, Russell who works as a packer. Both are Samoan.

1.   Russell: can you get me one please
2.   [in Samoan] :fa'amolemole: [please]

3.	Ginette:	you get one
4.	Russell:	ah you're not doing anything
5.	Ginette:	you go and get one
6.	Russell:	fuck it +++ fuck you
7.		get your fucking legs out here (fatters)
8.	Ginette:	why didn't you get one before
9.		I talked to you about that yesterday
10.	Russell:	because we're busy +
11.		I got to get all that out of the way

Source: Daly et al. (2004: 956).

From an outside perspective, the ways in which Russell talks to his superior (Ginette) in this example seem rather inappropriate: after Ginette refuses Russell's request (lines 1–3), Russell instead of accepting his boss's refusal, seems to almost attack her by accusing her of 'not doing anything' (line 4). These contestive and in-her-face challenges continue in lines 6 and 7 where Russell throws a range of expletives at Ginette: 'fuck it +++ fuck you' and an additional insult 'get your fucking legs out here (fatters)'.

However, while this kind of contestive and challenging in-your-face behaviour would probably be considered to be inappropriate in many workplace contexts, in particular when uttered by a subordinate towards his superior, in the factory context in which this example was recorded such behaviour is perfectly consistent with the interactional styles in which members of this particular team typically interact with each other (see Daly et al. 2004; Schnurr, Marra and Holmes 2008). This interpretation is not only supported by ethnographic data but is also shown in Ginette's responses to her subordinate's swearing. There is no indication in her responses that she is surprised or offended by Russell's behaviour. 'Rather she gives the kind of response one might expect between family members rather than co-workers' (Daly et al. 2004: 957): she is not going to help Russell because he got himself into the situation as he 'didn't get one before' when she actually reminded him of it (lines 8 and 9).

For members of this particular team (pseudonymed Power Rangers) frequent swearing, using insults and jocular abuse towards each other (including their boss) is normal, acceptable and appropriate behaviour. This observation can, at least partly, be explained by the type of workplace in which this behaviour occurs, namely a factory. However, although the fact that this workplace is blue-collar could have an impact on how people interact with each other, there is also some evidence that swearing (and other contestive and challenging behaviours) occurs in other kinds of workplaces including white-collar workplaces as the next two examples illustrate. The question of whether such behaviour is appropriate and acceptable is clearly more complex than simply distinguishing between different types of workplaces (such as blue-collar or white-collar).

Example 3.2

Context: A meeting of the senior management team at Company S, a white-collar IT company. The meeting is attended by five men. Victor is the managing director, Neil is new, but the others are well-established team members. Joel, another team member, is on a phone link.

1.	Shaun:	I get you two
2.		no nah I get you and Dean mixed up quite often mm
3.	Chester:	fuck off Shaun
4.	All:	//[laughter]\
5.	Chester:	/[laughs]: for the record:\\
6.	All:	[laughter]
7.	Neil:	Joel we're taping the session
8.		so we were trying to keep all four letter words out
9.		but that //hasn't really worked\
10.	Victor:	/[laughs]\\

[laughter throughout next turns]

11.	Shaun:	Chester was toning down his normal er
12.	Victor:	no they insist on us having //+ the normal meetings\
13.	Neil:	/yeah yeah\\ (yeah) yeah
14.	Chester:	oh right
15.	Neil:	it's two minutes thirty seconds into the
16.		discussion + they'll be thinking oh that's a record

Source: Schnurr and Holmes (2009: 109–10).

This brief exchange makes it clear that swearing is considered to be normal practice in this team. What is particularly interesting about this example is how interlocutors react to Chester's swearing (line 3). After some laughter, Neil (a newcomer) reminds Joel and the others, albeit tongue in-cheek, that they are recording the session and that thus they are 'trying to keep all four letter words out' (lines 7–9). This remark is then picked up by Shaun, who comments that Chester's swearing is actually toned down from his normal style (line 11). And Victor, the most senior person in the meeting, reinforces the view that Chester's behaviour is part of the normal (and thus acceptable) ways of talking in this team by reminding participants that they should not alter their behaviour just because they are being recorded for a research project (line 12). Even Neil's comment in the end further supports this interpretation when he humorously remarks that they had managed 'two minutes thirty seconds into the discussion' without producing a swear word, which for them is 'a record' (lines 15 and 16). In this white-collar workplace team, then, swearing (as well as jocular abuse and other contestive and challenging behaviours) is perceived as normal and appropriate ways of interacting with each other (see also Schnurr 2009b).

One more example is included here to show how swearing may be perceived in a workplace context. Example 3.3 is taken from the product review team in a manufacturing company.

Example 3.3

Context: At a meeting, staff of a manufacturing company are discussing how the company wastes money. Craig is the director, while Keith and Sharon are middle managers.

1.	Keith:	A form is a bloody form at the end of the day
2.		//for God's\ sake
3.	Craig:	/[laughs]\\
4.	Keith:	why do they //keep bloody changing it for all the
5.		time ( )\
6.	Sharon:	/[laughs]\\
7.	Keith:	because it pisses me off it really does

[laughter from all]

Source: Mullany (2007: 143).

In contrast to the examples above, in this workplace swearing does not seem to be part of how people normally communicate. At the beginning of the extract, Keith utters a series of expletives to express his frustration and anger over certain procedures (lines 1–2, 4–5, 7). However, unlike Russell's swearing in Example 3.1, Keith's choice of expletives seems a little weaker than Russell's (such as 'bloody' rather than 'fuck'), and Keith is complaining more generally about a form that 'they keep changing' (lines 4–5) rather than attacking an individual present during the meeting (as Russell does in Example 3.1). Moreover, in contrast to Example 3.1 Keith's swearing is perceived as inappropriate and marked in this particular workplace context, as the responses it receives illustrate. After each instance of swearing other participants laugh, thereby signalling that Keith is overstepping the boundaries of acceptable behaviour (Mullany 2007).

Clearly, different workplaces have developed specific norms of what counts as acceptable and unmarked behaviour, and what kinds of behaviour are unacceptable and hence marked. These workplace-specific differences are not only reflected in interlocutors' use of swearing and expletives but may involve virtually all aspects of communication, including transactional behaviours (such as making decisions and getting things done) as well as relational behaviours (such as appropriate ways of engaging in small talk) (see also Chapter 1).

Emails – why saying 'hi' may matter

Emails are another area where workplace-specific norms and expectations have an important impact on people's communication styles. As was mentioned in Chapter 2, workplaces vary considerably in terms of which medium of communication is considered to be most appropriate for what communicative purpose. This also includes norms about the frequency and style of emails.

In a comparative study of email styles in two New Zealand workplaces, Waldvogel (2007), for example, found remarkable differences in the extent to which staff in both workplaces included greetings and closings in their emails. The observed differences were linked to different norms and characteristics of the different workplaces. One of the workplaces, SCT, an educational institution, is a government-funded provider of distance education and the other workplace, Revelinu, is a manufacturing plant. While most members of SCT have teaching or administrative jobs, one-third of the Revelinu's staff work as administrators and the remaining two-thirds work on the factory floor. Moreover, SCT has recently undergone major restructuring which resulted in 'low staff morale and a mistrust of management' (Waldvogel 2007: 456). At Revelinu, by contrast, staff typically have 'open and positive relationships' with each other and with their management, and the atmosphere of the workplace is generally direct, friendly and familial (Waldvogel 2007: 456).

Exercise 3.1

Based on this information about SCT and Revelinu, which of the two emails below do you think was sent by a member of which workplace. What makes you think so?

Example 3.4

Colin
I don't know if this has been dealt with yet. Is there any reason why Michael should not leave at [date]?
Thanks
Cecilia

Source: Waldvogel (2007: 465).

Example 3.5

> Hi Julie
> Attached is the amended letter. I'll give this to Sarndra on
> Tuesday. Please let me know if you think it needs any changes.
> bye
> Fred

Source: Waldvogel (2007: 465).

Doing leadership differently

One aspect of workplace realities that is particularly affected by
workplace specific norms, practices, and expectations is leadership. In
Chapter 7 the complexities of leadership are discussed in more detail,
but here I will briefly mention how notions of what is considered to
be effective leadership behaviour may vary considerably across
workplaces. A particular focus is on the ways in which these differences
are reflected on the level of discourse. Differences in perceptions of
effective leadership affect virtually all aspects of leadership discourse,
including making decisions, getting things done, providing feedback
and developing a vision.

Marra, Schnurr and Holmes (2006), for example, compared the
ways in which leaders from two companies behaved rather differently
in the weekly meetings with their respective teams. The specific focus
of their study is how these leaders opened their meetings, what role
they played in decision-making episodes, and how they participated in
humour with the other team members. Findings indicate that the
leaders, Clara and Tricia, accomplished these goals differently by
displaying communicative behaviours that reflect (and at the same
time reinforce) the distinctive characteristics of their workplace and
norms of how members of their respective teams typically interacted
with each other.

More specifically, in line with Clara's hierarchical organisation
where relatively masculine ways of interacting were the norm (see
Chapter 6), she 'opened meetings smartly, with no waiting for
latecomers, and made non-contentious decisions crisply, without
waiting for everyone to contribute a view' (Marra et al. 2006: 254).
However, Clara also sometimes downplayed her experience and
status; she usually joined in the humour of her subordinates and
employed other ways of taking account of her subordinates' face
needs. Tricia's workplace, by contrast, was more democratic and
egalitarian, where a more feminine style of interaction was perceived
as normative. These characteristics of Tricia's workplace are also
reflected (and reinforced) in her leadership style. In contrast to Clara,
Tricia put more emphasis on consulting her subordinates before
making decisions and on empowering her team. In particular, her

rather different approach to leadership meant that 'she waited for all participants to arrive before starting the meeting; she negotiated through to a decision that was acceptable to, and reflected the views of all; and she tended to hedge decisions and make suggestions rather than give directives' (Marra et al. 2006: 255). These differences in leadership style were further reflected in the ways in which Clara and Tricia participated in humour with their team members: 'Clara's team is competitive and challenging; when she initiates the humour the team members compete to contribute wittily', while in Tricia's more democratic workplace 'Tricia tends to take a background role in humorous sequences, supporting, but generally allowing other team members to develop the humour' (Marra et al. 2006: 255).

These examples show how the specific ways in which Clara and Tricia do leadership by communicating with the members of their respective teams are influenced by the norms that characterise their respective workplaces. However, the relationship between a workplace and the communicative patterns staff typically display is complex, as discussed in more detail below. Not only do workplaces influence the ways members talk, but members' communicative behaviours, in turn, also actively contribute to developing, reinforcing, and even challenging specific workplace norms. Hence, expectations of leadership and effective ways of doing leadership are not only influenced by the norms of a particular workplace, but they also impact considerably on creating and shaping these norms and practices (see also Chapter 7).

As Examples 3.1 to 3.5 have illustrated, it is crucial to consider the specific norms that characterise a workplace in order to understand and make sense of people's behaviour. So, questions of whether it is appropriate for people to swear, as well as, for example, how decisions are normally made, whether it is acceptable to criticise superiors, and so on are crucially important when it comes to understanding the communicative behaviours of a particular workplace. These distinctive ways in which members of different workplaces typically communicate with each other are often linked to specific normative communicative patterns as well as practices (and even ideologies). These aspects are conceptualised and captured in the concept of workplace culture, an important notion for professional communication that is introduced in more detail in the next section.

Section B: What is workplace culture?

Introducing workplace culture

The metaphor of organisational or workplace culture derives from anthropology and has only relatively recently been adopted by business science (Hofstede et al. 1990; Miller 1999). The concept of culture was originally introduced to organisational sciences and management studies in order to account for the relationship between culture and management (Morgan 1997: 119), but its importance for understanding organisational behaviour started to fully surface in the 1980s, where this metaphor was used increasingly to explain the various forms of 'behaviors within organizations' as well as 'the vast differences among organizations' (Luthans 1989; Modaff and DeWine 2002: 83). Since then much research has been conducted with the aim of developing theories and methodologies to investigate workplace cultures.

Two major paradigms emerged in research on workplace culture: culture as variable or 'objective identities' and culture as metaphor (Brown 1995: 7). Supporters of the first predominately descriptive approach view culture as something a workplace has. This strand of research aims at utilising insights into the culture of a workplace as 'an objectified tool of management control' (Wright 1994: 4). Researchers pursuing the latter approach, by contrast, understand culture as a social phenomenon, and employ various metaphors to capture the essence of what a workplace is (Hofstede 2001; Smircich 1983). Some metaphors to describe the culture of a workplace include, for example, the metaphors MACHINE and ORGANISM (Brown 1995: 7).

More recent theories, however, that have begun to replace these initial paradigms, emphasise the performative and dynamic nature of workplace culture and argue that it is created and negotiated through the interaction of members (Miller 1999: 96; Riad 2005). This approach to workplace culture explicitly acknowledges the crucial importance of discourse in the process of developing, shaping, maintaining, reinforcing and enacting the culture of a workplace. Modaff and DeWine, for instance, note that workplace culture is 'a communicative construction' which is 'created and recreated as people interact (communicate) over time' (2002: 88). Based on this definition, the complex concept of workplace culture is treated here as a system of shared meanings and values as reflected in the discursive and behavioural norms typically displayed by members that distinguish their workplace from others (see also Schnurr 2009b: 80; Robbins et al. 1998: 562; Wright 1994). Consequently, the communicative patterns described in Section A (including swearing, email openings and closings, and decision-making processes) all crucially contribute to shaping the culture of the workplace where they are used. For example, the fact that Tricia tends to make decisions conjointly after consulting her team members, reflects and at the same time reinforces the overall collaborative and supportive nature of her workplace. In contrast to earlier notions, then, such a definition emphasises the performative and dynamic nature of workplace culture, and acknowledges that it is created and negotiated through the interaction of organisational members (Miller 1994; Riad 2005).

In addition to differences in people's communicative behaviours, such as those described in Section A, workplace culture is, perhaps even more obviously, also reflected in documents in which the organisation describes itself. Some of these documents were briefly mentioned in Chapter 1, such as organisational values and codes of conduct. Documents like these, regardless of whether they are made available to a wider public or specifically targeted at current (or future) employees or clients, provide useful insights into a workplace, and more specifically into how this workplace perceives and portrays itself. Example 3.6 shows an extract of one such document, the mission statement of a health service trust.

Example 3.6

Our mission is to provide a high quality, accessible and responsive service by putting our patients at the heart of everything we do. Our philosophy is to treat people how we would want to be treated and ensure that no-one tries harder for patients.
To us, 'Every Patient Matters'.

Mission statements like this one typically describe what an organisation is all about. They refer to the purpose and aim of the organisation (in this case, 'to provide a high quality, accessible and responsive service') and they describe how this is to be achieved ('by putting our patients at the heart of everything we do'). However, whether these documents are an accurate reflection of that organisation's reality is a different issue. Nonetheless, mission statements are important documents which can be utilised to create, shape and change an organisation's culture. In this respect, they are one of the central – and most visible – aspects of an organisation's culture (Kirkbride and Chaw 1987). Moreover, nowadays most organisations have a mission statement, which Koller interprets as 'undoubtedly a symptom of the "professionalisation", that is, marketisation, of the public and voluntary sector, which have adopted many genres and practices, including discourse practices, of the corporate sector' (2011: 107–8; see also Chapter 1).

Exercise 3.2

Search the internet to find and compare the mission statements of three to five different organisations of the same type. You could, for example, look at different supermarket chains, consulting companies, hospitals or voluntary organisations. Identify similarities and differences between these mission statements and discuss possible reasons for them.

Workplace culture and gender

One aspect of workplace culture that has received a lot of attention recently is gender. It has been argued that the notion of gender is a crucial aspect of the culture of a workplace, and is of importance for the functioning and organisation of workplaces (Alvesson and Billing 1997; Brewis 2001; Calás and Smircich 1999; Gherardi 1995). The impact of gender on workplace culture is manifested on several levels. Not only are workplaces gendered but they also have an impact on how their members construct their own gender and professional identities. Hence, specific ways, for example of doing leadership, getting things done or chairing a meeting, not only vary considerably across workplaces (as the examples in Section A have shown), but are also gendered in different ways. For example, Clara's relatively unilateral and crisp decision-making style points to the relatively masculine culture of her workplace, while Tricia's more collaborative and inclusive approach is in line with a more feminine workplace culture (the specific ways in which certain linguistic practices are linked to gender are explained in more detail in Chapter 6).

Specific and often very distinct ways of doing gender in different workplaces have led to the assumption that there exist to different degrees relatively masculine and feminine workplaces. The gender of a workplace is reflected in demographic factors, behavioural tendencies, and communicative patterns. Among the demographic factors that contribute to the gender of a workplace are the number of male and female employees and the types of their occupations, as well as the kind of organisation they are working for, the degree of organisational hierarchy, and the nature of rules within their workplace. Gender may be reflected in members' behaviour in terms of how decisions are being made, through what processes conflicts are being solved, and how power is being exercised. Equally important, albeit often overlooked, are the communicative patterns typically displayed by members of a workplace (Berryman-Fink 1997; Holmes and Stubbe, 2003a).

But what exactly is meant by masculine and feminine workplaces? Feminine workplaces are typically characterised by non-hierarchical structures, 'openness of feelings, supportive social relationships and the integration of private and work life' (Alvesson and Billing 1997: 116). The communication in these workplaces is typically characterised by 'a marked orientation towards collaborative styles and processes of interaction, together with a high level of attention to the interpersonal dimension' (Holmes and Stubbe 2003a: 587f). Masculine workplaces, on the other hand, are often associated with hierarchical structures, competitiveness and an emphasis on outcomes rather than relationships (Hofstede 1997: 93). Hard, direct, conversational tones are normative ways of communicating with each other (Alvesson and Billing 1997:

116), and the humour in masculine workplaces is often characterised by rough joking, swearing and jocular abuse (Holmes and Stubbe 2003a: 589; Schnurr 2009b). The swearing exchanges displayed in Examples 3.1 and 3.2 (in Section A) are taken from relatively masculine workplaces, and nicely illustrate this rather rough banter and swearing that characterise staff's interactional styles. The gender of a workplace is closely linked with the normative communicative practice of its members. In feminine workplaces elements ascribed to a feminine speech style are often viewed as normative ways of talking, while in masculine workplaces appropriate ways of interacting are often characterised by elements of a masculine speech style (as discussed in more detail in Chapter 6).

However, these characteristics describe stereotypes, and the gender of workplaces may be realised in a variety of ways and to different extents. Even within gendered workplaces people display a range of discursive strategies which are indexed for the opposite gender, and which are nevertheless perceived as normative and appropriate in this environment. Rather than constituting exclusive attributes of masculine and feminine workplaces, there is considerable overlap between those structures, practices and discourses that characterise the daily activities in which people engage (see Holmes and Stubbe 2003a; Schnurr 2009b). In other words, what counts as acceptable, normative feminine and masculine behaviour varies across workplaces and is negotiated in members' working groups.

A good example of a masculine workplace is Company S, a successful IT consulting company with headquarters in Wellington, New Zealand (see Schnurr 2009b). Example 3.2 in Section A is taken from this workplace. The masculine nature of this workplace is reflected on various levels including staff's perceptions and discourse, their everyday practices, and the overall make-up of the workforce. In interviews with the staff, for example, the workplace was described as a 'boys' club', and men were depicted as typical members, with women being 'marked' and to some extent singled out (see also Schnurr and Holmes 2009). This male dominance was further reflected in the fact that the vast majority of the staff were male, and most of the leadership positions were occupied by men. This was particularly true for the senior management team, which had exclusively male members. Stereotypical masculinity was also evident at various other levels, including dress and behaviours: women typically wore a suit and downplayed rather than emphasised their femininity through their clothing. The overall masculine nature of this workplace was also reflected in members' practices. For example, particular emphasis was put on individual achievements rather than on teamwork. This orientation towards outcomes (rather than processes or relationships) was reflected, for example, in the company's reward system: successful individuals literally rang a bell to make everyone aware of their success, and staff remuneration was based on individual performance (or 'talent management', as it was called by organisational members). These ways of rewarding and encouraging successful individuals rather than entire teams reflect the emphasis masculine workplaces put on result-based rewards rather than on processes.

The masculine nature of Company S was also shown in staff's discursive behaviours, and in particular their style of humour. Humour among members of Company S's senior management team, for example, was characterised by frequent use of challenging humour including 'biting' teasing (Boxer and Cortés-Conde 1997; Schnurr 2009a) and jocular abuse; the humour of organisational members was mostly constructed competitively with participants trying to outwit each other and fighting over who had the last word (for more details see Schnurr 2009b). Thus, the rather masculine and competitive nature of Company S was to some extent also reflected as well as maintained and reinforced in the ways in which interlocutors conjointly constructed humorous instances. However, although the overall nature of this company was clearly masculine, this would not necessarily exclude all feminine practices. And indeed, there is some evidence that participants also at times employed behaviours associated with femininity, such as mediating between people with differing views without explicitly agreeing with any of them. But what is interesting and noteworthy about these kinds of behaviour in Company S is that they were often perceived as marked behaviour, and such display of femininity was typically somewhat mitigated by subsequent displays of masculinity which seemed to reinstall norms of acceptable (normatively masculine) behaviour and the status quo (see Schnurr 2009b: 120–2).

The notion of gendered workplaces is also discussed by Baxter (2010), who observed three different types of gendered corporations among the British companies that she researched: the male-dominated corporation, the gender-divided corporation, and the gender-multiple corporation. Baxter's notion of male-dominated corporations is roughly equivalent with what I have described above as masculine workplace culture. These corporate environments are characterised by 'a patriarchal view of gender relations', which is, for example, reflected in the assumption that leaders are typically male and that women's role is limited to providing support functions (Baxter 2010: 17–18). Gender-divided corporations, on the other hand, are based on the assumption that men and women are inherently different but equal. This belief is, for example, instantiated in the different roles that men and women typically take on in these workplaces. While most senior management positions are occupied by men, women are typically found in administrative and clerical posts – because, as Baxter notes, 'they are deemed to be better equipped for these roles' (2010: 20). In gender-multiple corporations, by contrast, gender is not seen as the most important and distinguishing criterion along which individuals are characterised and assigned specific roles and positions. Rather, in these corporations, managerial positions are relatively equally shared between men and women, and women and men are treated equally, for example, in terms of promotion and mentoring opportunities.

Exercise 3.3

What do you think of Baxter's (2010) typology of gendered corporations? What are some of the advantages and disadvantages of categorising workplaces in this way? Do her observations reflect your own experience of places where you have worked?

Why workplace culture is important for professional communication

It is important to note that the culture of a workplace is not simply a negligible aspect of a company's performance but is one of the most significant aspects of any workplace, as it influences organisational life and members' behaviours on various levels. On one level, workplace culture has an impact on people's job satisfaction, which in turn may lead to higher job retention and higher productivity (Hagner and DiLeo 1993: 29). In addition to these benefits, which are ultimately measurable in transactional outcomes, workplace culture also performs a variety of other functions. For example, it provides mechanisms for sense-making and control, and it conveys a sense of identity (Robbins et al. 1998: 566). In this sense, the culture of a workplace provides the bigger framework for how actions and behaviours of its members are to be interpreted and understood.

In terms of research on professional communication this also means that it is crucial to always consider the culture of a workplace. Only if this level of context in which interactions occur is taken into account, can we understand the complexities of the communicative processes taking place. In other words, only if we know how things are typically done in a particular workplace can we make sense of people's communicative practices. Only if we know that staff typically expect to be consulted and have their say in decision-making processes can we understand why Tricia's decision-making episodes (as outlined in Section A) may appear rather lengthy and inefficient from an outsider perspective but are judged as absolutely normal and effective by insiders. Similarly, knowing that the workplace atmosphere at Revelinu is generally friendly and familial and that employees put a great effort into establishing and maintaining positive relationships with each other (as established in Section A) helps our interpretation of staff's email practices. Such information is particularly useful for understanding the implications if an email does not include a greeting or closing. Thus, being aware of the culture of a workplace is an important prerequisite for understanding of what is going on in that workplace.

Exercise 3.4

Based on your knowledge about the Power Rangers team (as discussed in Section A), how would you interpret Peter's final comment (line 8) in the exchange below?

Example 3.7

Context: Wellington factory packing floor. Ginette, the team coordinator, radios Peter (in the control room) to update the team on the packing line situation.

1. Ginette: copy control copy control
2. Peter: oh + good afternoon where have you been +
3. Ginette: who wants to know
4. Peter: well we do + + +
5. Ginette: um we're just gonna– run our fifth [product name]
6.   and see how this packaging holds if it's okay
7.   i– and then wait and we'll get back to you
8: Peter: ( ) thank you very much for your information
Source: Schnurr et al. (2008: 217).

Subcultures

Although the notion of workplace culture is quite intriguing, it is important to note that the assumption that a workplace is characterised by only one culture is rather misleading. Instead, workplaces, in particular larger ones, typically house multiple subcultures which all contribute to the overall culture of that workplace. These subcultures may 'co-exist in harmony, conflict or indifference to each other' (Frost et al. 1991 as cited in Miller 1999: 97; see also Schein 1992; Waddell, Cummings and Worley 2000).

Subcultures develop on different levels within a workplace and for various reasons. They emerge, for example, among members of specific departments (such as administrative departments and the factory floor), or they develop among people who do not necessarily work at the same workplace but who share the same occupation. The latter kind of subculture is often referred to as 'occupational culture'

(Hofstede 2001). Members of specific occupational cultures, such as people who work in IT, typically 'identify primarily with their type of job or occupation' rather than with their specific employer (Hofstede 2001: 414; Trice 1993). As a consequence, these people often feel more attached to their profession than to a specific workplace or employer, which could result in frequent workplace changes (as is, for example, typical for IT workers).

The existence of various subcultures is also reflected in the different discursive repertoires of members of different sections or departments within a workplace. In a study of humour at a lorry factory, for instance, Collinson (1988: 86) found that members of the various departments differed from each other with regard to the type of humour they typically employed. Staff working in the components division predominately used 'uncompromising banter ... which was permeated by uninhibited swearing, mutual ridicule, display of sexuality and "pranks"'. This rather challenging and often contestive humour was in stark contrast to the 'exaggerated and elevated above the middle class politeness, cleanliness and more restrained demeanour' displayed by the factory's administrative personnel (Collinson 1988: 86). In this workplace, then, the types of humour that are perceived as appropriate for performing particular functions, as well as the frequency with which they are employed, varied significantly across departments. By drawing on these distinctive ways of speaking, interlocutors at the same time signal their membership in these groups and contribute to maintaining and reinforcing the distinctive aspects of the subcultures at their workplaces.

In the next section three theoretical approaches are introduced that are frequently used to capture and describe the different practices, values and beliefs that contribute to the notion of workplace culture: the models of organisational culture[1] developed by Schein (1987, 1992) and Hofstede et al. (1990), and the concept of community of practice developed by Lave and Wenger (1991).

Section C: Theorising workplace culture

Schein's model of organisational culture

One of the most influential researchers on organisational culture is Edgar Schein, who developed a comprehensive definition of organisational culture which is still widely employed (e.g. Aaltio and Mills 2002; Hatch 1997). According to Schein (1987: 262) organisational culture consists of the:

> pattern of basic assumptions that a given group has invented, discovered, or developed in learning to cope with problems of

external adaptation and internal integration, and that have worked well enough to be considered valid, and, therefore, to be taught to new members as the correct way to perceive, think, and feel in relation to those problems.

Hence, organisational culture provides normative ways of thinking and behaving which members typically adopt and adapt to in order to make sense of the organisational environment and to deal with its challenges.

Schein (1987, 1992) claims that organisational culture is observable on three levels: artefacts, espoused values and basic assumptions. Artefacts reflect organisational culture on the surface level; they include perceptible phenomena of a particular organisation, such as language, architecture, technology, artistic creations, clothing styles, 'manners of address, emotional displays, myths, and stories told about the organization' (Schein 1992: 17). The following example of how artefacts reveal insights into an organisation's culture is provided by Brown (1995: 9–10):

> in most universities academics tend to be accommodated in individual offices, reflecting not only the nature of the work they conduct but an ethic of individual autonomy and independence. In contrast, in an organisation like Digital Equipment Company most office space is open-plan, reflecting a cultural inclination for cooperation and teamwork, and for control through peer pressure.

Further examples of organisational artefacts are corporate logos and mission statements (see Example 3.6 and Chapter 5). However, in contrast to artefacts, which are 'easy to observe and very difficult to decipher' (Schein 1992: 17), espoused values and basic assumptions are believed to constitute the 'core of an organization's culture' (Hatch 1997: 210).

According to Schein (1992: 9), an organisation's values typically describe 'what "ought to happen"' in the organisation in form of 'articulated, publicly announced principles and values that the group claims to be trying to achieve'. Common themes of values include 'satisfying customers, achieving excellence in products or services, providing an innovative product or service, developing and empowering employees, and making important contributions to society' (Yukl 2002: 284). However, as discussed in Chapter 1, these values are not necessarily consistent with what is actually happening. Nevertheless, they provide valuable insights into the culture of a workplace and in particular into how an organisation perceives itself and its members. They also help identifying what differentiates one workplace from another.

In contrast to values, basic assumptions are those beliefs which 'we neither confront nor debate and hence are extremely difficult to change' (Schein 1992: 22). They 'refer to the implicit, deeply rooted assumptions people share, and which guide their perceptions, feelings and emotions about things' (Brown 1995: 22). They often deal with fundamental issues of life, such as for example, the nature of interpersonal relationships. These assumptions thus not only form around aspects of a particular workplace, they also reflect more general beliefs about life.

Schein's model of organisational culture is summarised in Figure 3.1.

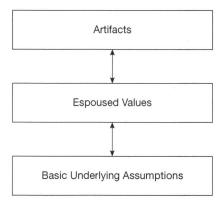

Figure 3.1 Levels of culture
Source: based on Schein (1992: 17).

According to Schein's approach, then, in order to assess an organisation's culture it is necessary to bring to the surface the characteristics of the organisation as manifested on the three levels of artefacts, espoused values and basic underlying assumptions. He suggests combining different methodological tools to achieve this, including conducting interviews and possibly surveys with organisational members and newcomers, ethnographic observation, analysing documents dealing with the organisation's history, and consulting organisational insiders regarding 'the anomalies or puzzling features observed or uncovered in interviews' (based on Schein 1987: 274–5). This qualitative approach to organisational culture is based on the assumption that 'culture is ubiquitous' and that organisational insiders constitute valuable resources for providing crucial support for the researcher in order to reveal and 'decipher what is really going on in a particular organization' (based on Schein 1992: 148; 2000: 130–1).

Hofstede et al.'s dimensions of organisational culture

A different approach to organisational culture is pursued by Geert Hofstede and his colleagues (Hofstede et al. 1990), who understand organisational culture as 'the collective programming of the mind that distinguishes the members of one organization from another' (Hofstede 2001: 391). According to this approach, organisational cultures are manifested and reinforced in symbols, heroes and rituals. Figure 3.2 illustrates Hofstede and his colleagues' conceptualisation of organisational culture.

In this model, symbols include 'words, gestures, pictures of objects that carry a particular meaning which is only recognised by those who share the culture' (Hofstede 1997: 7). Typical examples of symbols include corporate logos or particular behaviours that carry specific meanings in a particular workplace (such as working long hours to demonstrate commitment to the organisation). Heroes 'are persons, alive or dead, real or imaginary, who possess characteristics which are highly prized in a culture, and who serve as models for behavior' (Hofstede 1997: 8). Typical examples of heroes are the founders of an organisation and exceptional employees who embody the organisation's values particularly well. Rituals are certain collective activities which

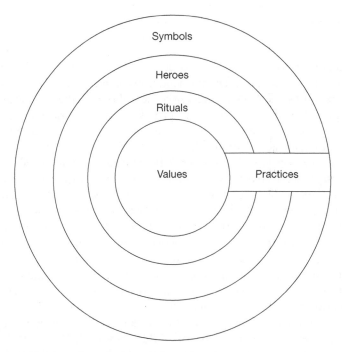

Figure 3.2 Manifestations of culture: from shallow to deep
Source: Hofstede et al. (1990: 291).

reflect and reinforce acceptable and expected behaviours. Examples of rituals are induction programmes, after-work parties and annual performance reviews. Due to the repetitive nature of these rituals they not only reflect but also reinforce an organisation's culture (see also Alvesson and Billing 1997; Robbins et al. 1998).

In contrast to Schein, Hofstede and colleagues argue that culture is quantitatively measurable (Hofstede et al. 1990: 287). In a classic study of ten organisations in the Netherlands and Denmark, he and his associates identified six dimensions along which cultures of different organisations can be compared. These dimensions, which describe differences with regard to the practices in which organisational members typically engage, are displayed in Table 3.1.

Table 3.1 Six dimensions of organisational culture

Dimension	
I	process-oriented vs results-oriented
II	employee-oriented vs job-oriented
III	parochial vs professional
IV	open system vs closed system
V	loose control vs tight control
VI	normative vs pragmatic

Source: Hofstede et al. (1990).

The six dimensions measure employees' perceptions regarding the degree to which they enact the different orientations of the various dimensions in their practices. The first dimension describes whether a particular workplace is more concerned with processes (process-oriented) or with outcomes (results-oriented). The second dimension measures whether an organisation focuses predominantly on its staff (employee-oriented) or on 'getting the job done' (job-oriented) (Hofstede et al. 1990: 303). Dimension three refers to different sources of members' identity: parochial means those 'units whose employees derive their identity largely from the organization' while professional describes those 'units in which people identify with their type of job' (Hofstede et al. 1990: 304). The fourth dimension distinguishes between open and closed systems regarding the organisation's communication habits, and the fifth dimension captures the amount of control mechanisms and internal structures that are in place. The sixth dimension measures an organisation's orientation towards its customers: '[p]ragmatic units are market-driven [whereas] normative units perceive their task toward the outside world as the implementation of inviolable rules' (Hofstede et al. 1990: 304).

According to Hofstede and colleagues, the degree to which these six dimensions are put into practice by organisational members is best examined in interviews with selected participants. These interviews could form the basis on which a questionnaire is developed, which is then further distributed to all organisational members. It is the responses from the questionnaires that eventually enable the researcher to assess and understand an organisation's culture. In this combination 'of a qualitative approach for depth and empathy with a quantitative approach for confirmation', Hofstede (2001: 393) sees a way to achieve 'objectivity and generalizability, plus pep talks and "war stories"'.

In spite of the appeal of the two models of organisational culture introduced here, it is crucial to bear in mind that 'actual organisational cultures are not as neat and tidy as the models seem to imply' (Brown 1995: 9). Rather, organisational realities are typically more complex and dynamic than these models suggest. Moreover, the cultures of workplaces are not static but change over time. For example, in a study of two leaders who succeeded each other in a New Zealand workplace, Holmes and colleagues (2007) show how the culture of the workplace changed as a consequence of the change in leadership. More specifically, differences in how the leaders managed meetings clearly reflected how the meaning of the specific cultural values of teamwork and individual accountability had changed with the arrival of the new leader. In particular, the first leader typically displayed a participative and democratic leadership style which reflected the emphasis she put on empowering staff, and ensuring collaboration and consultation. The succeeding leader's more report-like style and the fact that during the meetings individuals were selected to comment on particular issues, on the other hand, indicated his emphasis on individual accountability.

By describing a particular workplace in terms of the concepts introduced in the models described above, important aspects of its culture(s) – and of what makes this workplace special – can be captured. These characteristics, as we have seen in Sections A and B, may in turn provide valuable insights which are crucial for an understanding of people's communicative practices. These insights assist an interpretation of distinctive communicative practices within the specific context in which they appear, and they also provide explanations for why these practices sometimes vary considerably across workplaces (or even across teams within the same workplace).

Although both models of organisational culture introduced above acknowledge the role of language to some extent (for example in the form of artefacts, values and symbols), this does not go far enough in terms of explaining some of the differences in communicative practices displayed by members of different workplaces (as shown in the examples in Section A). Thus, a third model is introduced here which focuses more explicitly on the central role of language and

TC

Exercise 3.5

Choose one of the approaches to organisational culture introduced in this section and apply it to a real workplace. Describe as many aspects of the culture of your chosen workplace as possible. You could write about a place where you have worked previously (or where you are currently working) but you may also choose to write about any other workplace to which you have some access. Once you have identified a suitable workplace, think about ways of capturing its culture. The specific tools you use for doing so will depend on how familiar you are with that workplace and how much access you have. Depending on access, you could, for example, conduct interviews with staff, undertake ethnographic observation, consult organisational documents (including written versions of values and mission statements), administer surveys and so on.[2] Even if none of these options seem viable you should at least be able to obtain some relevant information about the culture of your chosen workplace through publically available sources such as the internet, brochures for clients and press releases. A good starting point for this exercise may be to explore the mission statement and values of your chosen workplace and to describe the overall ways in which the organisation presents itself, in particular to potential clients and staff.

communication: the community of practice (henceforth CofP). The CofP is particularly popular among research conducted within applied linguistics where it is specifically used to explore the communicative practices that characterise a particular workplace.

Community of practice

If we take as our starting point the assumption that '[t]he culture of a workplace is constantly being instantiated in on-going talk and action' (Holmes and Marra 2002c: 1685), none of the models outlined above go far enough in explaining the communicative processes through which language contributes to creating and shaping the culture of a workplace. The concept of CofP is particularly useful for exploring these processes.

The concept of a CofP was originally outlined by Lave and Wenger (1991) and further developed by Wenger (1998) to account for the processes involved in learning how to become a member in a new group (for instance when joining a new workplace). Based on this research Eckert and McConnell-Ginet (1992: 464) formulated a widely cited definition of a community of practice as:

> an aggregate of people who come together around mutual engagement in an endeavor. Ways of doing things, ways of talking,

beliefs, values, power relations – in short practices – emerge in the course of this mutual endeavor.

This definition is frequently adopted by research in applied linguistics, in particular in workplace contexts (e.g. Marra et al. 2006; Holmes and Stubbe 2003a; Mullany 2006). Joining a new workplace (or any other CofP) typically involves learning the behavioural and communicative practices that characterise this group and that distinguish it from another (see the swearing of the Power Rangers discussed in Section A). Since these behavioural and communicative practices (or the ways 'things are done here') form an integral aspect of the culture of this group or workplace, 'joining a community of practice inevitably involves acquiring the cultural norms of the community' (Holmes and Marra 2002c: 1685). In other words, learning to become a member of this group involves learning how to behave and communicate appropriately: that is, in ways that reflect this group's norms, values and practices.

In order to be classified as a community of practice, groups must fulfil three crucial requirements (Wenger 1998): members interact with each other regularly, in these encounters they negotiate a joint enterprise, and they develop a shared repertoire of discursive and behavioural norms. However, negotiating a joint enterprise does not necessarily imply that all members of a community of practice agree with each other. The focus is not so much on the sharing of a common goal, but rather on negotiating an enterprise which 'ought to contribute something meaningful to an understanding of the dynamics of the group involved' (Meyerhoff 2001: 528). The shared repertoire on the other hand, refers to the frequent use of certain discourse strategies, styles and behaviours which have become part of the distinct practices in which members of a community of practice engage (Wenger 1998: 83). Among the elements that may contribute to a shared repertoire are linguistic routines, gestures, and regular joint meals (Holmes and Meyerhoff 1999: 176).

Applied to a workplace context, the CofP model can explain why people at work have developed distinctive ways of communicating with each other (as the examples in Section A have shown). However, although applying the CofP concept to a workplace context is intriguing, the relationship between CofPs and the culture of the workplace in which they interact is complex. And not all workplaces can be characterised as CofPs. Relatively large workplaces, or those where staff of different departments or divisions do not frequently interact with each other, do not fulfil the three criteria outlined above. For example, not all members may interact regularly with each other. In fact, in many large organisations there may be relatively little communication among members of the different departments. In these cases, the workplace provides the wider context or background in which individual CofPs (such as departments or working groups) emerge. In these scenarios, the various aspects that characterise the culture of a workplace are incorporated and responded to in multiple ways in the various CofPs that make up a workplace.

In a study of humour in four New Zealand workplaces, for example, Holmes and Marra (2002c) show how different working teams or CofPs in these workplaces have developed distinct ways of using humour. The various CofPs differed from each other in the frequency, type and style of humour that people typically used in meetings. For example, some teams tended to use more or less supportive types of humour while others preferred more contestive humour (see also Schnurr 2009b Chapters 4 and 5). Holmes and Marra's observations illustrate that the specific ways in which members of these groups or CofPs use humour in their regular meetings are a reflection of the wider culture of their workplace. In other words, the practices, values, assumptions and so on that characterise a particular workplace are interpreted and given specific meaning in individual CofPs.

The concept of CofPs has also proven useful for capturing the notions of masculine and feminine workplaces (as outlined in Section B) and for understanding the (gendered) communicative practices displayed by members of these workplaces. In particular, a CofP approach enables researchers to explore how the gendered communication patterns that are regularly used by members of a particular group are linked to the shared practices of that group. For example, as was elaborated in Section B in more detail, the masculine nature of Company S is reflected in (and at the same time shaped through) the communicative patterns typically used by staff, which in turn are linked to some of the practices that characterise this particular group. In other words, the challenging and competitive humour, as well as the swearing and other contestive discursive practices that staff at Company S regularly draw on when interacting with each other, contribute to constructing the overall masculine and competitive nature of the workplace to a similar extent as women's rather masculine way of dressing, and the practice of individuals ringing a bell to make people aware of their success. Through these practices, then, the underlying values and assumptions that make up the culture of a workplace can be captured. Thus, by examining people's discursive behaviour within the context of specific CofPs it is possible to gain valuable insights into the various aspects of the culture and subcultures of a workplace.

Summary

This chapter has explored the concept of workplace culture and its relevance for professional communication. A particular focus was on the ways in which members of workplaces often develop distinctive ways of communicating with each other, which are reflected in, for example, interlocutors' use of swearing, appropriate ways of doing leadership, and normative ways of writing emails.

The metaphor of workplace culture aims to capture all those characteristics and practices that make a workplace what it is, and that distinguish it from similar workplaces. An important aspect of the culture of a workplace is whether it is more or less masculine or feminine. The gender of a workplace, like other aspects of workplace culture, is an important factor that impacts on the behaviour and experiences of individuals in a variety of ways. Thus, the culture of a workplace (including its various subcultures) needs to be taken into consideration when exploring any aspect of professional communication.

Three approaches to workplace culture have been introduced here. Schein's model of different levels of culture, and Hofstede and his colleagues' conceptualisation of culture as measurable along six different dimensions are useful for an understanding of workplace culture, but it is the concept of CofP which is particularly useful for investigations of the communicative practices that characterise a particular workplace culture.

Now that we have discussed some of the aspects that contribute to the culture of a particular workplace, the next chapter stays with the topic of culture and explores the role of national culture in professional encounters.

4 Culture and politeness at work

This chapter moves towards a more abstract conceptualisation of culture, and explores the role of (national) culture in professional encounters. A particular focus is on the complex relationship between national culture and politeness. A central concern of the chapter is to address the question whether culture is an issue at work – in particular in the increasingly multilingual and multicultural realities of many workplaces – and to explore what role politeness plays in these contexts. In line with recent research developments, this chapter challenges essentialist assumptions that tend to treat culture as the default explanation for a wide range of phenomena. Thus rather than assuming that in those situations where members from different countries interact and do business with each other, culture is relevant per se, I will start by exploring the question of whether culture is (really) an issue at work.

Section A: Is culture an issue at work?

Exercise 4.1

Read Example 4.1 and discuss whether or not you think this exchange occurred in an intercultural context. What makes you think so?

Example 4.1

Context: an internal management meeting.

1.	Terry:	yeah + does eighty minutes + include ATC
2.	Ron:	yes yes quite + but I mean that that's what the
3.		aeroplane physically exper
4.		I mean a purist would say that really we're looking
5.		for a twenty minute addition
6.		to the bloody sector time + not ten
7.	John:	[softly] don't swear like that
8.	[laughter]	

9. Chair: //yes\
10. Terry: /yes\\
11. Ron: so I mean we're still not really being honest with
12.   ourselves
13. Chair: //no\
14. Terry: /no\\
15. [general laughter]
16. Chair: no we are honest to ourselves for being realists +
17.   that's all it is
18. Ron: yeah + but don't be realists + be honest
19. [general laughter]

Source: Rogerson-Revell (2007: 19).

Answer Exercise 4.1 before reading on.

This data extract is taken from an internal management meeting at a large international airline corporation in South-East Asia. The meeting context can be characterised as intercultural since members have a range of different nationalities, including ethnic Chinese (Chair and Terry) and Anglophone expatriates (John and Ron). However, there is very little linguistic evidence in this exchange that marks it as intercultural despite the fact that the participants are from different countries. Rather, the ways in which interlocutors conjointly construct this humorous sequence indicates that they are a relatively close-knit group that has been working together for some time (and who may be classified as a community of practice (CofP) as discussed in the previous chapter). In particular, the frequent overlaps between Terry and the chair (lines 9/10 and 13/14) and the ways in which Ron skilfully draws on the chair's utterance and turns it into humour (lines 16–18) reflect that members have developed shared ways of interacting with each other.

This example has been included here to illustrate that, perhaps more often than not, communicating with members from different countries is not an issue but rather a normal part of the everyday realities in many workplaces around the world. This is particularly so since globalisation and the worldwide mobilisation of the workforce have led to an increased number of multicultural and multilingual workplaces (e.g. Lüdi, Höchle and Yanaprasart 2010). It has even been noted that 'the multilingual workplace is increasingly the norm in our evermore globalised economy' (Roberts and Campbell 2007: 415). It is thus common for many employees today to work and do business with members from a variety of different countries.

This multinational composition of the workforce is often seen as an asset rather than as an issue. In fact, some companies use the multinational profile of their members to portray themselves as global players. This is reflected, for example, in the 'who we are' rubric of the large international consulting company (also discussed in Chapter 5), which on its internet portal writes that

> We come from all over the world, with rich experience and all kinds of backgrounds and areas of expertise. We speak over 120 languages and represent over 100 nationalities.

Multicultural and multilingual aspects of a workforce may also have an impact on the ways in which members communicate with each other. On the most basic level this may include questions (and sometimes more or less explicit policies) about which languages are to be used in what function and what medium, and which language should be used as lingua franca between speakers with different native languages. The next example is an email from a highly multilingual workplace in Luxembourg where questions like these do not seem to be an issue.

Example 4.2[1]

> Liebe alle,
>
> wie angekuendigt treffen wir uns am [date and time] (thanks to Philippe for checking that the room – distributed by paper/pencil;) – is availalbe) ...
>
> afin de découvrir un travail de thèse de doctorant débutant (14-14:45) et de discuter des lectures faites (MAKE SURE YOU READ TO OF THE ARTICLES _PRIOR_ to the session.
>
> Message from Prof. [name]: Die artikel zur reading session on systems sind auf dem Blog verfügbar. http://xxx password: xxx
>
> NOTE – ALL active [name of system] useers (especially [other name] system) are invited to come at 13h as [name] will be available for discussing (the urgent) essentials! DONT FORGET!
>
> Happy Kleeschen!
>
> Petra

This email is quadrilingual: it starts off in German, then switches to English and to French before switching back to English, German and then English again. The sign-off or closing is in Luxembourgish (which is a reference to a Luxembourgish holiday celebrating St Nicholas at the beginning of December). Although multilingual communicative exchanges like this one may seem peculiar to an outsider, they constitute normal, appropriate and relatively unremarkable instances of communication for insiders who regularly and skilfully switch between languages when communicating with each other.

However, although multiculturalism has become an integral and often unremarkable aspect of many workplaces worldwide, in some instances it may become an issue and may be perceived as having an impact on various aspects of professional communication and behaviour, as the next example illustrates.

Cultural stereotypes and beyond

Example 4.3

Context: Interview with an Anglophone expatriate leader (Susan) in a major international corporation in Hong Kong. At the time of the interview Susan had worked and lived in China for just over two years.

What changed me I swore I'd never let this happen because when I arrived, I saw people, I saw managers and senior managers and partners doing things that I thought were really really not not appropriate and quite a dictatorial style and definitely power use, and powers came from, it was positional power. People are supposed to be using expert power. So I, you know, the use of relational power, I don't think it's effective.

Um, and coming to China what I realized is that the culture requires you in a way to do this, it actually requires you to act in ways that as a Westerner, foreigner, you find um, um, surprising. I don't think I'll have any difficulty when I return to work in other cultures. But you're always expected to act that way. If you don't, it confuses people, I think. It confuses the Chinese people who are working for you.

And I think what I learnt was that, um, that it worries the Chinese employees if you don't act this way. They actually don't know what to do if you don't use the hierarchical or positional power. Um, and they become worried and concerned and I call it, I call it 'the worried Chinese look' which is 'Oh my god, she's not doing what should be doing'. So you are forced in a way to change your management style and I find that odd. But then you have to do, what you have to do.

Source: Schnurr and Zayts (2012: 284).

In this quote, Susan, an expatriate who lives and works in Hong Kong, explicitly describes culture as having an impact on people's leadership performance. She recounts how she experienced that Western expatriates tend to change their leadership style in order to adapt to the culturally influenced expectations of the Chinese staff they are working with: 'the culture requires you in a way to do this, but actually requires you to act in ways that as a Westerner, foreigner, you find um, um, surprising'. Susan assigns these differences in leadership styles to what she perceives to be culturally motivated differences in exercising power: she believes that while Western cultures often appreciate expert power – that is, power which derives from an individual's 'knowledge, aptitude, and ability' (Dwyer 1993: 557; French and Raven 1959) – Eastern cultures tend to value positional power – that is, power that is based on an individual's position in an organisation (Northouse 1997, French and Raven 1959). According to Susan, in order to perform effectively as a leader she feels required to act in ways that take into consideration the specific expectations of her local Hong Kong Chinese staff which may often be in conflict with her own ideals of exercising power. Failure to adapt her leadership style to local cultural expectations may result in uncertainty and confusion among her subordinates, which she describes as 'the worried Chinese look'.

In cases like these, culture is often made an issue by participants and is used as an explanation for (perceived) differences in communicative and behavioural practices and expectations. The same applies to the following quotation which is taken from a book called *When Cultures Collide: Leading Across Cultures* which is targeted at practitioners (Lewis, 2006: 154):

> The purpose of a meeting depends on where one is coming from. Britons and Americans see a meeting as an opportunity to make decisions and get things done. The French see it as a forum where a briefing can be delivered to cover all aspects of a problem. They hunger for elegant processes. Germans, more concerned with precision and exactness, expect to gain compliance. Italians use meetings to evaluate support for their plans. The Japanese regard the first few sessions as occasions for establishing status and trust and finding out what possible sources of discord need to be eliminated from the outset.

While statements like these are clearly over-generalisations which tend to run the danger of stereotyping, there is often a perception, especially among practitioners, that members from different countries have remarkably different senses of what constitutes appropriate ways of doing business (see also Susan's quote above). Judged by the attention that business meetings have received, they seem to be one of the communicative events in which these cultural differences are perceived to be particularly relevant and obvious.

As was established in Chapter 2, meetings are a central aspect of many professional contexts. And although the proceedings and structures of meetings (as reflected for example in the various stages of a meeting) may follow relatively similar patterns in different countries, research studies have observed some variation among members of different countries regarding the purpose and function of meetings, as well as regarding what constitutes appropriate and expected behaviour in meeting contexts (Pan, Scollon and Scollon 2002: 109). For example, cross-cultural[2] research studies on meeting discourse (e.g. Miller 1994; Chan 2005; Yamada 1992; Bilbow 2002) have observed differences in terms of where decisions are made (in the meeting, before or after the meeting), who contributes to the discussions in the meeting and to what extent (and how this may be related to interlocutors' role and status), who has the right to decide when to move on with the agenda and to introduce a new topic, and when to engage in small talk on what topics and to what extent (see also Bubel 2006). In those instances where interlocutors may be unconscious of these differences in performing certain activities and communicative events, misunderstandings and sometimes even bewilderment and frustration may be the result.

For example, in a study of an American working in a Japanese advertising agency, Miller (1994) describes some of the difficulties the American and his Japanese colleagues were facing when discussing some of their clients. Recordings of an interaction show that a central source of interlocutors' misunderstanding was their different expectations of what kinds of activities should appropriately be performed in the meeting context in which their interaction took place. More specifically, some of the activities that the American would typically ascribe to meetings, such as establishing an agenda or solving problems and disagreements, were viewed by his Japanese colleagues as being more appropriate for pre-meeting interactions. As a consequence, the American's repeated questions and attempts to assign tasks to people and to set specific goals during the meeting were interpreted by his Japanese colleagues as being inappropriate and 'premature until they could conduct additional spadework activities, finding out what others felt about the account, what tasks and responsibilities people had in mind, and blocking out some of the outlines for a plan of action prior to scheduling a meeting' (Miller 1994: 234). The reactions and behaviours of the Japanese, in turn, were perceived by the American as 'being too indecisive' and as 'attempting to exclude him [the American] from participating in planning a meeting' (Miller 1994: 234).

Exercise 4.2

Have you ever encountered such a 'cultural misunderstanding'? If yes, describe what happened in this incident and discuss how you would explain what factors have led to this misunderstanding.

Some scholars have also described differences between members from different countries in terms of their non-verbal behaviour, for example in the way people dress, their facial expressions and other aspects of body language. Physical aspects of the workplace are also subject to such variation, which is, for example, reflected in the relative importance members of specific countries assign to office space and seating arrangements. Scollon and Scollon (2001: 203) outline the following scenario to illustrate differences in the use of space:

> An American who is visiting a Japanese business is likely to underestimate the importance of a Japanese corporate officer because he finds him seated at a desk in the middle of a busy room like he was a secretary. On the other hand, a Japanese business man consulting in an American company may well feel he has been shunted off the main flow of the discourse when he is taken to the corner office of one of the key corporate figures.

However, such generalisations (which are often based on anecdotal evidence) need to be treated with caution. One obvious problem with this example and with much cross-cultural research in general is that 'there is often an implicit assumption that cultural group is equivalent to national group or ethnic group' (Spencer-Oatey and Franklin 2009: 40; Sarangi 1994a; Poncini 2002; Shi-xu 2006). Moreover, there is a tendency to ascribe observed differences to cultural characteristics when they occur in intercultural encounters and to ignore the potential impact of other variables. These issues are discussed in more detail in Section B.

The next example is taken from a case study of American subsidiaries of Japanese companies (Clarke and Lipp 1998). It illustrates how people from different nationalities may have remarkably different expectations about what communicative behaviour is considered to be appropriate and perhaps even polite.

Example 4.4

Context: At the annual sales conference of a Japanese multimedia subsidiary in the United States. The conference takes place in Disneyland Resort Hotel and participants are mostly American sales personnel (many of whom had brought their spouses) and some high-ranking Japanese and American managers. The company has had a very successful year (with all goals being met or surpassed) which they wanted to celebrate at this occasion. The Japanese Vice-President of Sales gave the following speech.

Thank you for your hard work this fiscal year. We have broken many records, but ... we need to be careful and not to settle down so easily. We need to keep up our fighting spirit! Our competition is working to defeat us at this very minute while we are celebrating. You have done a good job ... but we must do more and aim higher. There is no time for frivolous activities. You must prepare yourselves to work twice as hard this coming year. The company has invested a lot of money in new manufacturing facilities. These facilities are producing our new product lines. It is your duty and loyalty to this company to sell these products as efficiently as possible. You must not fail! You must not let your guard down! You must not be content! I hope you will do a better job in the new fiscal year.

Thank you.

The speech was met with silence from the audience until the American Director of Sales stood up, turned away from the speaker and said with an awkward smile:

Disregard everything he just said. We are here to celebrate your fantastic achievements this year! We have out-performed all our competitors this past year and your success is far beyond expectations. So give yourselves a round of applause, and, let the festivities begin!

The audience applauded this speech.

Source: Ting-Toomey 2009: 236 based on
Clarke and Lipp 1998: 229–54

Exercise 4.3

Why do you think the speech of the Japanese Vice-President of Sales was met with silence? How do you think he felt when he heard the words of the American Director of Sales?

There are abundant examples like this one in the practitioner-oriented literature. Moreover, there is a wealth of 'how to' books targeted at practitioners that provide advice on effective intercultural communication between business partners from different nationalities. These guides are typically full of anecdotal evidence on which advice is based regarding how to avoid potentially harmful clashes of cultural expectations, norms and practices, and how to do business more effectively, as is often reflected in their title: *Doing Business in India for Dummies* (Manian 2007), *The No-Nonsense Guide to Doing Business in Japan* (Woronoff 2001), *China Uncovered: What You Need to Know to Do Business in China* (Story 2010).

However, as was shown in Example 4.1, culture is not always an issue in intercultural communication, and extreme cases like Example 4.4 tend to be the exception rather than the norm. Nevertheless, such examples are good illustrations of the different perceptions and expectations that people from different countries may have regarding what constitutes appropriate and polite behaviour. The next example further illustrates this point.

Example 4.5

Context: During the visit of a Chinese delegation to a British company. At the beginning of the visit the Chairman (CM) of the British company delivered a speech from which the following extract is taken.

CM: It is extremely important for us at [company] to make a special effort to welcome all of our Chinese friends and colleagues, as you and your company are very important to us. We we've over the last probably four or five years had quite quite a good relationship with with China, and have people from [company] and [place] and and the the various [industrial plants] in the various provinces of China, and we hope this will continue in the future.

Later on in the speech when providing some background information about his company, the Chairman made the following comments:

CM: So we are obviously very experienced eh in the design and the manufacture of these products … A lot of our trade now obviously goes to China and to the other Eastern countries, because that is obviously where a lot of the world trade now is and will be in the future.

Source: Spencer-Oatey and Xing (2000: 276–7).

While the British chairman presumably intended to make sure the Chinese delegation got a good impression of his company so that they would remember it when they went back to China, his speech was interpreted rather differently by the Chinese audience. They were particularly disappointed that the chairman praised his own company's products but did not compliment the Chinese strongly enough, nor did he express his gratitude towards the Chinese for allegedly saving the company from bankruptcy (the Chinese had heard on the grapevine that the chairman's company had been in financial difficulties, and they believed that their orders had significantly contributed to saving the company). As a consequence of this and other mismatches (not described here) between the expectations of the British chairman and the members of the Chinese delegation, both parties were dissatisfied with the visit.

So let us come back to our initial question 'is culture an issue at work?' Based on the evidence presented so far (in the form of authentic examples of professional communication and anecdotal evidence) we would probably have to say yes and no. Yes, because as the examples discussed above have shown, in some cases there seems to be an assumption that people from different countries bring with them a set of specific expectations about how things are supposed to be said and done, which can lead to misunderstandings (as in Examples 4.4 and 4.5). And, as Example 4.3 has illustrated, culture is sometimes even explicitly used by participants themselves as an explanation for some of the differences and difficulties they experience. However, based on some other examples, we would have to say no – culture does not seem to be an issue. In particular, as Examples 4.1 and 4.2 have demonstrated, in some workplaces, professionals from different nationalities communicate and do business with each other without culture appearing to be an issue. The next section attempts to disambiguate this yes-and-no answer by exploring in more detail the complex notion of culture and the question of how it may (or may not) be relevant in professional contexts.

Section B: Exploring culture

So what is culture?

As you will have realised by now, culture is a rather slippery concept that is 'notoriously difficult to define' (Spencer-Oatey and Franklin 2009: 13).

Exercise 4.4

Find five definitions of culture from different sources and compare them. Make a list of the features they have in common. How can you account for (potential) differences in the definitions?

Although researchers from different disciplines, including anthropology, psychology, history, philosophy, international business studies and applied linguistics – just to mention a few – have approached the question of what is culture, there is no agreement about what exactly culture is and how to capture it. It has even been claimed that 'the term means what we want it to mean' (Sarangi 2010). Drawing on a number of definitions of culture, Spencer-Oatey and Franklin (2009: 15) summarise the following four crucial characteristics of culture:

- Culture is manifested through different types of regularities, some of which are more explicit than others.
- Culture is associated with social groups, but no two individuals within a group share exactly the same cultural characteristics.
- Culture affects people's behaviour and interpretations of behaviour.
- Culture is acquired and/or constructed through interaction with others.

Exercise 4.5

What do you think about such a definition? Does it adequately capture the definitions of culture you found in response to Exercise 4.4?

The last point on their list is of particular interest to us here as it describes the crucial role of communication: rather than assuming that communication is 'just a carrier of cultural values and norms' it actively contributes to constructing and shaping cultural practices and assumptions (Sarangi 2010). More recent approaches thus conceptualise culture as a dynamic process and as something people do (Street 1993) rather than as a static and fixed concept. As a consequence, they focus on what cultures do and how they are enacted or performed (Sarangi 2010). According to this view, culture is clearly not an a priori variable that can explain people's behaviour. Rather, it is constructed, negotiated, and shaped in and through interaction.

Yes, but is it culture?

Although it may seem that the use of culture as an explanatory variable is pervasive when attempting to understand (perceived or actual) differences in behaviour of people from different countries, as some of the examples in Section A have indicated, it is crucial to question whether culture really is the most plausible explanation. While there may be systematic differences in communication patterns displayed by members of specific national groups (for example, in terms of preferences for performing specific speech acts such as complaints and criticisms), reducing an explanation of these observations to cultural differences is rather limiting and runs the danger of over-generalising and producing or reinforcing (often negative) stereotypes (Cheng 2003; Scollon and Scollon 2001; Sarangi 1994a; Hartog 2006). As Miller (1994: 235) remarks, when differences in interactions between members of the same country occur, 'participants are apt to ascribe the problem to individual or personality traits, while in interethnic encounters the problem is sometimes assigned to often polarized ethnic attributes' (see also Hartog 2006). The next example illustrates this tendency to over-use culture as an explanatory variable.

Example 4.6

Context: Interview for the position of librarian between Sandhu (Asian) and a panel of three British interviewees.
I = interviewer, S = Sandhu.

1.   I: you say you're very busy eh in your present job what
2.   exactly do you do
3.   I mean what are your duties day by day
4.   S: well we've to eh receive the visitors show them around
5.   and then we have to go out eh to the factories you know eh
6.   sometimes to attend the classes eh how to ehm cataloguing
7.   classification

Source: Gumperz, Jupp and Roberts (1979) as cited in
Sarangi (1994b: 165).

When asked about his current job, Sandhu (the Asian interviewee) mentions some activities which he typically performs (thereby answering the interviewer's first question) but he only marginally addresses the second question (about his daily duties). It could thus be questioned whether Sandhu's reply provides a 'relevant' and 'satisfactory' answer along the lines of what the interviewer had in mind (Sarangi 1994b: 165). And indeed, Gumperz and colleagues (1979), who first used this example, interpret it as an instance of miscommunication which they ascribe to different cultural norms and assumptions. More specifically, they view this exchange as a clash between different culturally motivated norms regarding the structuring of information: 'the British interviewer preferring a "direct and relevant" answer and the Asian interviewee opting for an "indirect and polite" response' moving from general (perhaps not so relevant information) to more specific and relevant information (Sarangi 1994b: 165). According to this line of argument, participants' different cultural expectations and assumptions with regard to the use of specific discourse strategies are the source for the mismatch in this exchange.

However, an alternative interpretation is provided by Sarangi (1994b: 187), who argues 'that Sandhu's response can alternatively be seen as reflecting his lack of knowledge of what constitutes an "allowable" contribution to the interviewer's question in the context of an interview for a librarian's post'. Thus, rather than ascribing observed differences in communicative behaviour to cultural norms (such as those regarding the structuring and presenting of information), they may also be explained in terms of interlocutors' awareness (or lack) of the norms that characterise a specific activity type, such as selection interviews (see also Roberts and Campbell 2005). According to this line of argument, we would not assume that Sandhu's response reflects rhetorical structures that are typical for Asian speakers, but rather interpret his communicative choices as showing a lack of awareness that in selection interviews in this specific context, answers are normally expected to be strictly relevant to the question (see also Campbell and Roberts 2007).

Enacting culture

One way of avoiding these pitfalls of over-emphasising the role of culture lies in taking a more 'dynamic view of "culture"' as outlined above (Sarangi 1994a: 416) and 'examining actual use of language by actual people from different cultures doing actual things with language in actual social situations' (Cheng 2003: 10). Thus, rather than relying on anecdotal evidence and identifying and describing cultural differences in what Sarangi (1994a: 416) calls 'an unproblematic way', it seems more promising to shift the analytic focus onto exploring how interlocutors 'mediate, negotiate and modify the values, beliefs, norms, attitudes and language that they bring along into the conversation' (Cheng 2003: 10). And rather than assuming that potential difficulties or mismatches in communication are based on cultural differences, we need to explore how culture is actually enacted in a particular encounter and how it may or may not be relevant. As was reflected in the examples in Section A, at some points in some interactions culture may indeed be relevant while in others it may not.

Akar (2002: 319), for example, identified a range of factors that have an impact on the form and function of written business texts produced in different Turkish companies. While he acknowledges 'ostensible influences that come from national, cultural ways of conducting business', other equally important factors were type of company (as for example reflected in the company's structure, size, age and industry), workplace culture, and the available communication technology. And in a study of several intercultural meetings between an Italian company and its international distributors, Poncini (2002: 367) observed some instances of conflict and negative evaluation, all of which she explained by 'factors unrelated to cultural differences'. She thus maintains that 'other factors besides cultural differences must be considered when investigating multiparty interaction in a multicultural business setting' (Poncini 2002: 367).

Clearly, there are other factors which have an impact on communicative practices that may be more relevant for explaining differences (or even mismatches) in intercultural encounters. Some of these factors include interlocutors' ethnicity, age, personality, gender, status and rank (Rogerson-Revell 2007: 11), as well as their 'organizational roles, the business context, or individual differences' (Poncini 2002: 349). At any point in an interaction, any of these variables may be more relevant than culture when accounting for differences or even miscommunication. As was elaborated in more detail in Chapter 3, two particularly important factors that may influence people's communicative performance are the norms that characterise the culture of a specific workplace and the norms agreed among members of individual CofPs. There is often considerable variation in the communicative practices that characterise specific workplaces or CofPs within the same cultural context. These distinctive practices, in turn, have a huge influence on what members consider to be appropriate and perhaps even polite ways of communicating and behaving. Thus, as was elaborated in the previous chapter, rather than ascribing certain practices (such as structuring information or decision-making processes) to national culture, it is crucial to understand how members of individual workplaces or CofPs negotiate and assign meaning to these practices which may or may not be in line with what is generally perceived as being the norm in a particular (national) culture. For example, in a study on leadership and politeness across cultures, Schnurr and Chan (2009) found that not all behaviours displayed by the leaders and their team members could be adequately explained by referring to the cultural values that characterised the wider context in which the interactions took place. Rather, the participants negotiated cultural norms and expectations of 'effective' leadership with the specific practices and expectations that characterised their workplaces or CofPs.

Culture and politeness

Research has shown that members of different workplaces or even members of different working teams within the same workplace often differ substantially from each other in the ways in which they do politeness (e.g. Holmes and Schnurr 2005). Hence, the specific ways in which individuals use certain discourse strategies to perform politeness depend on the norms of appropriate and polite behaviour that are developed and enacted on several levels, including specific CofPs, workplace culture, as well as the wider sociocultural context in which an interaction takes place (Rogerson-Revell 2007; Schnurr and Chan 2009).

Notions of politeness are closely linked to appropriate and normative ways of interacting (e.g. Watts 2003). For instance, as Examples 4.4 and 4.5 in Section A have shown, expectations about what constitutes appropriate ways of conducting particular speeches (such as a celebratory speech (Example 4.4) or a welcome speech (Example 4.5)) are often linked to issues of face and politeness. More specifically, they have demonstrated what may happen when these expectations are not met: people may feel surprised and uncomfortable (at best), and perhaps also shocked, and even offended.

These feelings have often been related to the notion of 'face'. For example, in analysing the encounter between the Chinese delegation and the British hosts displayed in Example 4.5, Spencer-Oatey and Xing (2000) maintain that '[w]hen the British chairman failed to express deep-felt gratitude towards them [the Chinese] for helping to save his company financially, they felt that their importance to the company had been underestimated and unacknowledged, and that their face had thus been insufficiently honoured'. In other words, members of the Chinese delegation not only felt uncomfortable and possibly offended, they specifically felt that they had not been given enough face in the speech of the British chairman. But what is face?

There is considerable controversy among researchers as to what exactly face means and what kinds of phenomena should fall under this term (Haugh and Hinze 2003: 1582). As Spencer-Oatey (2008: 14) notes, '[f]ace is a concept that is intuitively meaningful to people, but one that is difficult to define precisely. It is concerned with people's sense of worth, dignity and identity, and is associated with issues such as respect, honour, status, reputation and competence.' Most recent theorisations of face are based on Goffman (1969: 5), who describes face as 'the positive social value a person effectively claims for himself [sic] by the line others assume he [sic] has taken during a particular contact'. However, this conceptualisation of face has been criticised, for example for over-emphasising the individual aspect and describing face as essentially belonging to the self while not paying sufficient consideration to the ways in which face also depends on others (Yu 2003). There are several studies which describe differences in the face systems and politeness values across countries (e.g. Yu 2003; Matsumoto 1988; Haugh 2004; Cheng 2003).

Regardless of how the notion of face is defined, it seems to be general agreement that the processes of negotiating each other's face needs and doing face-work are central aspects of any social encounter. And as Examples 4.4 and 4.5 have indicated, expectations about what constitute appropriate ways of attending to each other's face needs are sometimes made particularly relevant in encounters among members from different countries. However, it is important to note that rather than constituting a static one-way process, the relationship between culture, face and politeness is a dynamic one which is constantly enacted in interactions. More specifically, cultural expectations about face and politeness not only influence interactive norms in complex ways, but by regularly drawing on these particular norms, interlocutors at the same time respond to and shape these notions of face and politeness by reinforcing as well as sometimes resisting and challenging them (e.g. Schnurr and Chan 2009).

Section C further elaborates the notions of face and politeness, and briefly introduces two theories of politeness which are frequently used in intercultural and cross-cultural research studies, politeness theory and rapport management.

Section C: Theorising politeness and face in cultural contexts

Politeness theory

One of the most comprehensive and most influential theories of politeness was developed by Brown and Levinson (1987). Their politeness theory revolves around the premise that all competent and rational adult members of a society, represented by a so-called 'model person' (henceforth: MP), have two types of face and generally tend to aim at maintaining their own and each other's face. Brown and Levinson's notion of face is based on Goffman's definition provided above. However, Brown and Levinson develop this conceptualisation further by distinguishing between negative and positive face: Positive face is the MPs' desire that their own self-image is appreciated and approved of by others, whereas negative face is the MPs' wish not to be imposed on and to maintain their freedom of action. The content of what exactly is involved in face varies across cultures, but the mutual knowledge of members' face and the social necessity of orienting to it are universal (Brown and Levinson 1987: 61–2).

These different types of face are often threatened in speech acts by so-called 'face-threatening acts' (henceforth: FTAs). According to Brown and Levinson, in order to minimise the threat of FTAs MPs may choose among a wide range of politeness strategies in an attempt to save their own as well as each other's face. Brown and Levinson (1987: 65) claim that certain speech acts are intrinsically face-threatening. More specifically, they believe that there are certain speech acts such as orders, requests, threats and warnings which in most contexts tend to threaten the addressee's negative face (by imposing on the addressee). Expressions of disapproval, criticism and contempt, as well as complaints, accusations, insults and disagreements, are described as typically threatening the addressee's positive face (in that they challenge the addressee's desire to be appreciated and approved of by others). Examples of FTAs that threaten the speaker's negative face include expressions of thanks, as well as acceptance of offers and apologies. In these speech acts the speaker needs to impose on their own freedom of action – often to conform to norms of appropriate and expected behaviour (for instance to accept an apology). And lastly, according to Brown and Levinson, FTAs that threaten the speaker's positive face include those utterances where the speaker admits to some kind of own fault, thereby threatening their own positive self-image, such as apologies.

From these elaborations it is clear that politeness theory conceptualises the notion of politeness in terms of conflict avoidance: MPs employ different politeness strategies in order to mitigate or avoid the face-threat of FTAs. The various strategies for performing FTAs among which speakers have to choose are summarised in Figure 4.1.

As the figure illustrates, speakers have various options when it comes to performing FTAs. They can decide either to 'Do the FTA' or 'Don't do the FTA'. In other words, they can either utter the FTA (and thus potentially threaten their own and/or the addressee's face(s)) or they can decide to avoid performing the FTA. Once they have decided to 'Do the FTA', they have the options of doing it on record or off record: they could perform the FTA implicitly, for example by hinting at something rather than formulating a directive. A classic example is to say 'It's cold in here' rather than 'Can you please shut the window'. They can also do the FTA on record – that is, they can actually utter it. In this case, speakers have two further choices: they may either issue the FTA baldly and without redressive action or they may issue it with redressive action. In other words, they can either directly utter the FTA in an unmitigated way, such as 'You need to write the report again', or they can employ positive and/or negative politeness strategies to minimise the face-threat of their FTA. One way of doing this is on

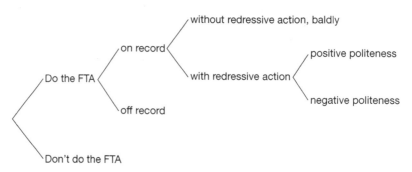

Figure 4.1 Strategies for performing FTAs
Source: based on Brown and Levinson (1987: 60).

the lines of 'Thanks for sending me the report on time. We might just have to change a few minor things before we circulate it to everyone.' By thanking the addressee for sending the report on time the speaker performs positive politeness (and makes the addressee feel good about themselves) before indicating that certain things need to be changed. The criticism is hedged not only by the use of positive politeness (the compliment) but also by the use of a range of negative politeness strategies, including the modal 'might', the formulation 'a few minor things', and the use of the inclusive pronoun 'we'.

To summarise, positive politeness is understood as attending to interlocutors' positive face needs. It is often related to an expression of solidarity, and it is generally approach-based: that is, interlocutors need to do something in order to be positively polite. Negative politeness, on the other hand, tends to be avoidance-based: that is, interlocutors refrain from doing something in order not to impose on each other. It attends to interlocutors' negative face needs, for example by expressing restraint and minimally interfering with the addressee.

Example 4.7[3]

Context: Email sent from a prospective student from an Arab country to a German academic who is the course coordinator of an undergraduate course at a university.

Hi Dear!

I am an English language teacher and i want to get admission in ur institution for a three months course in linguistics and/or phonetics. Please send me detail of the programmes ur institution offers in the year 2007 with admission process, fees and all other relevant material.

I hope u will not disappoint me.

[name]

Exercise 4.6

How would you feel if you received an email like Example 4.7? How would you react? Can you explain why the addressee might have perceived this email as rude and inappropriate? Which of his face needs might have been threatened, and how was this accomplished?

What annoyed the receiver of this email the most was that he considered it inappropriate in a variety of ways. In particular, considering the status differences between the student and himself he would have expected a more formal and impersonal and perhaps even more carefully composed email. Moreover, he considered the student's request to be unreasonable because first, all the information the student requested was available online, and second, sending out application and information material are tasks that fall under the responsibility of specific administrative staff at his institution, and would not normally be done by someone in his position.

As this example and some of the examples displayed in Section A illustrate, in determining appropriate levels of politeness, social factors play an important role. Three such social factors have been identified by Brown and Levinson as having a particularly crucial impact on the level of politeness employed in an interaction. More specifically, Brown and Levinson argue that MPs calculate the seriousness of the FTA they are about to perform in order to choose appropriate politeness strategies to mitigate potential face threats. The three factors they propose are perceived solidarity or social distance between interlocutors (D), perceived status or power difference between interlocutors (P), and cultural ranking of the imposition (R) (how threatening a particular speech act is perceived to be in a particular cultural context). Based on interlocutors' assessment of these three factors they calculate 'the seriousness or weightiness of a particular FTA' (Brown and Levinson 1987: 76) and decide which politeness strategies to employ. Brown and Levinson maintain that D, P and R are independent factors and that all other potentially relevant factors can be subsumed under them (Brown and Levinson 1978: 80). Moreover, D, P and R are culture-specific and depend on the specific context in which an interaction occurs.

The theoretical conceptualisation of positive and negative politeness and the notion of face-threat and its mitigation are assumed to be universally applicable. Nevertheless, Brown and Levinson also acknowledge some cultural variation, for example in terms of what kinds of speech acts may be perceived by MPs to be face-threatening, what kinds of social relationship engender which politeness strategies, and what politeness strategies are preferred in a specific cultural context (Eelen 2001: 5).

Politeness theory has received a lot of criticism, in particular for its notion of face, which has been challenged for having a Western bias and for not capturing Asian meanings of the concept (e.g. Matsumoto 1988; Fraser 2005). If we try to apply politeness theory to the examples discussed in Sections A and B we also encounter some limitations. For example, if we apply Brown and Levinson's categories to Example 4.5, we notice that their notions of negative and positive face cannot adequately explain why the members of the Chinese delegation felt offended when the British chairman 'failed to express deep-felt gratitude towards them for helping to save his company financially' and when he did not sufficiently emphasise 'their importance to the company' (Spencer-Oatey and Xing 2000: 280). While one could argue that the Chinese felt threatened in their positive face (for not being appreciated sufficiently), such an explanation does not account for the fact that they felt treated unfairly and unacknowledged in the role their company had played. Thus, rather than feeling personally offended, they felt not appreciated or treated fairly as a group.

There is abundant research on politeness in Asian contexts which challenge various aspects of Brown and Levinson's politeness theory, in particular their concept of negative face. Some people have argued that the desire to be unimpeded by others is not perceived as a face issue, for example, in Japan and China (Matsumoto 1988; Gu 1990). Rather, in countries where individualism is less pronounced and group membership is generally perceived as being a central aspect of societal relations, the notion of negative face needs as proposed by Brown and Levinson appears to be much less of an issue. Other aspects for which politeness theory have been criticised include the conflation of deference with politeness (for example as reflected in the use of honorifics in some languages, which is viewed as an acknowledgement of interlocutors' sociocultural relationships rather than an expression of negative politeness), and the omission of impoliteness in the theory. For a comprehensive summary of the major criticisms see Fraser (2005).

However, although politeness theory has been criticised and challenged by a range of researchers, it remains one of the most comprehensive and frequently used approaches to politeness. The next section introduces rapport management, a more recent development of politeness theory which takes into consideration some of these criticisms and which is particularly useful for an understanding of intercultural communication.

Rapport management

Rapport management is based, among others, on the work of Brown and Levinson (1987) and Leech (1983). In a nutshell, it 'examines the way that language is used to construct, maintain and/or threaten social relationships' (Spencer-Oatey 2000: 12). Thus, in contrast to politeness theory, which assumes that MPs generally aim at maintaining smooth relations, rapport management is more generally concerned with 'any kind of behaviour that has an impact on rapport, whether positive, negative, or neutral' (Spencer-Oatey 2005: 96). Moreover, although the notion of face is also central to rapport management, this framework entails more than the management of face, and includes the management of so-called sociality rights and goals, as outlined below.

Like politeness theory, rapport management draws on Goffman's notion of face. However, rather than distinguishing between negative and positive face, in its earlier version rapport management conceptualised face as consisting of two (interrelated) aspects: quality face and identity face. Quality face refers to everyone's desire to be positively evaluated by others 'in terms of our personal qualities' (comparable to Brown and Levinson's positive face), whereas identity face describes our desire for others 'to acknowledge and uphold our social identities or role' (Spencer-Oatey 2000: 14). More recently, another type of face, respectability face, was added to the framework. This kind of face 'refers to the prestige, honor or "good name" that a person or social group holds and claims within a (broader) community' (Spencer-Oatey 2005: 102). However, in its most recent form rapport management does not seem to make this distinction between the different kinds of face any more, but rather generally acknowledges that '[f]ace is closely related to a person's sense of identity or self-concept' (Spencer-Oatey 2008: 14).

As a consequence of this shift towards a focus on identity, the three different types of face are replaced by three different types of identity: individual identity (self as an individual), group or collective identity (self as a group member), and relational identity (self in relationship with others). And although the links between the different types of face proposed in the earlier version are not exactly the same as the different kinds of identities suggested in the most recent version of rapport management, there appears to be some overlap: a person's individual identity, for example, seems to be closely related to their quality face (that is, their desire to be evaluated positively for their personal qualities or attributes). Similarly, a person's group or collective identity could be interpreted as being specifically related to their identity face since it is closely linked to one's role or status within a group. And lastly, the overlap between the notion of relational identity and respectability face is reflected in the emphasis that both put on the relationship between self and others (for example, with regards to one's prestige and honour). Due to these similarities between the different types of face and identity, I will use the terminology introduced in the earlier version of rapport management and will continue to talk about different kinds of face, as this terminology also makes the links to our discussions of face issues throughout the chapter more obvious.

In addition to face, the other aspect of rapport management is sociality rights, which are 'concerned with personal/social expectancies, and reflect on people's concerns over fairness, consideration, social inclusion/exclusion and so on' (Spencer-Oatey 2000: 14). They are made up of two components: equity rights and association rights. Equity rights refer to people's 'fundamental belief that we are entitled to personal consideration from others, so that we are treated fairly', while association rights capture people's 'fundamental belief that we are entitled to an association with others that is in keeping with the type of relationship that we have with them' (Spencer-Oatey 2000: 14). These notions of face and sociality rights can help explain some of the mismatches that occurred during the visit of the Chinese delegation to the British company displayed in Example 4.5: members of the Chinese delegation may have felt upset about the British chairman's speech because he did not sufficiently honour their identity face by not highlighting enough their (in their own eyes) crucial contribution to saving his company, and he thereby possibly also threatened their association rights.

(TC)

Exercise 4.7

In Example 4.4 (discussed in Section A), identify which types of face needs and sociality rights have been threatened by the two speeches of the Japanese Vice-President of Sales and the American Director of Sales.

An important difference between Politeness theory and rapport management is that the former mainly remains on the level of speech acts (such as complaints, criticisms, promises etc. as described above), while the latter acknowledges that politeness is more than performing speech acts. Moving away from such a focus on speech acts, Spencer-Oatey (2000: 19) mentions five 'domains of politeness' which are crucial for the management of rapport:

- The illocutionary domain describes the illocutionary effects of performing certain speech acts, that is, whether they are threatening, enhancing or maintaining interlocutors' face needs.
- The discourse domain deals with content and structure of discourse in an interaction. For example, topic choice and topic management and the ways in which information is organised and presented, may all be relevant in any encounter.
- The participation domain refers to 'the procedural aspects of an interchange', including turn-taking, inclusion or exclusion of interlocutors, and the occurrence of listener responses.
- The stylistic domain describes 'the stylistic aspects of an interchange', such as the tone, and genre-specific characteristics (such as appropriate choice of words).

- The non-verbal domain captures non-verbal aspects of an interaction, including facial expressions, gestures, and other body movements.

Managing these interrelated domains appropriately in any encounter is a crucial aspect of rapport management.

Another difference between rapport management and politeness theory lies in their different conceptualisations of face. As we have seen above, in rapport management, the management of face and sociality rights both have a personal as well as a social component (Spencer-Oatey 2000: 15). Thus, in contrast to Brown and Levinson's politeness theory (which perceives face primarily as a personal issue located within the individual), this framework acknowledges that there is also a social component to face which is located not in the individual but in the wider societal relations (this is particularly true for identity face and respectability face). Moreover, rapport management makes 'a distinction between face needs (where our sense of personal/social value is at stake), and sociality rights (where our sense of personal/social entitlements is at stake)' (Spencer-Oatey 2000: 15). As we have seen these differences are important for explaining possible mismatches in intercultural communication, such as the ones that occurred during the Chinese–British meetings described in Example 4.5 in Section A.

There is often variation in the ways in which these components of rapport management are perceived, oriented to and enacted in an ongoing interaction. For example, Spencer-Oatey has shown that members of different countries may differ from each other in the emphasis they put on some of these components, such as whether identity face or quality face is considered to be more important (e.g. Spencer-Oatey and Xing 2000). And there may also be some variation in terms of what are considered to be normative ways of orienting to these components, which is ultimately reflected in the strategies used to do rapport management (Spencer-Oatey 2000: 15).

In addition to culture, Spencer-Oatey (2000) outlines several other factors that have an impact on the strategies used by interlocutors to manage rapport. These factors are related to rapport orientation, contextual variables and pragmatic conventions. Rapport orientation describes whether interlocutors aim to enhance, maintain, neglect or challenge each other's face needs and sociality rights. Contextual variables capture the specific characteristics of the context in which an interaction takes place, and include participants' relations (including for example, power relations), message content (for instance, how face-threatening the proposition of a particular utterance is), social and interactional roles of interlocutors (which may be reflected in interlocutors' rights and obligations), the type of communicative activity (such as a board meeting, job interview or medical examination), and an overall assessment of the context.

Rapport management has also been criticised. For example, Schnurr and Chan (2011) have shown that some aspects of the framework may be more easily applied to certain sociocultural contexts. In particular, in an analysis of humour responses in professional contexts in New Zealand and Hong Kong, we observed that the distinction between quality and identity face was more obvious in the Hong Kong data but was much harder to uphold in the New Zealand data. More specifically, it was not always possible to decide which kind of face was threatened in the New Zealand examples, as the concepts of identity and quality face seemed to overlap to a great extent.

In addition to the variables described by Spencer-Oatey (2000) as having an impact on how interlocutors perform rapport management and orient to each others' face needs and sociality rights (as outlined above), Schnurr and Chan (2011) thus propose that the specific norms that characterise the practices and discursive performance of individual CofPs also play a crucial role in how people manage rapport. More specifically, in order to account for interlocutors' different discursive choices when managing rapport, we found that it was crucial to consider both the norms of participants' CofPs, and cultural values and idealisations (for example of professional role relationships) that may have informed interlocutors' performance. Only if we understand the norms and practices of specific CofPs can we understand how their members do face-work and negotiate sociality rights in specific situations in specific sociocultural contexts. Clearly, ascribing observed differences in participants' practices and discursive behaviour to cultural values and assumptions and using culture as an explanatory variable does not always do justice to intracultural variation, and often runs the risk of overgeneralisation and perhaps even stereotyping (see Section B). As was discussed in great detail in Chapter 3, even within the same culture, individual groups or CofPs differ significantly in what their members consider to be normative and appropriate ways of behaving and communicating. A possible way to address these issues is to combine rapport management with a CofP approach and to explore the ways in which cultural values are actually enacted and responded to on the micro-level of everyday (professional) interaction (Schnurr and Chan 2011). Such an approach would enable us to view culture not as a static concept but more productively as a dynamic performance which is created and shaped in and through discourse.

Summary

This chapter has explored the complex topic of culture and politeness at work. Several examples of authentic professional communication from a wide range of multicultural and multilingual workplaces have illustrated some of the ways in which culture may be reflected and responded to in the communicative performance of professionals. However, rather than assuming that culture is always an issue in any kind of intercultural encounter, the examples have demonstrated that culture is often just an unremarkable aspect of people's everyday workplace reality (in particular in multicultural and multilingual workplaces), while in other cases culture may be perceived as the source of miscommunication and misunderstandings.

These diverse ways in which culture is realised and responded to in workplace settings are also to some extent reflected in the difficulties researchers face when attempting to define the slippery concept of culture. However, recent research rejects the idea that culture is an a priori variable that can explain people's behaviour, and rather conceives culture as a performance and as being dynamically constructed, negotiated, and shaped in and through interaction. Any attempt to explain observed differences by reference to culture runs the risk of over-generalising and stereotyping. This is particularly true for cross-cultural research that aims at identifying and describing differences in communication patterns by members of different countries. Thus, in order to avoid some of the pitfalls of stereotyping, it is crucial to critically ask whether culture provides indeed the most plausible explanation or whether other variables may more adequately account for the observed phenomenon.

Two theoretical frameworks were introduced which both provide useful tools for analysing the ways in which culture and politeness are enacted on the micro level of communication: politeness theory and rapport management. While politeness theory is mainly concerned with strategies that are used to mitigate potential face-threats and to maintain smooth interpersonal relations, rapport management looks more broadly at any kind of behaviour that may influence rapport. And while both theories revolve around the notion of face, they differ in the types of face they consider interlocutors to possess and orient to in an encounter. In spite of some criticisms and shortcomings of these frameworks, they both provide useful angles from which communication across cultures may be approached.

Building on some of the discussions in this and the previous chapters around the concepts of group membership, face and identity, the next chapter elaborates the complex notion of identity, and explores some of the ways in which notions of 'who we are' are particularly relevant in a professional context.

5 Identities at work

The discussions of workplace culture and national culture in the previous chapters have established that the ways in which we perceive ourselves and others as members of particular groups (such as workplaces, departments, countries or professions) are an important aspect of professional communication. This chapter further explores this crucial role of 'who we are' in professional contexts, and illustrates some of the ways in which issues of identity are enacted and reflected in and through professional communication.

Section A: Exploring identities at work

Identity is everywhere. Every time we engage in communication, we orient to and construct identities. This may be implicit or explicit, involve deliberate and conscious efforts, or it may be unconscious and happen almost by accident. But as the examples in this and the other chapters illustrate, we always do identity work when we communicate: for example, we may construct our own identity, that of our interlocutors or audience, and also that of the company or organisation that we represent. The examples below illustrate just some of the multiple ways in which identity is relevant and may be an issue in workplace contexts – sometimes very explicitly and at other times rather implicitly.

Example 5.1

Who we are

We are problem solvers with a passion for excellence. We are intellectually curious and highly collaborative. We minimise hierarchy. ... We come from all over the world, with rich experience and all kinds of backgrounds and areas of expertise. We speak over 120 languages and represent over 100 nationalities. ... We are a network of leaders. ...

This excerpt is taken from a rubric entitled 'Who we are' which was displayed on the website of a large international consulting company.

Exercise 5.1

How are company members portrayed in Example 5.1? Which aspects of their identities are mentioned and why do you think these aspects are particularly relevant in the specific context of the company's website?

The mere fact that these kinds of 'who we are' rubrics exist and that they often form an integral part of the kinds of information a company wants to communicate to outsiders (including potential clients and job applicants) illustrates the high relevance of identity in this context. It is relatively common for companies to include information about who they are in their forums of public communication. This does not necessarily have to be an entire rubric on their internet portal (as in the example above), but it could take various forms. It could be a paragraph in the (often glossy) information brochures targeted at potential clients, possibly accompanied by a picture of staff members; it could even be part of the company's motto, such as the slogan of an auto insurer: The 'no problem' people. The ways in which companies want to (in this case deliberately) portray themselves to the outside world are also manifested in the name, logo or motto of a company.

Exercise 5.2

Find three to five examples of logos and mottos from different companies – ideally within the same industry (for example, you might want to look at banks, restaurant chains, delivery companies). How do the organisations portray themselves in and through these channels of communication? What do you think are the intended purposes of these logos and mottos?

Clearly, communication plays a crucial role in the processes involved in establishing and maintaining an organisation's identity: it is through communication via various channels that identities are created and introduced to different audiences. As the example and exercises above have shown, these channels may include, among others, the company's website, marketing material, logos, mottos and slogans, and many more. For example, in a study of HSBC, Koller (2007: 111) explored how 'the banking group represented themselves in their externally oriented discourse as a brand combining the global and the local'. She analysed the visual and linguistic elements used in HSBC's external communications (for instance, on its websites and in brochures) and identified several strategies which contributed to creating the HSBC brand as 'the world's local bank'. Through its branding strategy which draws on local and global schemas, HSBC 'position[s] itself as a provider of both global amenities and local "authenticity"' (Koller 2007: 115). Such a self-portrayal can be linked to the (perceived) identity of consumers who presumably find such a branding attractive. And indeed, regardless of 'whether the HSBC brand indeed reflects global or even local identities, its branding strategy has so far been successful in terms of increased brand value (Treanor)' (Koller 2007: 128–9).

Clearly, the notions of brand, identity or 'who we are' are perceived as an important aspects of what makes a particular company (or us) successful and potentially appealing to the addressees (who are often clients or stakeholders). It is thus perhaps not surprising that many companies spend a lot of money on creating and maintaining their corporate identity or corporate branding. However, if you Google individual phrases of the self-portrayal of the company in Example 5.1 you may be surprised by the number of hits such a search generates. Apparently, there are many other companies whose staff is described in similar terms. These findings are supported by Koller (2011), who analysed the mission statements of 100 Fortune Global 500 companies and identified several domains of meaning that are overused in her corpus of mission statements when compared to a general reference corpus. In the mission statements that she looked at, employees were often described as 'talented', 'professional', 'committed' or 'dedicated' and as 'people who accomplish extraordinary things'.

Hence, mission statements or 'who we are' rubrics are often relatively generic, and seem to primarily function as a promotional tool rather than providing actual information about a company's staff – for example, in terms of what percent of staff members have which kinds of (cultural, educational, and expertise) backgrounds. (Some of these points are elaborated in more detail in Section B.) They thus crucially contribute to the ways in which an organisation portrays (and idealises) itself and how it perceives and is perceived by its members, stakeholders and clients. In this way, the identity of an organisation (which has often been referred to as 'corporate identity') is closely related to the culture of an organisation (see Chapter 3). Corporate identity has been defined as 'the sum of all the factors that define and project "what the organisation is", "what it stands for", "what it does", "how it does it" and "where it's going"' (Melewar 2003: 197). This definition bears some similarities with the definition of workplace culture that was introduced in Chapter 3 as all those characteristics and practices that make a workplace what it is, and that distinguish it from similar workplaces. The two concepts of corporate identity and workplace culture are thus related and inform each other in complex ways. For example, some of the values, artefacts, symbols and behaviours that characterise the culture of an organisation also contribute to shaping an organisation's corporate identity. And an organisation's identity may be an important aspect or manifestation of the culture of a workplace.

So far we have looked at how organisations construct their identity or that of their staff. But what about individuals? How do staff members themselves portray themselves, each other and their company? As Example 5.2 shows, one of the strategies frequently employed by interlocutors to construct their identity is to emphasise membership in a specific group, for example by positioning oneself in opposition to another group. In other words, by describing who they are *not*, interlocutors at the same time construct themselves as members of a particular in-group which is set up in opposition to a specific out-group. Example 5.2 is taken from an interview with Susan, Head of one of the departments in a major international consulting company in Hong Kong. Susan talks about her experiences when first working with a team from China.

Example 5.2

Susan:

Every country is different. Each partnership is different. So, you do have a radically different em working environment. I mean I (would think of) a beautiful story I have (just to summarise this). I (worked) with the China team (who was) complaining about one of the Australians ((inaudible)). They're saying oh you know he gets to six thirty, you know, he leaves. And I said oh (did he complete his work)? Yeah yeah he has completed his work. So why shouldn't he leave? Oh no, you should stay back and be with the team 'cause the rest of the team is working. That's to do things in China. And I, to me, I find that quite amusing yeah. Finished his work, and it's done, what you're meant to do? But you shouldn't leave because the people in the team haven't done. So you should be there and you should stay at work. That summarises the difference. In Australia, everyone leaves at whatever time. You finish your work, it's done.

Source: Schnurr and Zayts (2012: 291)

The anecdote that Susan recounts here shows how her expectations about working hours and team membership have clashed with the expectations and practices of some of the people she used to work with some time ago in Australia: Susan comments that she found it 'quite amusing' when the members of the Chinese team were surprised to see a member of the Australian team leave the office once he had finished his work. While there is a lot to say about this example in terms of cultural stereotyping and culturally influenced expectations, assumptions and practices (these issues are dealt with in more detail in Chapter 4), it has been included here because it is a good example of how identity categories may become particularly obvious when people talk about who they are not.

In this anecdote Susan portrays herself as a team leader (of an Australian-Chinese team) who is aware of and at the same time amused by cultural differences regarding working hours and teamwork. In this narrative Susan actively sets up a relatively explicit and distinct subject position for herself almost in opposition to her Chinese colleagues: she portrays herself as a leader and as someone who believes in specific, and according to her, culturally influenced, values and practices, including flexible working hours, as well as employee independence and responsibility for their work. Susan thereby constructs her own complex identity – including her professional identity as a leader and her group identity, which in this case is closely related to her cultural identity of being a member of the Australian team. In this short excerpt, various different kinds of identity (including professional identity, cultural identity and group identity) are constructed and become relevant at different points in the interaction.

The examples and exercises discussed so far have shown relatively obvious instances of identity construction where companies and individuals appear almost deliberately and intentionally to portray themselves in a particular way. However, identity construction is often a rather subtle process which may take place without the speaker intending it. The next two examples show that even apparently unremarkable stretches of interaction contribute to identity construction.

Exercise 5.3

Read through the interaction in Example 5.3 and think about who the interlocutors are and in which context the encounter might have taken place. What factors helped you make your decision?

Example 5.3

1. M: how are you?
[1.5 sec pause]
2. EM: [drawls] : well : I am fairly fine I guess
3. M: you are
4. EM: Yes
5. M: hm (0.3) now + you've started to feel movements of
6.   the foetus?

7. EM: Yes
8. M: for how long have you felt them?
9. EM: well I have felt it for a couple of weeks
10. M: Mm
11. EM: though it's more now in the //last\
12. M: /it's\\ more evident now yes
13. EM: Yes

Source: Bredmar and Linell (1999: 243f)

The specific processes of identity construction that are at play in this example and that assist interlocutors in setting up their own and each other's identities are discussed in more detail in Sections B and C. The next example illustrates that roles and identities are not fixed labels which are attached to an individual. Rather, they are dynamic processes which may shift throughout an interaction.

Example 5.4

Context: Interaction between Tricia and Evelyn in the latter's office. Members of the department have submitted baby photos of themselves which are displayed on the wall in Evelyn's office. Staff are now trying to identify their colleagues in the baby photos.

1. T: oh hello [laughs] //[laughs]\
2. E: /we've just sent\\ Tina back to do the photos
    [laughs]
3.   [laughs]: she came in with the sheet
4.   and I went //+\
5. T: /look at the sheet\\
6. E: how could you get this one wrong and she's
7.   going well you know
[several turns omitted]
8. T: [drawls]: oh: poor thing //[laughs]\
9. E: /([name]) had marked the one she had wrong\\ and
10. T: I said now go away and come back later
11.   [laughs] //[laughs]\
12.   /(if you'd seen) man she was [drawls]: so: funny\\
13.   [laughs]
14.   um can you tell me the principles and values thing
15.   where they handed out at (those) manager's
16.   meeting the other day +
17.   I need you to get me about forty copies of them
18.   [sighs]
19. E: oh yep that's fine

20.	T:	for our meeting at three o'clock that I've just
21.		discovered that I've got
22.		and not //long ago\ found out what I'm supposed
23.		to be saying at
24.	E:	/[laughs]\\

In the beginning of this excerpt Tricia and Evelyn portray themselves as equals and as colleagues who get on well with each other: there is a lot of laughter (lines 1, 2, 3, 8, 11, 13) and overlap between the two (lines 1 and 2, 4 and 5, 8 and 9, 11 and 12) which could be interpreted as heightened involvement; and Tricia provides minimal responses throughout Evelyn's humorous anecdote, thereby signalling her interest and encouraging Evelyn to continue (e.g. lines 5 and 8). There is no indication of status differences between interlocutors in this part of the conversation. In fact, a similar exchange could have equally well taken place between two friends or people who know each other well.

However, from line 14 onwards the interaction takes a turn and Tricia and Evelyn are portrayed rather differently: after the hesitation marker 'um' which introduces a change in topic (line 14) Tricia switches back to 'work mode': she asks Evelyn to do several work-related things for her (lines 14). And judging by her response Evelyn seems happy to comply with her. In this second part of the extract, the women's interaction becomes more transactionally oriented and interlocutors' professional roles and identities take centre stage: Tricia is constructed as the one in charge while Evelyn is portrayed as her subordinate and, judged by the tasks Tricia asks her to perform, her personal assistant. This shift in identities also affects the women's relationship, which shifts from being friendly and primarily relationally oriented to being professional and clearly task-oriented (albeit still friendly in nature).

These dynamics of identity construction also apply to other encounters that take place in professional contexts. As I explained in Chapter 1, the fact that an interaction occurs in a professional setting does not automatically make it an instance of professional communication. And similarly, although interlocutors may carry certain titles (such as midwife, lawyer or managing director), it does not automatically mean that they construct the professional identities of a midwife, a lawyer or a managing director. Thus, as Schegloff (1987: 219) notes, 'the fact that they are "in fact" respectively a doctor and a patient does not make those characterisations ipso facto relevant (as is especially clear when the patient is also a doctor)'. Rather, interlocutors jointly construct their relevant identities as their interaction unfolds. Through their use of language they portray themselves as particular kinds of (professional – among others) personas. For example, using the technical term 'foetus' (rather than baby) in Example 5.3 contributes to constructing the professional identity of a nurse.

The examples discussed in this section have shown that identity is omnipresent in workplace contexts: it is not only reflected in the diverse ways in which organisations portray themselves to their clients and the wider public, but identity work is also done in relatively unremarkable everyday workplace interactions. The next section explores in more detail some of the various processes through which identities are constructed.

Section B: Constructing identities at work

Considering that most people spend a good deal of their time at work, it becomes clear that workplaces are important sites of identity construction. Not only are institutions 'sources and sites of identification for individuals' as Jenkins (1996: 134) maintains, the processes involved in the negotiation of members' identities in turn also contribute to creating and shaping the image of their profession and the specific workplace environment in which they regularly interact.

While the examples and discussions in Section A have shown that identity is more than a category developed by researchers to help understand communication (and other social activities), the question remains of how identities are constructed. And which processes contribute to this? As the examples in Section A have demonstrated, identity construction is not a straightforward one-way undertaking but is typically characterised by multiple and complex interactional processes. Since identities are interrelational constructs and typically involve various interlocutors, it is not surprising that they often gain their meaning in relation to each other: a doctor identity is often created simultaneously to a patient identity, a teacher identity is established in relation to student identities, leader identities usually require follower or subordinate identities and so on. In this sense, then, the different identities 'cannot be separated in an institutional context, but have to be regarded as mutually dependent' (Hall, Sarangi and Slembrouk 1999: 295). In fact, it is often through the very process of creating one identity that another one is shaped at the same time. And through constructing certain professional identities, the specific types of work (in the context of which these identities are shaped) are also created and formed (see Hall et al. 1999).

One of the processes through which identity is actively created and enacted is indexicality. The notion of indexicality describes how through their use of language interlocutors index particular stances which in turn are associated with certain roles or identities (Ochs 1992: 341). For example, by using tag questions and hesitation markers, speakers may evoke the stance of uncertainty. This stance, in turn, may be associated with certain identities, such as the identity of somebody who is new to an organisation and who is in the process of learning how to do things in a new workplace. As De Fina (2010: 215) summarises,

> [i]ndexicality relates signs, in our case linguistic signs such as words, utterances, accents, etc., to complex systems of meaning such as ideologies, social representations about group membership, social roles and attributes, presuppositions about all aspects of social reality, individual and collective stances, practices and organisation structures.

However, it is important to emphasise that linguistic forms do not directly index specific identities. Rather they are implicitly associated with certain identities via the interactional stances that they evoke (Mullany 2007; Ochs, 1992, 1993; Tannen 1999). Moreover, any particular utterance may contribute 'to the construction of more than one aspect of an individual's identity, whether institutional (such as their professional identity as a manager), social (such as their gender identity as a woman) or personal (such as their wish to be considered friendly or well-informed)' (Holmes, Stubbe and Vine 1999: 353). In other words, by drawing on particular linguistic resources, such as using interruptions, interlocutors may portray themselves as powerful and aggressive, perhaps even rude, but also as experts (who may know better than the person they are interrupting), and they may also evoke associations of masculinity. (The link between certain discursive strategies and gender is discussed in more detail in Chapter 6.)

Example 5.5

Context: In a courtroom: Q = Counsel, A = witness.

1. Q: Miss Bush could you please tell the court what happened
2. when you were riding back from the beach
3. on the 4th April this year?
4. A: well I was ... [detailed eyewitness narrative of the crime
5. follows]
6. Q: thank you Miss Bush
    Source: Heffer (2005: 78); based on official court transcripts.

Through their use of specific linguistic strategies which are indexed for specific stances, the interlocutors in this example construct their identities and roles. For example, Counsel's question and the rather formal and precise way in which it is formulated, such as the specification of the day (line 3) as well as his (formal) response to Miss Bush's narrative (line 6), could be interpreted as indexing a relatively (at least at this stage) objective yet powerful stance that in turn may be associated with the identity or role of Counsel. Miss Bush, in turn, complies with Counsel's request and provides a detailed narrative of the crime (lines 4 and 5). She thereby contributes to constructing Counsel as the more powerful interlocutor and collaborates with him in setting up her own subject position as that of the eyewitness.

But since there is no one-to-one relationship between any linguistic form and the stances and identities it is linked to, linguistic forms may evoke different stances and may be associated with different identities in different contexts and different communities of practice (Ochs 1993). That is, being quiet, listening actively and letting others do most of the talking may be interpreted as being supportive and facilitative in some counselling contexts, and may thus create the identity of a successful and experienced counsellor. However, the same behaviours may be interpreted as being passive, not prepared, and perhaps even uninterested in a white-collar workplace where members are expected to actively (in this case, verbally) participate in discussions. In these different professional contexts, the same linguistic behaviour evokes very different stances and indexes very different kinds of identities. As Holmes, Marra and Vine (2011: 16) maintain:

[b]y activating different stances participants dynamically construct complex workplace identities which take account of the norms of the specific discourse context in which they are interacting as well as the specific interactional goals they wish to achieve from moment to moment.

Negotiating group and individual identities

Identities are not created in isolation. Rather, any identity is influenced and shaped by a variety of other identities, including collective/group identities as well as personal or individual identities. As illustrated in some of the examples in Section A, collective or group identities may, for example, refer to membership in a particular organisation, occupation, or a specific working team within the organisation, while personal identities refer to unique qualities, such as one's sense of humour or the ability to multi-task. However, rather than viewing collective and individual identities as two distinct entities, Jenkins (2008: 35–6) maintains that 'the individual and the collective are routinely entangled with each other' and that 'the theorisation of identification must therefore accommodate the individual and the collective in equal terms'. This intricate relationship between the individual and the collective is particularly obvious in what Jenkins calls 'institutionalised identities', which include the identities created in organisations.

Good examples of how individual and group identities are intertwined with each other are mission statements. As Koller (2011: 108) notes, 'mission statements serve to communicate an ideal professional identity to employees to achieve identification and internal cohesion'. However, as her study of 100 mission statements shows, the ways in which employees are portrayed are often relatively generic: they 'tend to be represented with exclusively positive and often superlative attributes, which serves to flatter them as a stakeholder group but also to persuade external stakeholders of the company's value' (Koller 2011: 121). And although the ways in which staff view and construct themselves and each other on the micro level of their everyday workplace interactions may differ remarkably from these kinds of idealised portrayals, mission statements and other channels of a company's self-portrayal provide valuable insight into the company's workplace culture, which in turn forms the backdrop against which the identity construction of its members has to be understood.

Exercise 5.4

Choose a workplace that you know fairly well – for example, because you have worked there – and compare the external and internal representations of that workplace. In doing so, you could look at the ways in which the company portrays itself in publicly available material (such as its website and information brochures) and compare this with your own experience of the company. Describe similarities and differences.

Another point about the close link between group and individual identity is made by Meyerhoff and Niedzielski (1994: 318), who argue that the two are 'inextricably linked, and ... both are defined in terms of "more or less" of the other'. Thus, if a specific group identity is highlighted at a particular point in an interaction, then aspects of interlocutors' individual identities may take a back seat, and vice versa. For example, membership in a particular organisation may be very salient for a company representative who is pitching the company's services to a client, whereas it may be considerably less prominent during an email exchange with another colleague from the same company where other aspects of identity (perhaps related to interlocutors' roles) become more relevant. But as Example 5.6 shows, the emphasis on different identities may shift throughout an interaction and sometimes even within an utterance.

Example 5.6

> *Context: Excerpts from a speech given at a business seminar. The speech was originally in Dutch and has been translated into English.*
>
> We worked erm seriously on that, I think
>
> ... So, I think, and I mean it, that we really will have to sit down around the table with the government and the private partners during the next years ...
>
> So probably this was my last speech, uh, as project leader of the strategic project on, uh, this theme. ... Five years ago, when I arrived at the department of water we had just developed the triad method and we had actually built a good base, I would say. ...
>
> There has been a lot of chopping and changing and in my opinion it has become a boat after five years. So I hope we were able to build that hull into some sort of boat. ...
>
> Source: Van de Mieroop (2007: 1127, 1139).

In analysing the pronoun use in this speech, Van de Mieroop (2007: 1126) shows that 'the speaker and the organisation he represents are linked closely' in the speaker's institutional identity. This link is particularly reflected in the speaker's use of the inclusive 'we' referring to the wider company (including himself as one of its members), and his use of 'I' referring only to himself. Combining these two pronouns throughout his speech, the speaker manages to elaborate on the achievements and future plans of the company (thereby portraying it in a particular way) while at the same time expressing his own stance towards these aspects. Moreover, as the extracts show, the speaker's identity shifts throughout the speech from a focus on the speaker (as an individual who takes a certain stance towards the subsequent proposition, as reflected in 'I think', 'I would say', 'I hope' and so on) towards his institutional identity which emphasises his membership in the company.

However, it is important to note that the identities of individuals or groups who are part of a particular organisation are not always inextricably tied to the identity of the larger organisation in an unproblematic way (Richards 2006: 47), and that the processes involved in the construction of professional identities are often characterised by a 'tension between the individual and the collective level' (Van de Mieroop and Clifton 2012: 1). Individuals often have to find and negotiate ways of portraying themselves as members of a larger group while at the same time emphasising their uniqueness.

Another important aspect of identity construction relates to the ways in which interlocutors' identities and roles interact with each other.

Identity versus role

Identities are often understood as 'the reflexive enactment of roles in social interactional terms' (Hall et al. 1999: 293). In other words, by enacting and performing specific roles, people construct their identities. Such conceptualisations view roles as rather static and as comprising of 'fixed sets of expectations and responsibilities associated with particular social positions, for example, occupation, class, gender or family' (Hall et al. 1999: 293). More recent approaches, however, acknowledge that role, like identity, is not a stable category but a discursive construct (Holmes et al. 1999; Roberts and Sarangi 1999). In fact, in most situations the two concepts are closely related, or as Hall and colleagues (1999: 294) put it, they are 'mutually sustaining'. In other words, the identities that individuals construct for themselves and each other are closely related to the expectations associated with their respective roles in a specific context, and at the same time individuals either adapt and reinforce or challenge and reject the roles that they are assigned to in this specific context.

In this view, identities are 'negotiated through the differentiation and delineation of role expectations, whilst always recognizing that the opposite is also taking place, i.e. specific role models are confirmed/disconfirmed through situated identity work' (Hall et al. 1999: 295).

There is also considerable variation in the ways in which individuals enact their institutional roles in different contexts: for example, leaders may present themselves (through their talk and their actions) not only as leaders, but also as advisers, experts, learners, ordinary team members, and many other roles. In other words, although their official role or title may describe people as director, team leader, secretary, apprentice, head of department and so on, in actual practice roles and identities are not a priori constructs but emerge throughout the encounter. Tensions may thus arise between interlocutors' institutional roles (as, for example, reflected in their job titles) and the identity that is dynamically created and constructed in actual discourse (e.g. Schnurr and Zayts 2011). Clearly, everyone (regardless of their official job title) may potentially take on leadership roles and display leadership behaviours, for example in a specific meeting. (The notion of leadership and various ways of doing leadership are discussed in more detail in Chapter 7.)

The next example demonstrates how roles and identities are interactionally accomplished.

Example 5.7

Context: Police interview between A, a woman complainant who is making a complaint of rape, and B and C (two male police officers).

1.	B:	listen to me + I've been sitting here twenty minutes
2.		half an hour listening to you +
3.		some of it's the biggest lot of bollocks I've ever heard +
4.		I can get very annoyed very shortly
5.		+ one minute you're saying it's Coley next
6.		minute you're saying it's the Meadways
7.	A:	we passed Coley Park
8.	B:	what //happened\
9.	C?:	/happened\\
10.	B:	I'm sick and tired of the ups and downs and the ins and
11.		outs + some of this is better fairytales
12.		than bloody + Gretel can do (2.9)
13.		now stop mucking us all about
14.	A:	I'm not mucking you about
15.	B:	well I'm not saying to you as you're lying
16.		get rid of the fruitiness
17.		get rid of all the beauty about it
18.		and let's get down to facts and //figures\
19.	A:	/it's not beautiful\\ at all is it
20.	B:	well some of it is all crap about bus stops and +
21.		numbers and blue and white tea towels
22.		to wipe myself down with +
23.		what the hell's gone on
24.		if nothing's gone on let's all pack it off and go home

Source: Thornborrow (2002: 54).

This short extract from a police interview shows how particular roles, such as the roles of a police officer and a complainant, are associated with certain discursive expectations, obligations and rights. In this example the police officer B does most of the talking, he challenges the complainant at several occasions (e.g. lines 3 and 10–13), he is the one to ask the questions (e.g. line 8), he issues directives (e.g. lines 13 and 17–18), and he plays a crucial role in constructing reality (i.e. he 'decides' which versions of the woman's account describe what actually happened the night of the rape). He also interrupts the woman (line 8), he threatens her (e.g. lines 1–6), and he swears (e.g. lines 3, 12 and 20). By drawing on these discursive practices that are associated with power and authority, Speaker B at the same time constructs and enacts his role as a police officer, and portrays himself as a tough and experienced professional who is determined to establish 'what really happened'.

Another noteworthy aspect of this example is how Speaker A constructs herself. Rather than being overly intimidated by the police officers' display of power, she insists on her version of reality (line 14) and she even challenges the officers for questioning her account (line 19). By drawing on discursive practices that are associated with a powerful stance, Speaker A thus to some extent rejects the role that the police officers try to project onto her. Rather than playing along with the police officers' attempt to structure the interaction in a particular way, she presents and insists on an alternative, less asymmetrical, format of a police interview. In this sequence Speaker A thus portrays herself as a powerful person who stands her ground.

This example shows how the various expectations associated with specific roles are crucial for identity construction: it is through orienting to the expectations associated with certain roles, and by adapting to or rejecting them, that individuals at the same time construct identities for themselves and for others (Hall et al.1999: 296).

Issues of power

Professional identities are always to some extent related to power (Van de Mieroop and Clifton 2012). They 'exist and are acquired, claimed and allocated within power relations' (Jenkins 1996: 25). In other words, who we are to each other, how we present ourselves and how we are perceived by the people we work with is closely related to issues of power. This intricate relationship between identity and power is also reflected in the examples in Section A. For example, in the brief encounter between Tricia and Evelyn (Example 5.4), through the specific ways in which Tricia gets Evelyn to assist her in preparing the upcoming meeting Tricia has to attend, she portrays herself as a friendly and forgetful leader who downplays rather than emphasises status differences. This is shown, for example, in Tricia's use of strategies to minimise the impact of her directives (she uses a need-statement and a question form (lines 14 and 17) rather than uttering more explicit and bold directives). Moreover, by providing explanations (lines 20–23) and portraying herself as a 'last-minute' person Tricia further downplays the power asymmetry between herself and Evelyn. And Evelyn's responses (her informal 'oh yep that's fine' (line 19) and her laughter (line 9) further contribute to this.

A rather different way of exercising power is demonstrated in the next example where power is displayed rather overtly.

Example 5.8

1.	Constable:	[makes a very long complaint about what the
2.		Inspector has said]
3.		and I'm afraid Sir I'm just absolutely staggered
4.	Inspector:	yeah well yes well
5.		what you're basically saying is that um Detective
6.		Inspector Jenkins is wrong
7.		Detective Inspector er Miller is wrong er
8.		Acting Superintendent until recently Chief
9.		Inspector Butler is wrong
10.		Chief Inspector Walker is wrong
11.		all these people are wrong
12.		but Barry you are right
13.	Constable:	no you know I can't take them on sir

Source: Thomas (1984: 230).

By referring to all these people with their complete titles (sometimes even including previous titles) the inspector constructs the constable (to whom he refers by his first name only) in stark contrast to these other more senior people who hold hierarchically higher positions than Barry. Through the inspector's use of the titles and the reference to what others have said, he not only disregards his subordinate's complaint but cumulatively his repetition of 'wrong' creates the rhetorical effect of hammering Barry into the ground. The inspector's display of power is particularly strong and potentially threatening to Barry because of its syntactic structure and the challenging and ironic (or possibly even sarcastic) question at the end (lines 11 and 12). And although the inspector does not explicitly reject his subordinate's complaint, Barry's comment in the last line makes it clear that he has understood his boss.

This and the previous example have shown that by drawing on certain discursive strategies, interlocutors do power and identity work. However, it is important to remember that there are no linguistic strategies that always index power. Rather, the interactional context in which specific strategies (such as interruptions and silence) occur impacts on their function and effect, and results in their being interpreted as more or less powerful or powerless.

Defining power

Power, like identity, is not a fixed attribute attached to certain roles and positions, but is dynamically enacted and negotiated in interaction. Rather than defining power in traditional terms as the ability to influence the behaviour of someone else, post-structuralist approaches view power as 'a systemic characteristic' and focus 'on the system of common, everyday assumptions that create reality' (Fletcher 1999: 16, 17). In contrast to traditional theories of power, post-structural approaches conceptualise power as 'a complex and continuously evolving web of social and discursive relations' which influences all social interactions (Thornborrow 2002: 7; Foucault 1980). So what does this mean for workplace contexts?

Power at work is manifested and enacted in a complex web of relationships and realities. Power relations are often not overtly recognisable as they are not always linked to role relationships and hierarchical levels. Rather, as a result of the new work order that emerged due to changes in professional ideology (as described in more detail in Chapter 1), power relations and role-relationships between interactants have changed and moved away from strictly hierarchical structures characterised by distinct power asymmetries towards more subtle ways of manifesting and enacting power (Sarangi and Roberts 1999). This more subtle way of enacting power is also reflected in workplace discourse – for example in the observation that in many Western workplaces people tend to address each other by their first names and to drop titles and overt reference to organisational positions (but see Example 5.8 for a counter-example). Example 5.9 is a good illustration of how power may be exercised in relatively subtle ways, for instance by employing humour.

Example 5.9

Context: a small meeting between three colleagues who are on the same hierarchical level.

1. Noel: [to Patrick] you're clearly the most important person
2. Isabelle: oh definitely
3. Patrick: cool do I get veto rights
4. Noel: [voc] well yes but you get to do all the work
5.   as [laughs]: well:
6. Patrick: oh (great what a move up) +

Source: Schnurr (2009b: 31).

Rather than directly telling his colleague Patrick that he has to take over a large part of the work on a particular project, Noel wraps this message in some humour and laughter: he teases Patrick as being 'clearly the most important person' (line 1) and he laughs in a friendly way when he reminds him that with this special status come certain obligations and that he has 'to do all the work as well' (lines 4–5). Since Noel and his colleagues Isabelle and Patrick are all on the same hierarchical level it would have presumably been rather inappropriate if Noel had exercised power more directly, for example by reminding his colleague more explicitly about his duties. Instead of displaying power overtly, with his humorous comment Noel manages to get all meeting participants involved while at the same time getting his message across to Patrick.

By enacting power in relatively subtle ways, Noel and the other participants also do identity work. In particular, they exploit the humorous potential of identity and status for the purpose of gentle coercion, that is, as a way to 'convince' Patrick of his responsibilities in this project. In assigning the identity 'important person' to Patrick they also assign certain activities to him which are associated with that identity (taking over the main workload). Patrick recognises this and plays along by suggesting to use his veto rights (which come with his new identity/role) (line 3), which is then countered by Noel (lines 4 and 5). The humour and laughter, as well as the overall friendly tone of the interaction and the high collaboration between participants further contribute to constructing interlocutors as colleagues who get on well with each other.

However, in spite of these apparently equalising tendencies, power is still often an issue, and people are usually aware of power relations even though they may be more hidden and may typically not be manifested on the surface.

In the next section we return to the question of what identity is from a more theoretical perspective, and explore how identity construction may be theorised within a social constructionist paradigm.

Section C: Theorising identity construction

Questions of identity have long been of interest to scholars and lay people alike. It is thus perhaps not surprising that a considerable amount of research has been conducted on issues of identity, including work in sociology, anthropology, organisation sciences, social psychology and applied linguistics. This section introduces some more recent approaches to and conceptualisations of identity.

Most theories of identity can be described as either essentialist or constructionist. As Benwell and Stokoe (2006: 9) explain:

> [e]ssentialist theories locate identity 'inside' persons, as a product of minds, cognition, the psyche, or socialisation practices [whereas] ... constructionist theories treat the term 'identity' itself as a socially constructed category: it is whatever people agree it to be in any given historical and cultural context.

Moving from essentialist to more constructionist approaches, conceptualisations of identity have changed dramatically from viewing identity as a fixed set of categories which basically describe 'who we really are' to more discursively constructed views of identity as being constantly created and enacted in interactions (Benwell and Stokoe 2006; De Fina 2010). According to the latter view, identity is not perceived as being merely reflected in discourse, but rather as actively and dynamically constructed in and through discourse in ways that involve numerous interlocutors (e.g. Bucholtz and Hall, 2005; Hall et al. 1999). Identity is thus 'something that people *do* which is embedded in some other social activity, and not something they *'are''* (Widdicombe 1998: 191; my emphasis). In this sense, identity is a performance or a verb (Butler 1990). It is something that people conjointly (although not always necessarily in harmony) construct, negotiate and enact when engaging with each other. As a consequence, identity construction is conceptualised as a never-ending process (Hall 1996), and there is thus no stable identity in the sense of who we are. Thus, the various identities that interlocutors set up for themselves and each other are fluid and change frequently as an interaction unfolds.

As was demonstrated by the examples in Sections A and B, when communicating with each other, interlocutors constantly set up and negotiate various subject positions or identities for themselves and each other – whether very explicitly in 'who we are' rubrics in internet portals (Example 5.1) or more implicitly in routine face-to-face interactions (Examples 5.4 and 5.5). Identity is thus a complex concept which is hard to pin down. A rather broad but useful definition of identity which captures this complexity is proposed by Jenkins (2008: 5; emphasis in original):

> As a very basic starting point, identity is the human capacity – rooted in language – to know 'who's who' (and hence 'what's what'). This involves knowing who we are, knowing who others are, them knowing who we are, us knowing who they think we are, and so on: a multi-dimensional classification or mapping of the human world and our places in it, as individuals and as members of collectivities (cf. Ashton et al. 2004). It is a process – *identification* – not a thing. It is not something that one can *have*, or not; it is something that one does.

As a consequence of this dynamic concept of identity, it has become 'necessary to speak of identities in the plural, considering that every social agent – whether individual or collective – can actualize, mobilize or produce identities according to the context' (Deschamps and Devos 1998: 3). In other words, when interacting with each other, people construct and enact not only one but numerous identities. This dynamic and complex nature of identities is nicely illustrated in

Example 5.4, which shows how Tricia and Evelyn's identities shift throughout the interaction.[1]

Exercise 5.5

Read the quote below and discuss how the notion of identity is conceptualised in this text.

[I]dentities are never unified and, in late modern times, increasingly fragmented and fractured: never singular but multiply constructed across different, often intersecting and antagonistic, discourses, practices and positions. They are subject to a radical historicisation, and are constantly in the process of change and transformation.

(Hall 1996: 4)

Such a conceptualisation of identity falls within the realms of social constructionism, which has been claimed to be 'the single most important influence on the construction of a new paradigm in identity studies' (De Fina 2010: 206).

Social constructionism

Social constructionism was introduced to linguistics in the 1990s and since then has frequently been used by sociolinguists who are interested in exploring the complex processes of identity construction in interaction (Holmes 2003). This approach is based on the assumption that language is a crucial means on which individuals draw in order to construct and perform various identities. As Benwell and Stokoe (2006: 10) succinctly summarise, 'constructionist approaches investigate how people perform, ascribe and resist identity, and how what it means to "have an identity" is produced in talk and text of all kinds'.

Social constructionism is built on three theoretical premises (De Fina 2010: 207):

- Essentialist views of identity are rejected in favour of more dynamic conceptualisations of identity as a process which is constantly enacted in interaction and social practices.
- Identities are constructs rather than 'mental products or sets of properties'.
- Identities must be understood in the context of the concrete social interaction and practices in which interlocutors construct them through their use of language.

In line with the conceptualisations of identity described above, social constructionism views identity construction as an ongoing process which takes places in and through discourse. More specifically, it treats language as 'a set of strategies for negotiating the social landscape' on which speakers readily draw in order to construct different identities (Crawford, 1995: 17; see also Widdicombe 1998; Zimmermann 1998). One of the advantages of using a social constructionist approach to professional communication is that it becomes possible to understand and explain that individuals may behave differently in different situations by assuming they are constructing different social identities. Social constructionism is thus particularly useful for an investigation of the ways in which individuals set up and negotiate their various professional and other identities in a workplace context.

Research conducted in the social constructionist paradigm typically employs qualitative research methods and looks at authentic discourse data such as interviews, focus group discussions, and interactional data such as recordings of conversations and business meetings. Analyses of how participants construct and negotiate their various identities tend to focus on participants' discursive behaviour at the micro level, and look at how their linguistic choices contribute to creating particular identities in the specific context in which an interaction takes place. Researchers have analysed, for example, participants' use of certain styles, vernacular and standard pronunciations, pronouns, use of humour, and many more aspects.

So how are identities constructed? One of the most comprehensive frameworks of identity construction that is firmly grounded within the social constructionist paradigm is the framework for studying identity construction proposed by Bucholtz and Hall (2005).

A framework for studying identity construction

Drawing on work on identity conducted in a wide variety of linguistic and anthropologic traditions, Bucholtz and Hall (2005) propose five principles of identity construction in interaction: the emergence principle, the positionality principle, the indexicality principle, the relationality principle, and the partialness principle.

The emergence principle

In this principle, identity is conceptualised as emerging from linguistic (and other) practices rather than being a pre-determined category that impacts on people's language use:

> Identity is best viewed as the emergent product rather than the pre-existing source of linguistic and other semiotic practices and therefore as fundamentally a social and cultural phenomenon.
>
> (Bucholtz and Hall 2005: 588)

The emergence principle captures some of the processes outlined above, such as the notions of performativity (Butler 1990) and of interlocutors doing identity work (Fenstermaker and West 2002). In line with this work, identity is viewed as being constructed in and through discourse.

The positionality principle

This principle states that:

> [i]dentities encompass (a) macro-level demographic categories; (b) local, ethnographically specific cultural positions; and (c) temporary and interactionally specific stances and participant roles.
>
> (Bucholtz and Hall 2005: 592)

This view of identities maintains that they are complex constructions which incorporate macro- and micro-level categories, roles, and positions. Through their use of language, interlocutors not only position themselves in certain ways in relation to the ongoing interaction (for instance as joke teller or listener) but they thereby at the same time evoke more abstract identity categories (such as gender and age). Some examples that nicely illustrate how different kinds of identities or subject positions are created simultaneously in an interaction can be found in Chapter 6, which discusses how interlocutors' language use indexes both professional and gender identities.

The indexicality principle

The indexicality principle summarises some of the processes and mechanisms through which identities are formed. It highlights the fact that interlocutors are constantly engaged in identity work – not only when they explicitly refer to identity categories, roles and positions, but also more implicitly in positioning themselves and each other throughout an interaction. An example of indexicality is the midwife's use of term of 'foetus' (rather than the non-technical term baby) in Example 5.3., which indexes or points to her professional role or identity as outlined above.

Identity relations emerge in interaction through several related indexical processes, including overt mention of identity categories and labels; implicatures and presuppositions regarding one's own or others' identity position; displayed evaluative and epistemic orientations to ongoing talk, as well as interactional footings and participant roles; and the use of linguistic structures and systems that are ideologically associated with specific personas and groups. (Bucholtz and Hall 2005: 594).

> ### Exercise 5.6
>
> Some of these processes of identity creation are also reflected in the examples in Sections A and B. Look again at the examples discussed in this chapter and identify which of the processes described by the indexicality principle are used by interlocutors to construct their identities in these encounters.

TC

The relationality principle

This principle constitutes the heart of the framework for identity construction (Bucholtz and Hall 2005: 587). It posits that identities are relational phenomena which are not constructed in isolation but in relation to other identities:

> Identities are intersubjectively constructed through several, often overlapping, complementary relations, including similarity/difference, genuineness/artifice, and authority/delegitimacy.
>
> (Bucholtz and Hall 2005: 598)

The first pair of relations through which identities may be constructed is similarity/difference, which refers to the processes through which similarities with or differences from other individuals or groups are constructed by interlocutors (see also Locher 2008: 513). This process is at play, for example, in Susan's description of her Chinese colleagues (Example 5.2) and also in the interaction between the midwife and the expectant mother (Example 5.3).

The second set of intersubjective identity relations, genuineness/artifice, captures how the identities that individuals (or groups) claim for themselves are perceived by others, and more specifically, whether they are viewed as being genuine or artificially crafted or false. The third pair of identity relations, authority/delegitimacy, describe the ways in which institutionalised notions of power and ideology either affirm and impose identities (in the case of authority), or how they dismiss, censor and ignore them (in the case of delegitimacy). In the police interview described in Section B (Example 5.7), for example, the officers' professional identities are not only reflected in their assertive, direct and confrontational language use, these practices are also affirmed and reinforced by the institutional power and authority which is associated with the professional roles of police officers. However, these various relations through which identities may be created are not mutually exclusive but often occur conjointly.

The partialness principle

Drawing on the poststructuralist view of identity as fragmented and fractured (as described above), this principle states that identity construction is not always fully rational and conscious but may also be habitual. Moreover, the complex processes of identity construction are always performed conjointly between self and other in specific situational and ideological contexts.

> Any given construction of identity may be in part deliberate and intentional, in part habitual and hence often less than fully conscious, in part an outcome of interactional negotiation and contestation, in part an outcome of others' perceptions and representations, and in part an effect of larger ideological processes and material structures that may become relevant to interaction. It is therefore constantly shifting both as interaction unfolds and across discourse contexts.
>
> (Bucholtz and Hall 2005: 606)

This principle conceptualises agency as much broader than simply referring to an individual's (deliberate) actions. Rather, agency is viewed as encompassing a wide range of aspects including intentional and habitual processes, as well as 'interactional negotiation [and] ... representations and ideologies' (Bucholtz and Hall 2005: 608).

These five principles of identity construction proposed by Bucholtz and Hall's framework provide a comprehensive summary of recent trends and developments in identity research within the social constructionist paradigm. They outline an approach to understanding the intricate processes involved in identity construction based on the premise that identity is enacted and created in interaction. And by acknowledging the crucial role of language in these processes, such a conceptualisation is particularly useful for research in applied linguistics.

Summary

This chapter has discussed the notion of identity in a workplace context with a specific focus on some of the processes through which identities are created through professional communication. Issues of identity, it seems, are particularly relevant in a workplace setting: notions of who we are constitute important aspects of an organisation's self-perception and self-representation, which in turn affect members' identities in multiple ways. Equally, individuals' identities, in particular their professional roles and identities, play an important part in understanding any communicative encounter as interlocutors constantly set up and negotiate their own as well as each other's identities.

Rather than viewing identities as static attributes assigned to individuals (and larger entities, such as groups and organisations), identities are conceptualised as performances which are dynamically enacted by interlocutors. As a consequence, who we are (to each other) is fluid and may change throughout an interaction. One of the processes through which identities are created is indexicality, which links communicative practices with identities via interactional stances. It was also shown that identities acquire their meaning in relation to other identities, and that the notion of power plays a crucial role in this process. Not only are professional identities always to some extent related to power issues, institutionalised ways of enacting (or (de-) emphasising) power relations also impact on organisational structures, which in turn may have an influence on members' performance.

One of the most recent and arguably most important paradigms that have significantly influenced conceptualisations of identity is social constructionism. The main tenets of this paradigm posit that identity is a dynamic performance which is constantly constructed among interlocutors in specific contexts. One of the most comprehensive frameworks to analyse identities within in this paradigm is Bucholtz and Hall's (2005) work on five principles of identity construction in interaction. Their emergence principle, positionality principle, indexicality principle, relationality principle and partialness principle provide a useful conceptual framework for identity construction, and outline some specific mechanisms involved in these processes.

Now that we have explored the complex notion of identity in professional contexts, the next chapter zooms in on one specific type of identity that is particularly relevant in professional interactions, gender identity. Some of the ways through which professional identities and gender identities interact with each other are illustrated, and the role of gender at work is discussed.

6 Gender

In the previous chapter it was mentioned that professional and gender identities are intertwined with each other in complex ways. This chapter follows up on this observation and illustrates the crucial role of gender in professional communication – not only with regards to identity construction but also in terms of various other aspects of workplace realities which may impact on how people interact at work.

Section A: Gender stereotypes and reality

Exercise 6.1

Read through Example 6.1. Try to assign a name to each speaker and to replace the letters with proper names. Think about why you have given particular speakers female and others male names. What influenced your decision?

Example 6.1

Context: a regular weekly meeting of a project team in a multinational white-collar commercial organisation in New Zealand. C is the leader of the group, and H, P and M are subordinates. Participants in the meeting have been discussing ways of providing information about computer processing to other members of the organisation. The expression 'screendumps' refers to printing off material directly from the computer screen.

1.	H:	look's like there's been actually a request for
2.		screendumps
3.		I know it was outside of the scope
4.		but people will be pretty worried about it
5.	C:	no screendumps
6.	M:	we-
7.	C:	no screendumps
8.	P:	[sarcastically]: thank you C:

9.   C: /no screendumps\
10. M: /we know\ we know you didn't want them and we um er
11.   /we've\
12. C: /that does not\ meet the criteria
13.   [several reasons provided why screendumps should be
14.   allowed]
15. C: thanks for looking at that though
16. S: so that's a clear well maybe no
17. C: it's a no
18. S: it's a no a royal no
19. C: did people feel disempowered by that decision
20. P: [sarcastically]: no:

Source: Holmes and Stubbe (2003b: 1).

Regardless of the specific names you have assigned to the speakers above, there are two important aspects to this exercise: first, people find it generally not too hard to assign names to speakers and thereby to decide whether they are men or women. And secondly, there is often considerable agreement in the gender that people ascribe to the speakers in this example. This exercise, and more specifically, the reasons that you may have put forward for assigning certain names (and hence genders) to speakers has illustrated that there exist stereotypical ideas about how men and women supposedly talk.

These ideas, of course, may or may not coincide with reality. And although a lot of our assumptions are, in fact, stereotypical, they nevertheless often inform our perceptions and expectations, for example about what constitutes appropriate and acceptable behaviour. As Holmes (2006: 2) notes, 'we bring to every interaction our familiarity with societal gender stereotypes and the gendered norms to which women and men are expected to conform'. Take swearing as an example. Swearing is typically associated with masculinities since, as Coates (2003: 46) maintains, it has 'historically been used by men in the company of other men as a sign of their toughness and their manhood'. As a consequence, women who swear are often perceived negatively and as overstepping the boundaries of acceptable behaviour, as Example 6.2 illustrates.

Example 6.2[1]

Context: Two female security guards talk to each about one of their female colleagues who behaved inappropriately (in their eyes).

1. Joey: she's gone too far
2. Lillian: cheap

3. Joey: she talks so baldly + also uses bad language
4. Lillian: {she} got used to it! what kind of person she is

This example shows how women may be perceived negatively (by their colleagues) when displaying behaviours typically associated with masculinities. Here, Lillian and Joey complain about how one of their female colleagues has 'gone too far' (line 1). They not only complain about her inappropriate behaviour (such as flirting with their boss, as the women remark earlier, which is not shown in the transcript) but also about her inappropriate use of swearing and the use of taboo language (line 3). The women are particularly upset about the fact that their colleague has 'got used to it' (line 4), that is, that she has adapted to the masculine culture of their workplace where swearing and jocular abuse (and other elements typically associated with masculine ways of talking) are the norm (see also Chapter 3).

In addition to specific communicative practices which are typically associated with masculinities and femininities, people also tend to have expectations about what men and women want to achieve in their jobs and in life in general. These kinds of gendered stereotypes, in turn, may have an impact on the specific workplace realities that people create, as the next example shows.

Example 6.3

Context: An interview with a female stockbroker.

I have sat on female recruitment committees but I warn them this is not an easy place to work. The simple fact is that fewer women want this lifestyle than men. Women quite rightly often have other priorities. If a man is more committed to the job puts in more hours and effort then he is going to be more successful. If you want to last in this industry [finance] you need to behave like a man.

Source: Luyendijk (2011).

This example illustrates not only that the interviewee believes that men and women have substantially different aims and priorities in their (professional) lives, but it also makes it very obvious that she thinks that the industry in which she works (finance) is a masculine domain and thus for women to survive and be successful they 'need to behave like a man.'

Gender problems in reality: the double bind and the glass ceiling

These preconceived and often stereotypical ideas about how men and women supposedly talk and act, and what their skills and aims are, become particularly relevant in workplace contexts where these kinds of stereotypes may have serious implications for the perception and treatment of men and women. As Mullany and Litosseliti (2006: 137) note, 'stereotypes have a strong influence on workplace communication, and ... gendered social evaluations and stigmas may contribute to limiting women's options with language'. This seems to be particularly dramatic in those workplace contexts where assumptions and expectations about being successful are associated with masculinities (such as in the quote above), and where norms of effective and appropriate communication are often 'equated with the ways in which men (allegedly) communicate' (Pauwels 2000: 137).

This is particularly true for workplaces that are 'traditionally seen as the province of white-collar male professionals' (Pauwels 2000: 137), such as those in finance (as in the quote above) and for blue-collar workplaces. In these workplace environments, many of the behaviours associated with power and authority (such as being decisive, assertive and making decisions autonomously) are at the same time associated with masculinities. Tannen (1994: 167), for example, claims that even 'the very notion of authority is associated with maleness'. This also means that certain professional roles and positions of power and authority (such as leadership roles) are associated with masculinities. As a consequence, women may find it particularly hard to get access to some of these male-dominated positions and practices. These difficulties are, for example, reflected in the observation that women who aim to reach positions of power and influence are often faced with particular challenges, which have been described as the 'double bind' and the 'glass ceiling'.

The double bind refers to the observation that women who display more assertive speech styles typically associated with masculinities tend to be evaluated negatively for being too aggressive and unfeminine. However, if they display more feminine behaviours, they are often perceived as unprofessional and even weak (see also Mullany and Litosseliti 2006; Pauwels 2000; Brewis 2001). In order to escape this double bind, women have to find ways of overcoming the dilemma of being required to display behaviours associated with power and authority (and thus hegemonic masculinity) while avoiding the dangers of being perceived negatively or as 'unfeminine' by the people they work with. Peck (2000: 223) recounts how the professional women she interviewed frequently complained that they are in a no-win situation: they are 'expected to be assertive but condemned as being

Figure 6.1 Essential qualifications

castrating bitches when they are'. Professional women who are 'too feminine' may be perceived as unprofessional, while women who are assertive and decisive are often perceived, as Bergvall (1999: 278) notes, as 'doubly deviant': they are 'not male nor yet fully female'.

However, these negative evaluations of women in positions of power and authority seem to be changing, and there is an increasing recognition of the values and benefits of more inclusive, empowering, other-oriented, and hence feminine approaches to doing things at work. This may be particularly true in organisations with a specific kind of workplace culture, which Baxter (2010) describes as a 'gender-multiple' corporation: that is, those corporations where gender is not viewed as a distinguishing criteria according to which positions and roles are distributed (as elaborated in Chapter 3).

Recent research on leadership, for example, has started to observe a 'feminization of leadership' (Eagly and Carli 2003), and some industries have identified a 'female advantage' (Fletcher 2004), acknowledging that ways of doing leadership traditionally associated with femininities offer valuable alternatives (e.g. Pauwels 2000). According to gendered stereotypes, feminine styles of leadership are characterised by an orientation towards relationships rather than tasks (Fletcher 1999; Holmes and Marra 2004), by nurturing and caring (Bass 1998: 72), and by a particular interest in 'the well-being of the collective' (Martin 1993: 275). Due to these positive facilitative elements, Bass (1998: 79) argues that '[a]lthough traditional hierarchical organizations of the past may have required "masculine" leader behaviour, today's flatter organizations may call for a more "feminine" approach' (see also Ferrario 1994; Olsson 1996; Parry and Proctor-Thomson 2000). But in spite of this so-called 'female advantage' (that is, the observation that 'effective leadership is congruent with the ways in which women lead' (Eagly and Carli 2003: 810), women have not really been advantaged, in particular in male-dominated organisations (Fletcher 2004: 654). Instead, women's performance of leadership is often evaluated less positively than men's (see e.g. Geis, Brown and Wolfe 1990) and is sometimes even viewed as something other than leadership (Sinclair 1998; Rutherford 2001).

Another barrier that many women in the workplace encounter at some stage during their careers has been referred to as the glass ceiling effect. The glass ceiling describes an invisible barrier that prevents women from moving into the top positions in their workplaces (see e.g. Berryman-Fink 1997; Burke and Davidson 1994; Humphries and Gatenby 1996). The following quote is taken from an article in the *Guardian* which reported on interviews with women who work in finance in the United Kingdom.

Example 6.4

Context: Woman interviewee who works in the finance sector in the United Kingdom.

There is a glass ceiling in finance but not in a formal sense. If you want to get to a real senior position, you have to become buddies with the senior managers, who are still all male. These men constantly hold meetings together, travel together, eat together .... They need you to fit in. You need to play golf, blend in with the casual banter .... When a woman joins such a team, its dynamics change. This is a very important barrier.

Source: Luyendijk (2011).

Although feminism and equal opportunity legislations have led to significant increases in women's status and rights in the workplace in many countries and cultures, this quote nicely illustrates that stereotypical and often discriminatory practices and assumptions still persist and disadvantage women. In particular, in many workplaces in different countries, women in senior positions are still exceptions (Baxter 2010; Mahtani, Vernon and Sealy 2009), women tend to receive less pay than men for the same kind of work (e.g. Schnurr and Mak 2011; Calás and Smircich 1999), they are less likely to receive or benefit from mentoring (Berryman-Fink 1997), and they are often excluded from informal networks (e.g. Berryman-Fink 1997; Humphries and Gatenby 1996). Thus, in spite of various improvements, for women in some professions, the glass ceiling is still an important issue, which prevents them from enacting their full potential.

Section B describes some potential ways out of this 'Catch-22' situation of the double bind and the glass ceiling, for example by combining elements of speech styles that are ascribed to femininities as well as elements that are associated with masculinities; and by resisting and challenging gendered discourses. Before exploring in more detail the question of how gender is relevant in professional communication, I briefly discuss what exactly gender is and how it is conceptualised in applied linguistic research.

Section B: Engaging with gender

This section looks in more detail at the concept of gender, with a particular focus on how gender is done in a workplace context, and more specifically how it is enacted, reflected and sometimes resisted and challenged in workplace talk.

What is gender?

Researchers have noted that gender is always potentially relevant in any social encounter, not only at the workplace.

> We are surrounded by gender lore from the time we are very small. It is ever-present in conversation, humor, and conflict, and it is called upon to explain everything from driving styles to food preferences. Gender is so thoroughly embedded in our institutions, our actions, our beliefs, and our desires, that it appears to us to be completely natural.
>
> (Eckert and McConnell-Ginet 2003: 9)

Gender is an omnipresent social category. It is not only something that speakers themselves may make relevant in their interaction (such as Example 6.3 in Section A has shown), but it is also 'a latent, omnipresent, background factor in every communicative encounter, with the potential to move into the foreground at any moment, to creep into our talk in subtle and not-so-subtle ways', as Holmes (2006: 2) notes. So, what is gender?

Eckert and McConnell-Ginet (2003: 10), two prominent language and gender researchers, note that '[g]ender is not something we are born with, and not something we have, but something we do (West and Zimmerman 1987) – something we perform (Butler 1990)'. In other words, gender is an activity rather than an attribute: people behave in ways that are associated with masculinities and femininities, and they thereby do gender. However, which specific behaviours or practices are associated with masculinities and femininities may vary considerably across workplaces (see also Chapter 3). Moreover, the notions of masculinity and femininity are clearly 'anything but monolithic' (Eckert and McConnell-Ginet 2003: 47). And rather than assuming that 'they are experienced or defined the same ways everywhere' (Eckert and McConnell-Ginet 2003: 47), it is crucial to acknowledge their multiplicity.

Clearly, multiple masculinities and femininities exist in addition to the often hegemonic white middle-class versions. An example of different kinds of masculinities is provided by Connell (1995, as cited in Eckert and McConnell-Ginet 2003) who distinguishes between the physical masculinity which is associated with the exercise of physical power and the technical masculinity which tends to be associated with scientific and political power. And while the former is typically ascribed to the working class, the latter is normally associated with the upper-middle class. As a consequence of this multiplicity, it seems more productive to conceptualise and talk about masculinities and femininities in the plural.

The term 'gender' is often used in opposition to sex, whereby sex refers to biological differences between men and women (differences based on hormones, genes and so on), whereas gender is socially constructed and acquired as people learn what it means to behave and talk like a man or a woman (Talbot 1998: 7; see also Litosseliti 2006). This distinction between gender and sex is important, since as Litosseliti (2006: 11) notes, '[b]iological explanations of socially constructed differences between men and women are often used to justify male privileges or reassert traditional family and gender roles, for example, women's so co-called 'natural' role as mother and nurtures'. These biological differences are thus sometimes used to support discriminatory practices. In a workplace context, for example, they may be used to justify the pay gap between male and female employees or why men are (allegedly) more suitable for certain jobs than women and vice versa (see also Litosseliti 2006). As Eckert and McConnell-Ginet (2003: 45) explain, '[t]he "rational" and "impassive" male has been seen as more suited to managerial work'. Women, on the other hand, have traditionally been viewed as being particularly good at jobs that require nurturing and caring (such as nursing). These beliefs and assumptions about men and women being particularly suitable for certain professions, albeit clearly being stereotypical, are often reflected in the gendered discourses (that is, the specific ways in which people talk about women and men) that prevail in many workplaces (as shown in Example 6.3 in Section A). These gendered discourses, in turn, contribute 'to ensur[ing] that women stay in low-status low-paid jobs, such as call centre jobs', as Litosseliti (2006: 64) notes. These aspects are discussed in more detail below.

In the next sections two of the ways in which gender is performed in professional contexts are discussed in more detail. I first explore how some speech styles are gendered (such as C's behaviour displayed in Example 6.1) before looking in more detail at some of the gendered discourses – or gendered ways of talking about men and women – that exist in many workplaces (see Example 6.3). A third way in which gender is relevant for professional communication was discussed in Chapter 3, where it was shown that the workplace context in which interactions take place is already gendered, which in turn has an impact on how people talk and act, and how they are perceived by others.

Gendered speech styles

Exercise 6.1 and Example 6.2 in Section A have illustrated that people often make a connection between certain ways of doing and saying things and gender. For example, C's direct and perhaps even confrontational way of refusing to allow 'screendumps' (for instance, by interrupting others to make her point) tends to be associated with masculinity, while H's indirect way of making a request (as reflected in the frequent use of mitigation strategies) is often ascribed to more feminine ways of doing things. These and other features that are often associated with feminine and masculine interactional styles are summarised in Table 6.1.

A masculine speech style is characterised by direct, often confrontational, and aggressive contributions, which are outcome-oriented rather than relationally oriented (Coates 1994; Holmes and Stubbe 2003a; Tannen 1995). This masculine orientation is expressed

Table 6.1 Widely cited features of feminine and masculine interactional styles

Feminine interactional style	Masculine interactional style
Facilitative	Competitive
Supportive feedback	Aggressive interruptions
Conciliatory	Confrontational
Indirect	Direct
Collaborative	Autonomous
Minor contribution (in public)	Dominates (public) talking time
Person/process-oriented	Task/outcome-oriented
Affectively oriented	Referentially oriented

Source: Holmes (2000c).

linguistically in a variety of ways, for instance, in one-at-a-time construction of the floor (Coates 1997), the 'use of competitive and confrontational devices' (Case 1988: 56), and frequent interruptions (Case 1988). A feminine interactional style, on the other hand, predominantly focuses on person- or process-oriented aspects, and is typically associated with indirectness, collaboration and supportive feedback (Coates 1996; Holmes and Stubbe 2003a; Romaine 1999; Talbot 1998; Tannen 1993). This is achieved linguistically, for example, in collaborative construction of the floor (Coates 1996), through supportive feedback (Holmes 1998), and frequent use of negative and positive politeness features (Coates 1993).

However, it is important to note that this distinction between feminine and masculine speech styles is also problematic, as it neglects the impact of other social factors on language use, such as variation in styles in different contexts depending on interlocutors' goals. Moreover, such a distinction seems to suggest that feminine and masculine speech styles are dichotomous and that certain speech elements are directly linked to gender, none of which is the case, as is explained below. But in spite of these drawbacks, the distinction between gendered ways of talking is useful since it captures quite well the discursive elements people typically associate with feminine and masculine speech behaviours (Holmes and Stubbe 2003a: 575). As was shown in Exercise 6.1 and Example 6.2, these stereotypes often inform judgements about appropriate behaviour for men and women (see also e.g. Mills 2003: 184; Philips 2003). This distinction between feminine and masculine styles is thus particularly useful for an understanding how people at work are being perceived and judged by others.

In their everyday interactions at work (and in many other contexts) people tend to draw on a wide range of speech styles when interacting with each other. In some situations they may be very decisive and perhaps even confrontational, while in others they may be more conciliatory and indirect. By using elements of different speech styles, speakers evoke different stances and create different identities or roles for themselves. As was discussed in more detail in Chapter 5, this way of linking particular speech styles to particular stances, which in turn are associated with certain identities or roles, has been referred to as indexing (Ochs 1992, 1993). For example, by using speech elements that are indexed for masculinity, such as being decisive, direct, and perhaps even confrontational when making decisions unilaterally and autonomously, a speaker may evoke the stances of power and authority. These stances, in turn, are indexed for certain professional roles, such as leadership. In other words, by being decisive, direct, and perhaps even confrontational, a speaker constructs themself as the one in charge of what is happening and may also take over leadership roles.

What has this got to do with gender? Gender comes into play in a rather implicit way here: as was elaborated above, certain speech elements (such as being decisive and direct) are typically associated with a masculine interactional style (as summarised in Table 6.1). Hence, by using these speech elements to create certain professional roles (such as the role of a leader), speakers at the same time also do gender because certain speech elements are indexed for power and authority *and* for masculinity. By evoking powerful stances, associations with certain masculinities are created. In other words, by doing power and constructing powerful professional identities, speakers simultaneously enact hegemonic masculinities. In this way, then, speech elements are not only indexed for certain stances (which in turn are associated with specific identities and roles) but they are also associated with gender.

Exercise 6.2

Identify elements of masculine and feminine speech styles (as summarised in Table 6.1) in Sabitha's contributions in Example 6.5. Describe the stances they evoke and the social categories and roles these stances are associated with. Are there any problems with this?

Example 6.5

Context: Weekly meeting at a non-profit organisation. Participants discuss the new layout of their office. Sabitha, the CEO of the company, chairs the meeting.

1.	Sabitha:	or we move this along THAT way +++
2.	Beth:	(we just move up there there there)
3.	Faye:	But if we leave to move this I think it's pretty
4.		still (if we move this) along there but if you wanna
5.		get extra space then ( )

[Faye outlines her view disagreeing with Sabitha] +++

6.	Sabitha:	I would prefer to get another desk in and do a
7.		purpose built here
8.		move this forward flat stuff along here cause again
9.		you're using a whole wall for this er half a //+ \ half
10.		a wall ++
11.	??	/yeah \\
12.	Beth:	( ) because I don't think the copier
13.		can move from here
14.		and take this over and and [some lines omitted]
15.	Sabitha:	(okay) repeat

16. Beth: the the copier can come over here
17. Sabitha: [drawls] :okay:
18. Beth: and then the ( ) can come over here and then
19.   yeah on top of each other and then the desk can
20.   move from here to be there
21.   (and the other there and there) and up here
22. Sabitha: the problem with putting a desk here is
23.   I agree with Beth
24.   I think we should have noth-
25.   no bloody fitting over here
26.   because remember the meeting
[some discussion omitted]
27. Sabitha: okay I think what we're required I tell you
28.   the third stage is get rid of [drawls] :all: the
29.   publications
30.   okay just keep few hundreds of each ...
31. ??   you know when I //( )\
32. Sabitha: /and what\\ I would like to recommend if possible is
33.   to try and store it [drawls] :in boxes:
34.   do we have boxes or no
[some discussion omitted]
35. Sabitha: so if you can do that by next Monday // \ okay
36.   that's the preference
37. ??   /yeah\\

Source: Schnurr (2010: 122–3), slightly modified and shortened.

Example 6.5 illustrates some of the ways in which people at work do gender while achieving their workplace objectives: while Sabitha is discussing with her team various ways of reorganising their office, her language choices are associated with gendered speech styles via the stances that they evoke. Hence, by primarily engaging in discussions and making decisions, Sabitha (and her colleagues) not only construct their professional identities (see Chapter 5) but also perform gender and portray themselves as more or less masculine and/or feminine at different points in the interaction. In this way, all language use is already gendered to some extent, and, as was argued earlier, it seems impossible to separate enacting gender from performing work-related activities because the same stances may be indexed for both professional and gender identities.

The next section explores another way through which gender becomes relevant for professional communication, namely through the gendered (and often discriminatory) discourses that exist in many workplaces to describe men and women.

Gendered discourses

As we have seen in Section A, gendered discourses exist in many workplace contexts. Gendered discourses refer to those instances where people talk about or make assumptions about men and women and about what constitutes gender appropriate ways of behaving and talking. As Litosseliti (2006: 58) notes, 'gendered discourses are discourses that represent and (re)constitute, maintain, and contest gendered social practices'. In explaining your choices of names in Exercise 6.1, for instance, it is very likely that you have drawn on a variety of gendered discourses. You may, for example, have argued that you think C is a man because he is very direct, says what he wants and does not take any prisoners. In assigning certain behaviours and ways of talking to men and women, respectively, people at the same time draw on and reinforce gendered discourses; that is, gendered ways of talking about men and women. In doing this, as Litosseliti maintains, '[g]endered discourses position women and men in certain ways, and at the same time, people take up particular gendered subject positions that constitute gender more widely. In this sense, discourses can be gendered as well as gendering' (2006: 58 referring to Sunderland 2004: 22). In other words, by talking about men and women in certain ways, speakers create, maintain and sometimes challenge specific subject positions or roles for men and women, which are based on and reflect or challenge generally acceptable norms of masculinities and femininities.

A range of gendered discourses in workplace contexts are identified by Mullany (2007). In interviews with male and female managers in a retail company and a manufacturing company she encountered, for example, discourses of gender difference and the double bind, discourses of female emotionality/irrationality, discourses of motherhood and family, and discourses of femininities. An analysis of these discourses indicated that the women managers in this study were 'judged and evaluated differently from their male counterparts' (Mullany 2007: 205), which was particularly reflected in the discourse of gender difference, as Example 6.6a illustrates.

Example 6.6a

Context: An interview with Martin, one of the employees of a manufacturing company.

When I did have a woman boss do they do tend to be a bit more emotional than men you know I think men can be pretty hard but probably straighter whereas women tend to be I don't know some some women can play the fact that they are women and other

women erm just tend to be more emotional I've found th- than
men which isn't someone I particularly want to wor- I I don't
particularly want to be working for a person who's got emotional
highs and lows you know I want to be working for someone that I
know where I am when I'm with them.

Source: Mullany (2007: 186).

In explaining why he prefers to work for men rather than women,
Martin draws on the discourse of gender differences depicting men
and women as essentially different. According to him, women 'tend to
be a bit more emotional' and they sometimes exploit their femininity,
whereas men 'can be pretty hard but probably straighter'. What is
particularly interesting about Martin's comment is not only the fact
that he neatly distinguishes between men and women but also that he
'views women in positions of authority as inappropriate due to their
"emotional highs and lows", which is seen in direct opposition to the
rational and efficient characteristics which he indirectly attributes to
men', as Mullany (2007: 186) notes.

> ### Exercise 6.3
>
> Read some more of Martin's interview in Example 6.6b, and identify the
> gendered discourses he uses.

Example 6.6b

I just find men in general I mean in the workplace and in general I
just find them to be more stable and straight really than women
.... if you look at sort of even just on the biological clock you
know you've got one week of the month you know not as they are
the other three weeks of the month you know and that is bound to
have an effect I mean that is whatever people say about men and
women are the same they're not because we- you know men don't
go through that women do it's very rare a woman who says she
isn't affected for that week of the month so if you're working for
someone and you get them in that week you know it's they will be
emotionally they will be more susceptible to emotional swings and
not making decisions erm with the kind of same sort of accuracy
that they normally would.

Another area where gendered discourses are particularly relevant are
metaphors. In a study of UK and US business magazines, for example,
Koller (2004) found that the metaphor BUSINESS IS WAR is frequently
used to describe male and female business people. Using this metaphor,
she argues, contributes to creating and maintaining the business world

as a masculine domain, and reflects and reinforces the hegemonic masculinity of business discourse. Koller (2004) observed two ways in which women reacted to these masculine war metaphors. Some women displayed an 'emphasized femininity' (Connell 1987: 187 as quoted in Koller 2004: 6) by drawing on complementary metaphors, such as metaphors of CARE AND AFFECTION. For example, one business woman described herself as a gardener: 'I ... will water [the corporate culture], fertilise it, and see that it takes roots' (Koller 2004: 19). On the other hand, some women also adapted the WAR metaphor in their own discourse: one woman manager, for example, remarked 'I am ruthless in using every bullet I have', and another commented that 'I think [being] a woman helps when you're out in the field' (Koller 2004: 19). These ways of talking and conceptualising successful women managers and, equally important, the ways in which these women managers view and describe themselves contribute to the persistence of gendered discourses, in this case, discourses of hegemonic masculinity.

Challenging gendered discourses and shattering the glass ceiling

In addition to drawing on gendered discourses, and thereby reinforcing underlying (often stereotypical) assumptions and ideologies, people may also resist these discourses and thereby challenge taken for granted assumptions and offer alternative interpretations. Humour is an excellent means to achieve this, as Example 6.7 illustrates.

Example 6.7

> *Context: An interaction at an IT company. Jill is a director and Lucy is a project manager. The women currently share an office, and Donald, who is the company's CEO, is in their office to set up Jill's computer.*

> 1. Lucy: and you're not gonna have a monitor
> 2. Jill: I'm not gonna have a monitor
> 3.   I'm not //gonna have\
> 4. Lucy: /now you've got\\ room for a pot plant
> 5. Jill: ( ) perfect //there you go\
> 6.   laughs]\\
> 7. Jill: you can tell the (girly) office can't you
> 8. Donald: yes //(yeah)\
> 9. Lucy: /[laughs]\\

> Source: Schnurr (2009b: 104).

This example not only shows that gender is indeed a dynamic activity, something that speakers do and produce as they talk (for instance by portraying themselves as 'girls'), it also demonstrates how Jill and Lucy send up the gendered stereotypes they are confronted with on a daily basis, thereby resisting and challenging the gendered discourses that prevail in their workplace. Like the women studied in Speer (2002: 368), Jill and Lucy 'resist and ironise the (masculine) interpretation' of what women's offices stereotypically look like. This results in what Speer (2002: 368) describes as 'a collaboratively produced stereotyped version of femininity'.

A similar observation is made by Mullany (2007: 202), who found that some of the women managers she studied also used the expressions 'girly' and 'girls' as means to 'deliberately mark themselves out as different from their male colleagues'. Like Jill and Lucy in Example 6.7 the women in her study thereby 'draw attention to gender differences in a positive, celebratory way in order to invoke humour and enhance solidarity and collegiality amongst themselves' (Mullany 2007: 202).

Examples 6.6 and 6.7 have shown how by talking about men and in women in certain ways, speakers at the same time contribute to creating certain positions and roles for men and women. These gendered discourses that are reflected in how people talk about and position men and women are particularly meaningful (and powerful) as they create boundaries for normative and expected and hence acceptable behaviour, and this in turn creates certain positions or roles for men and women.

Hence challenging, resisting and ultimately changing these gendered stereotypical and often discriminatory discourses are important steps to be taken 'if the workplace is ever to become a more egalitarian environment in which women will achieve equality, including equal numbers of men and women advancing through the glass ceiling into the higher ranks of management' (Mullany 2007: 210). One way of achieving this gender equality, as Mullany and Litosseliti (2006) suggest, is to raise the gender awareness of people in the workplace. In particular, they mention several avenues where 'linguistic intervention' can be evidenced in the workplace environment, including 'guidelines, codes of practice, and equal opportunity policies in industry; in awareness training seminars in organizations; in the promotion of gender-neutral terms in job advertisements, and so on' (Mullany and Litosseliti 2006: 143). However, these steps are just a few examples of raising people's gender awareness. More effort needs to be taken in order to challenge and replace the stereotypical and discriminatory practices, beliefs and assumptions that characterise many workplaces. Only if the discourses of hegemonic masculinities are replaced by more egalitarian and gender-neutral ones can the workplace domain become an egalitarian environment in which both men and women can equally flourish and achieve their goals.

The next section introduces critical discourse analysis, a discourse-analytical approach which is often used to analyse and explain the various aspects of gender performance in a workplace context.

Section C: Researching gender issues at work

This section provides a brief overview of critical discourse analysis (CDA). It outlines the major aims of this approach to discourse analysis, and describes how it may help address some of the issues outlined in Sections A and B. As Litosseliti (2006: 58) maintains, CDA, or related forms of it (such as feminist CDA), put an emphasis on 'critically examining the ways in which women and men do gender, or construct particular gendered relations and identities through discourse'. CDA researchers typically have a political agenda and an interest in discourse and social change, and thus use CDA for identifying and changing some of the hidden agendas that may contribute to creating and maintaining gender inequalities and discriminatory practices. In particular, CDA assists researchers in exploring how gender and power are constructed in and through discourse. It thereby contributes to challenging and ultimately changing social inequalities.

What is CDA?

In contrast to some of the theories and approaches introduced in earlier chapters, CDA is 'not a linguistic theory' (Huckin 1997: 80), and therefore the focus of CDA is 'not upon language or the use of language in and for themselves, but upon the partially linguistic character of social and cultural processes and structures' (Fairclough and Wodak 1997: 271). And although there is no unified way of doing CDA among scholars, I will try to outline here some of the major ideas and principles that inform and motivate research conducted under the umbrella of CDA.

Van Dijk (2001b: 352) summarises CDA as 'a type of discourse analytical research that primarily studies the way social power abuse, dominance, and inequality are enacted, reproduced, and resisted by text and talk in the social and political context'. CDA can thus be used for analyses of both spoken and written texts.

The main tenets of CDA are summarised by Fairclough and Wodak (1997: 271-280) as:

- CDA addresses social problems.
- Power relations are discursive.

- Discourse constitutes society and culture.
- Discourse does ideological work.
- Discourse is historical.
- The link between text and society is mediated.
- Discourse analysis is interpretative and explanatory.
- Discourse is a form of social action.

I shall discuss just some of these points, with a specific focus on the notions of power and ideology which are particularly relevant in a workplace context, and which are crucial aspects of CDA researchers' political and committed agendas.

Workplaces and institutions in general are important sites where power is constantly enacted, reinforced, and sometimes also challenged in and through discourse (see Chapter 5). In these contexts, CDA is often used as a tool for examining how asymmetrical power relations are produced and reproduced in social practice and in and through discourse. CDA may, for example, explore how power relations are constructed and enacted in interactions, how more powerful groups or speakers exercise their power and how thereby certain ideologies (or particular ways of doing and seeing things) are being reinforced. Over time, these ideologies that underlie existing power relations become 'naturalised' or taken for granted and seem like the only plausible arrangements because they are not questioned any more (see also Cameron 2001; Fairclough 1989). They constitute ways of reinforcing and legitimising the dominance of those in power (e.g. Van Dijk 1997).

Examples of naturalised or taken-for-granted ways of talking about women are shown in Examples 6.3 and 6.6. By portraying women as the exception who have to adapt to masculine ways of doing things if they want to be successful (Example 6.3) and by describing women as being emotional and having mood swings (Martin in Example 6.6), speakers at the same time reinforce the hegemonic masculinities that prevail in their workplaces and perhaps even in the wider society.

CDA proposes that discourse is the most influential factor in producing and reproducing ideologies. Hence, CDA research aims to reveal how power and dominance are enacted in specific contexts. In workplace settings, CDA research may show, for example, how less powerful members are regularly silenced or excluded from decision-making processes, while more powerful members typically get to decide which direction an interaction takes (see e.g. Example 6.1 where C insists on her decision without giving the other participants the opportunity to participate). These findings regarding discourse practices (as observed on the micro level) then need to be linked to social realities or problems (as observed on the macro level). So for example, by silencing less powerful members and thereby excluding them from decision-making processes, their voices are also silenced (and may simply not be considered) in the final decision or its implementation, and the specific reality this decision may create. These elaborations show that CDA views discourse as 'a form of social practice' (Fairclough 1995: 7): that is, as something that people do and that actively contributes to creating certain realities.

Another example of how discourse can be viewed as a form of social practice is guidelines for non-discriminatory language use, which are promoted and implemented by many institutions. The role of CDA scholars in this context is to identify and criticise discriminatory (such as sexist) use of language and help devising guidelines for non-discriminatory language use with the aim of making minorities (such as women) visible not only in language use but also in social practice. These discourse practices of talking with and about disadvantaged groups may then lead to changes in people's consciousness (Fairclough and Wodak 1997: 280).

These examples have made it clear that one of the main aims of CDA is to identify and expose 'hidden agendas' of discourse. In other words, CDA scholars have a specific agenda with a commitment to 'understand, expose, and ultimately resist social inequality' (Van Dijk 2001b: 352). They not only identify social inequalities and problems but they also aim to explain and ultimately contribute to changing these realities by making people aware of them and by demonstrating how they are reflected, embedded and constantly enacted in and through discourse. In this sense, CDA is 'a form of intervention, in practice or social relationships' (Fairclough and Wodak 1997: 258).

However, CDA has also been criticised, in particular for its 'openly 'committed' agenda, which challenges the orthodox academic belief in objective neutral description' (Cameron 2001: 140). As a consequence, as Stubbs (1997: 102) claims, 'the textual interpretations of critical linguists are political rather than linguistically motivated, and ... analysts find what they expect to find'. Another criticism of CDA has been that it is circular in certain aspects. In particular, conversation analysis (CA) scholars (see Chapter 7) point out that CDA research tends to assume that dominance and power are omnipresent and crucially relevant categories for analysis. The relevance of these categories is then demonstrated in the analysis, where it is shown how patterns of dominance and power are reflected and reinforced in texts and talk. CDA scholars thus simply assume the relevance of these categories regardless of whether interlocutors consider them to be relevant or, to use Schegloff's words, whether they are 'demonstrably relevant for the parties' (1997: 183). For a more detailed discussion of criticisms of CDA see, for example, Schegloff (1997), Stubbs (1997),

Wetherell (1998), and see Chouliaraki and Fairclough (1999) for a reply.

CDA in research on language and gender in the workplace

In spite of these criticisms, CDA is a framework that is frequently used in language and gender research. For example, using CDA to analyse interviews with women managers in an Australian bank, Beck (1999) found that power relations are constantly expressed in the management context in the bank in and through a variety of managerial discourses as well as through the discursive performance by the managers themselves. More specifically, the discourse practices in the management context in this workplace are highly masculinised, thereby propagating a strong link between masculinities and management. This masculinisation of management forms and discourses has become naturalised and is rarely questioned. As Beck (1999: 60) argues, it 'has become so deeply entrenched in theory and practice that it is easy to overlook the fundamentally gendered nature of supposedly gender-neutral managerial attributes'. As a consequence, women who want to make their ways into top positions in their workplace are forced to negotiate a juggling act of competing and conflicting demands of being perceived as managerial and feminine in their everyday workplace performances (Beck 1999: 203).

When applied to some of the examples in Section A, a CDA analysis would, for example, identify and describe some of the gendered and discriminatory assumptions that underlie the discourse of participants, for example Jill's comment describing Lucy and herself as 'girls' which marks them as outsiders in an otherwise predominantly masculine workplace (Example 6.7). CDA would also prove useful for an interpretation of the stereotypical and highly derogatory ideologies that inform Martin's description of women managers (Examples 6.6a and 6.6b). If these discourses were recurrent in the context of this specific workplace (or perhaps even across a range of workplaces), such an analysis could provide strong arguments for attempting to change the culture of this workplace and others (that is, make them more (gender) inclusive), for example by implementing codes of practice, equal opportunity policies, and perhaps offering awareness-training seminars. Through these measures, CDA scholars would aim to make the gendered nature of workplace realities visible and thereby to instigate change and to make the work domain a more (gender-) inclusive place in which both men and women could enact their full potential without having to face discriminatory practices (as reflected, for example, in discourse).

Exercise 6.4

Analyse and compare the ways in which men and women are portrayed on the internet sites of two to three companies of the same kind. In analysing the internet sites of your chosen companies you should pay attention to lexical choices as well as visual representations. You may want to consider, for example, how the sites utilise pictures, slogans, quotes, captions and other types of texts and images to portray men and women. It may also be interesting to think about what kinds of information they do not provide. How could a CDA approach support your analysis? What kinds of questions would you ask and what kinds of issues would you focus on if you were to do a CDA analysis of the ways in which men and women are portrayed on these sites?

Summary

This chapter has demonstrated that gender is indeed an important aspect of workplace realities which impacts on professional communication in a variety of different ways. In particular, the existence of gender stereotypes about how men and women (supposedly) talk may be reflected (more or less overtly) in people's discourse, and may also have serious implications for the (often discriminatory) perception and treatment of women (and sometimes men) in specific professions and workplace environments. Two of these gender-related issues that affect women in many workplaces, in particular as they try to advance their careers, are the double-bind and the glass ceiling.

Gender is conceptualised as a performance rather than an attribute. And it has been argued that gender is always potentially relevant in any encounter – it may be relatively hidden in the background or it may be something that interlocutors themselves comment on and make relevant in various ways throughout their interaction. Two specific ways in which gender is enacted in workplace contexts are the use of gendered speech styles and the existence of certain gendered discourses. By drawing on elements of masculine and feminine speech styles, interlocutors not only evoke certain stances which contribute to constructing certain professional roles and identities, at the same time they do gender. Equally, by talking about men and women in certain ways, interlocutors simultaneously respond to (and reinforce or challenge) specific notions of masculinities and femininities.

One of the approaches frequently used to investigate language and gender at work is CDA. With its openly political agenda, CDA is primarily interested in showing how asymmetrical power relations are produced and reproduced through discourse, and how the ideologies underlying these power relations become naturalised and taken for granted. The main aim of CDA, then, is to expose hidden agendas of discourse and to contribute to changing social inequalities and problems by making people aware of them and by pointing to the discursive mechanisms through which they are recreated and constantly reinforced.

In the next chapter some of the issues discussed here are picked up and applied to leadership – a complex concept which is inherently gendered and which has a male bias in most professional contexts. A particular focus is on leadership discourse and the ways in which leadership is performed through language.

7 Leadership

This chapter deals with a particularly complex and highly relevant aspect of professional communication, leadership. It approaches the question of what leadership is from the perspective of applied linguistics, and focuses primarily on the crucial role of communication for leadership performance. In doing this, some of the benefits of taking a discursive approach to leadership are illustrated.

Section A: Exploring leadership discourse

Almost everybody has an idea about what leadership is, which behaviours constitute good and effective leadership, and how people should be led. However, when it comes to actually defining what leadership is, things are far from straightforward. In fact, some people have argued that there are almost as many definitions of leadership as there are people who have attempted to define it (Bass 1981: 71; see also Decker and Rotondo 2001). However, before adding yet another definition to the increasing pile (in Section B), we will explore what doing leadership means from the perspective of applied linguistics.

Exercise 7.1

Think about someone you consider to be a good leader in the work domain. This could be somebody famous, someone you have heard about in the media, or somebody you have worked for or are still working for. Once you have identified a leader, make a list of the activities you think this person regularly performs throughout their typical everyday working day. In making this list, try to be as specific and concrete as possible.

Answer Exercise 7.1 before reading on.

Although the items on your list may vary, it is likely that they will include activities such as envisioning goals and motivating others; getting things done by making decisions, organising, coordinating, and directing other's performances while at the same time allowing subordinates some autonomy; developing group cohesiveness; creating and maintaining a productive work climate; guiding and supporting subordinates; ensuring effective communication within the team and across the wider organisation.

These are just some of the activities typically associated with leadership in the literature (e.g. Dwyer 1993, Gardner 1990, Yukl 2002). A closer look at these items shows that most (if not all) of them in one way or another involve communicating with others. Take decision making as an example. Communication is clearly a crucial part of this complex activity: most decisions are not made out of thin air but are complex processes which typically involve consultations and discussions with others, as well as some kind of information seeking – all of which involve communication. Even those decisions that are made unilaterally, that is, without consultation and discussion with others, involve communication – at the very least when it comes to informing those who are affected by the repercussions of that decision. Communication is thus at the heart of decision-making processes and is also crucially relevant for other aspects of leadership performance, as this chapter illustrates.

Examples of leadership discourse

So how do leaders talk at work and how is leadership actually done? This section approaches these questions by discussing some examples of leadership in action. All examples are taken from authentic workplace discourse including different media, such as face-to-face interactions, emails, and an ongoing interaction on a wiki[1] platform. While these different channels or media are clearly not exhaustive in terms of where and how leadership can be enacted, they nevertheless provide a good picture of the complexities of leadership discourse.

Example 7.1 was recorded in a team meeting at the beginning of a project. Clara, the team leader in a New Zealand corporation, expresses her appreciation of and her confidence in her team's abilities.

Example 7.1

Context: Meeting of project team at beginning of project. Clara is the senior manager and section head.

1. Clara: a couple of things about the project
2.   we really expecting a high performance work team
3.   and I'm I'm really confident that we've got that
4   with the make up of the people we've got here.

Source: Vine et al.(2008: 348).

With this brief comment, Clara accomplishes a range of leadership tasks: she not only motivates and perhaps even inspires her team to perform well on their new project, she also expresses her high expectations. She thus creates team spirit and a good atmosphere in the team while at the same time communicating her expectations. Behaviours such as those displayed by Clara that are targeted towards encouraging and motivating subordinates and which aim at maintaining harmony and good relationships within the team are often associated with leadership performance (Yukl 2002).

Although motivating subordinates is an important leadership activity, in everyday workplace interactions the focus may sometimes be on more transactional behaviours, such as ensuring people know what they are supposed to be doing: for example, what exactly their role is in a particular project, what tasks they are responsible for, what deadlines to meet and so on. The next example shows how this aim of making sure people are on track can be achieved. Example 7.2 is taken from the same working team as Example 7.1.

Example 7.2

Context: Update meeting of project team. Smithy is the deputy section head and special project manager. Clara is the most senior person in the team.

1.	Smithy:	action items from last week's meeting um
2.		Clara Banks was to arrange [systems] access with
3.		Keely Cooling
4.		and you've done that?
5.		[brief discussion about this item]
6.	Smithy:	okay training meeting with Fraser um
7.		re the customer satisfaction course
8.	Tessa:	yep + (we did that)
9.	Smithy:	Tessa to follow up [name] for notification of the
10.		training system for [system]
11.	Tessa:	yep we've done that ++

Source: Vine et al. (2008: 348).

At the beginning of a project meeting Smithy checks that team members have done the jobs they had been assigned at the last meeting (lines 1–4, 6–7, 9–10). His utterances are clearly task-oriented, their main aim being to ensure tasks have been completed so that 'the next step of the project can be initiated' (Vine et al. 2008: 348). Checking up on team members' progress and ensuring targets are met is an important activity that is routinely performed by leaders or meeting chairs, often at the initial stages of a meeting. In contrast to Example 7.1 this short excerpt does not contain any behaviours explicitly targeted at creating or maintaining group harmony and positive interpersonal relationships.

While Examples 7.1 and 7.2 are instances of spoken interaction, Examples 7.3 to 7.6 are taken from written communication, namely from emails collected in a non-profit workplace. As discussed in Chapter 2, emails are becoming increasingly important in workplace communication, and in many workplaces (in particular, in corporate environments) leaders often spend a considerable amount of their time communicating via emails. The emails displayed here were sent by Sabitha, the CEO and owner of a small non-profit organisation in Hong Kong, to her subordinates (7.3–7.5) and to an external client (7.6). They are representative of the ways in which Sabitha typically communicates with her subordinates and clients.

Example 7.3

Subject: FW: Meeting with [client name]
           Can you work on this?
           <Electronic signature>
           <Public Company link and motto>

Example 7.4

Subject: FW: ENGAGE in Hong Kong
           What are you doing about this?
           <Electronic signature>
           <Public Company link and motto>

Example 7.5

Subject: FW: Meeting with [client name]

           Bonnie

           An you pls write a blurb about this in Other events for
           our website
           <Electronic signature>
           <Public Company link and motto>
Source: Examples 7.3–7.5 are from Schnurr and Mak (2011).

What is perhaps most striking about these emails, compared with the examples of spoken interaction discussed above, is their short and explicit style. The first two emails do not contain a greeting and the third one has only a minimal greeting (the name of one of the addressee). There are no mitigating constructions such as 'I was wondering whether' or 'could you perhaps', and even Sabitha's use of 'pls' (an abbreviated version of 'please') in Email 7.5 seems to function as a conventionalised politeness marker or even a booster (Waldvogel 2005), leaving little doubt about the fact that the addressee (Bonnie) does not really have an option about complying. All three emails are relatively direct and thus potentially face-threatening to the addressee. However, the relative directness of the emails is mitigated to some extent by the question form of the directives and by face-to-face interactions that typically precede the emails, as members of this workplace have commented in interviews after the data collection (see Schnurr and Mak 2011). In all emails Sabitha effectively ensures that her subordinates know what they are supposed to be working on. A rather different email style is shown in Example 7.6, an email which has been sent by Sabitha to an external client.

Example 7.6

Subject: Thank you

Dear Daisy
Many thanks for the wonderful moon cakes which I received this afternoon. They are yummy!

I would like to set up a telecom with you to see how best we can move forward with our working with [company name] and my colleague Betty will be in touch with you to set up a time for us to talk.
Thank you again
Sabitha
<Electronic signature>
<Public Company link and motto>

What is perhaps most interesting about this email from Sabitha to an external client is the remarkably different tone from the emails to her subordinates. This email contains a 'proper' greeting ('Dear Daisy') and closing ('Thank you again'), and it starts off with some small talk establishing common ground before moving on to the aim of the email, namely to set up a teleconference. In this email, then, Sabitha skilfully combines both relational and transactional aspects: she does relational work and creates a positive ground for future collaborations with this client while at the same time achieving her transactional goals.

These differences in email style may be due to a variety of factors including participants, purpose and context. In particular, it is clearly important to create and maintain good relationships with clients, which may be one of the reasons why the email to Daisy includes more relational work than Sabitha's internal emails. Moreover, as mentioned above, Sabitha and her colleagues work together very closely in the same open-plan office. Hence, emails are often sent as reminders or record-keeping devices which follow up on oral discussions (Vine 2004). And since people at this company have been working together for a while, it is quite likely that they have developed shared ways of communicating with each other (see the discussion of communities of practice in Chapter 3). Other factors that might have an impact on Sabitha's different leadership styles in the emails could be different purposes of the emails, different time constraints when writing them, different degrees of urgency, and many more.

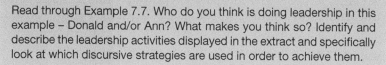

Exercise 7.2

Read through Example 7.7. Who do you think is doing leadership in this example – Donald and/or Ann? What makes you think so? Identify and describe the leadership activities displayed in the extract and specifically look at which discursive strategies are used in order to achieve them.

Example 7.7

Context: Interaction between Donald and Ann after a successful interview with a job applicant (Beverley).

1.	Donald:	yep + okay alright
2.		do you wanna write do up a letter of offer
3.	Ann:	//[laughs]\
4.	Donald:	/[laughs]\\
5.		(are) you the project manager
6.		//[laughs]\
7.	Ann:	/how do I\\ do that
8.	Donald:	eh? [laughs]
9.		there's standard templates
10.	Ann:	for letters of offers?
11.	Donald:	yep
12.	Ann:	oh hell
13.	Donald:	so but what you're gonna have to do is work out
14.		what you're asking her to do and what the
15.		what the position is +
16.		cos we don't have a position for (her) + [laughs]
17.	Ann:	okay so what's that then
18.	Donald:	so I would think you'd write as you know [voc]
19.		project assistant or something or +++
20.		technical assistant +++
21.		I think I'm sorry I'm not very good at euphemisms

22.   for roles
23.   [laughs]
24. Ann: [laughs]
25. Donald: chief coffee //maker\
26. Ann: /[laughs]\\
27. Donald: we didn't ask her how well she makes coffee
28.   [laughs]

Source: Schnurr (2009b: 28–9).

The next example illustrates leadership of a rather different kind. Example 7.8 is an extract from a wiki[2] collaboration among members of a research community. The aim of this particular wiki is to create an entry (an article, as the interlocutors call it) for an online resource. The entries from the wiki collaboration below provide the name of the participant, as well as the time and date of when the wiki was posted.

Example 7.8

Lukas M. Kline 14:50, 7 January 200X (CST): I'm going to try to build some more information into this article. There are a number of a ways to precipitate DNA [... names a few methods]. I'll research it in a few of the protocol books and try to type up something on this page. Perhaps we should make sub-pages for each method of extraction? We could also make an outline type system for each method. Let me know what you all think--I'm rather new to the [name] community.

Nena 14:55, 7 January 200X (CST): Sounds great. There is some relevant info at Purification of DNA ... specifically the section on alcohol purification. Perhaps you could move that content here ... and expand it? And then link to [other topics].

Lukas M. Kline 15:27, 7 January 200X (CST): That sounds great. I think that DNA Precipitation is something of a subset of Purification of DNA, so that link definitely makes sense.

WilliamH 24 November 200X: With all due respect but is there a reason why we need 2 protocols for the same? Maybe they could be merged? See also: http://xxx

The exchange starts with a suggestion by Lukas M. Kline to add more information to an article (on which members of this online community are working). He explains what he thinks needs to be done, makes a few concrete suggestions for improvement and explicitly invites his colleagues' feedback. A few minutes later a first reply is posted in which Nena supports Lukas' proposed changes ('sounds great'), making further concrete suggestions herself: 'Perhaps you could move that content here ... and expand it? And then link to [other topics].' About 30 minutes later Lukas posts a reply agreeing with her suggestions: 'That sounds great' and 'definitely makes sense'. The next reply by a third member of the team, WilliamH, is posted more than 10 months later. It questions and challenges the usefulness of the proposed (and presumably by that time already implemented) changes. WilliamH's contribution is relatively short (considering that this is a disagreement which questions what had previously been agreed upon): it consists of two questions and a link. At the time of writing this was the last contribution made by members of the community, but since the issue of what to include in the article and which links to make has not yet been resolved, it is likely that the discussion will continue.

The ways in which leadership is performed in this extract are less straightforward and perhaps more complex than in the previous examples: none of the participants has been 'officially' assigned a leadership role. So who is doing leadership in this extract? We will come back to this question in Section B.

The examples discussed in this section have illustrated a wide range of leadership activities which may be performed very differently. Leaders may, for example, put great emphasis on motivating their subordinates before expressing their expectations and explaining what they are required to perform (as Clara did in Example 7.1); they may be more or less explicit and direct in what exactly their expectations are and how they are supposed to be met (like Sabitha in Examples 7.3–7.5). However, leadership may also mean conjointly negotiating what needs to be done (as in Example 7.8) rather than one person making the decisions. These different ways of doing leadership are explored in more detail in the next section.

Section B: Conceptualising leadership

As discussed in Chapter 1, changes in organisational structures have led to different and increasingly complex ways of communicating in many workplace contexts. These changes are also reflected in ways of doing leadership. In particular, changes from strictly hierarchical structures to more horizontal structures have resulted in various diverse leadership constellations which increasingly replace traditional top-down models. As Jackson and Parry (2008: 55) maintain, '[t]raditional command-and-control, hierarchically-based organizations are seen as being no match for the flat, laterally-integrated network organizations in the context of a rapidly changing competitive global economy'. As a consequence of these structural changes, ways and patterns of communication (in particular, leadership communication) have changed as well. And it seems that people are very aware of these changes, as Example 7.9 illustrates.

Example 7.9

Context: Two leaders discuss some problems they are having with another manager who is more senior in the organisational hierarchy and who they describe as 'old style'.

1.	Pat:	I guess I know [name of person higher up in the
2.		hierarchy] (1.3)
3.		and I know a little how he he operates ++ and
4.	Jane:	okay tell me about that
5.	Pat:	I just think //he's\
6.	Jane:	/how does he operate? What do you know?\\
7.		++
8.	Pat:	He is just erm to me a good old boyish ++
9.		kind of erm + you know
10.		he sat behind me at June meeting and was very much
11.		in the old style of the division manager and ++
12.		not like Skip at all ( ) participative
13.	Jane:	( )
14.	Pat:	no
15.	Jane:	[laughs]
16.	Pat:	erm ++ not like- he's not like Skip where he can work
17.		through I mean
18.		he's very much in the old style of it + traditional +
19.		so ++ you know he'll play the- he'll play the game
20.		he'll play the politics
21.		he'll put the pressure on
22.		he'll put the fear in
23.		he'll- he'll make the comments and
24.		he's very much with the comments
25.		and the jabs and things
26.		and that will forever be out in the system
27.		and we don't need that
28.		so we have to either + have to go and solve it
29.		or we need to send someone to UT (for the training
30.		session)

Source: Fairhurst (2007: 111).

Jane and Pat describe one of the leaders higher up in their organisation as 'the old style division manager' (line 11). They complain about his leadership style which is 'not … participative' (lines 11 and 12) and which seems to rely on traditional command-and-control approaches, as is reflected in the women's complains: 'he'll play the game, the- he'll play the politics, he'll put the pressure on, he'll put the fear in, he'll-he'll make the comments' (lines 19–23). The women make it clear what they think about these kinds of behaviours: 'we don't need that' (line 25). Their comments show that there is an expectation that more participative and empowering ways of doing leadership, in particular by sharing leadership responsibilities, are the more appropriate way forward. Some of these less 'leader-centred' and more 'follower-centred' approaches to leadership are introduced next.

Different leadership constellations

In addition to typical (more or less hierarchical) leadership constellations in which the leader holds a hierarchically higher and typically more powerful position than their followers, there are numerous other possible constellations of individuals who are involved in the performance of leadership. And recent research is developing an increasing interest in these 'other' non-leadership centred constellations of leadership (e.g. Jackson and Parry 2008; Raelin 2003; Nielsen 2004). One of these so-called follower-centred perspectives on leadership which has been researched from a linguistic perspective is co-leadership (e.g. Schnurr and Chan 2011; Vine et al. 2008).

Co-leadership has been described as 'two leaders in vertically contiguous positions who share the responsibilities of leadership' (Jackson and Parry 2008: 82). First introduced by Heenan and Bennis (1999: 6), the notion of co-leadership can be applied to various constellations. As O'Toole, Galbraith and Lawler (2002: 78) observe, co-leaders may divide their roles and tasks in various ways, such as 'Mr. Inside and Mr. Outside; Mr. Business Line A and Ms. Business Line B; Ms Operations and Ms. Acquisitions'. However, sharing leadership 'is not just an issue at the top of corporations' (O'Toole et al. 2002: 79); rather, empirical evidence suggests that in many organisations, leadership tasks are shared among employees at all levels (see also Day, Gronn and Salas 2004). Although co-leadership has various benefits and usually involves the effective sharing of various leadership responsibilities, potential difficulties may arise in those situations where co-leaders disagree with each other, as in the following example. Example 7.10 was recorded during a meeting at a consulting company in Hong Kong. It illustrates how co-leadership is enacted between Danny (the managing director and assigned chair of these meetings) and QS (the company's CEO) who is also present during these meetings.

Example 7.10

> *Context: After a weekly meeting at a Hong Kong-based consulting company. Participants are starting to leave the room but several people continue their discussions. QS and Danny (the co-leaders) and Lilly (one of the other meeting participants) are discussing an upcoming marketing event that Lilly is supposed to prepare.*

1.	QS:	so I was just suggesting um Lilly's upcoming
2.		marketing activity
3.	Danny:	uh they she is not ready
4.		so this oh she wouldn't
5.	Lilly:	I'm not ready yet
6.	QS:	[laughing]: no I know you're not ready:
7.		but if I if I there are lots of them that are coming up
8.	Danny:	yeah we need to at first see the marketing event
9.		er calendar
10.		looking for ( )
11.	QS:	I'm I'm talking to the VP of marketing
12.	Danny:	I'm talking to my help-
13.	QS:	[in agitated tone of voice]: I don't care I I'm talking to
14.		//VP of marketing\:
15.	Danny:	[in agitated tone of voice]: /( )\\:

[8 second pause before researchers come in to collect equipment]

Source: Schnurr and Chan 2011: 198).

Although most of the co-leadership activities between QS and Danny take place harmoniously, this example shows another less harmonious side, namely how they deal with disagreements. In this instance the co-leaders disagree on whether one of their staff members (Lilly) should attend a particular marketing event (lines 1–4). What is particularly interesting about this exchange is how the disagreement becomes increasingly explicit and aggravated (e.g. lines 11–15) so that in the end the co-leaders do not talk with each other (see the silence after line 15). In disagreeing with each other, Danny and QS challenge each other's role and authority, and ultimately also their position within the co-leadership constellation. Responding with silence to this (at this stage) unsolvable disagreement seems to be an effective means for them to insist on their different views while at the same time avoiding more confrontation in front of their subordinates (Kjaerbeck 2008; Laforest 2002). Thus, by remaining silent for a remarkably long period (8 seconds), QS and Danny seem to acknowledge their disagreement without wanting to further elaborate on it in this situation.

Other follower-centred perspectives on leadership are shared leadership and distributed leadership. Shared leadership refers to situations in which leadership responsibilities are shared and rotate among team members. In these constellations, the person whose abilities best match the specific (and often changing) requirements of the situation takes on the leadership responsibilities, for example for a specific phase in a project. Once the phase is completed or different skills and abilities are required, the leadership responsibilities (and thus leadership role) gets passed on. This kind of actively participating in the leadership processes can be viewed as genuinely empowering members (Jackson and Parry 2008: 56) as they are been given the opportunity to share and exercise leadership activities conjointly (see also Raelin 2003).

Distributed leadership describes those constellations in which teams lead their work 'collectively and independently of formal leaders' (Vine et al. 2008: 341). In these 'leader-less' constellations, there are no (more or less) 'officially' assigned leaders; rather, the various leadership activities (including making sure deadlines are met and things are getting done, as well as encouraging and motivating other team members) are performed by team members who are often on the same hierarchical level within their organisation (see also Nielsen 2004; Day et al. 2004; Gronn 2002). Typical examples of distributed leadership are schools where administrative work is often shared among different teams (Grace 1995 as cited in Gronn 2002; Spillane et al. 2000 as cited in Day et al. 2004).

It has been suggested that these various leadership constellations can be placed along a continuum with co-leadership at one end and distributed leadership at the other end (see e.g. Jackson and Parry 2008). However, it should be noted that in spite of some advantages of these 'other' leadership constellations, sharing leadership between different individuals does not always provide the most effective way of doing leadership. Instead, as will be elaborated below in more detail, different constellations of leadership and different ways of doing leadership are best suited to address the specific demands of different workplaces, different working teams, different projects, and even different phases within a project.

What then is leadership?

As mentioned earlier, because leadership is a multifaceted concept which often mystifies (Yukl 1989: 276), there is little agreement among scholars regarding its meaning and definition (Hosking 1997: 293) and there is, in fact, an ongoing debate among scholars as to what exactly constitutes leadership (e.g. Alvesson and Spicer 2012; Grint 2005). As Yukl (2002: 3) laments, '[r]esearchers usually define leadership according to their individual perspectives and the aspect of the phenomenon of most interest to them'. It is thus perhaps not surprising that multiple conceptualisations of leadership exist, including those that 'define leadership in terms of traits, behaviours, influence, interaction patterns, role relationships, and occupation of an administrative position.' (Yukl 2002: 3). However, in spite of these differences, most researchers agree that in order to capture the complex and multifunctional nature of leadership, it is useful to view it as a process or an activity rather than as a position of authority or as a personal characteristic (Heifertz 1998: 347; see also Hosking 1997; Northouse 1997).

As we have seen in Section A, the activities in which leaders typically engage span a wide continuum including achieving transactional objectives and performing relationally oriented behaviour (for a more detailed discussion see also Dwyer 1993; Robbins et al. 1998; Sayers 1997; Smith and Peterson 1988). As was described in Chapter 1, generally speaking, transactional behaviours describe activities that primarily aim to get things done, solve problems and achieve set goals, while relationally oriented behaviours centre around ensuring group harmony and creating a productive working atmosphere. Both activities are integral aspects of the leadership process and cannot always be separated from each other (see Ferch and Mitchell 2001). Instead, leaders often skilfully combine transactional and relational objectives in their discourse (see Examples 7.5 and 7.7).

Taking into account the central role of language in achieving these various transactional and relational goals (as established in Section A), leadership can productively be viewed as a discursive performance, which by influencing others advances the goals of the organisation (transactional behaviour) while also maintaining harmony within the group (relational behaviour). This relatively broad discourse-based definition of leadership has proved useful for discourse analytical approaches to different types of leadership in diverse contexts (for example Schnurr and Chan 2009; Holmes 2006; Marra, Schnurr and Holmes 2006; Schnurr 2009b). Most importantly, though, this definition takes into account that leadership may take different forms in different contexts.

Exercise 7.3

Have another look at Examples 7.1–7.8 discussed in Section A. Based on the definition of leadership provided above, identify who performs leadership in each example and explain why you think so. What leadership constellation is depicted in each of the examples, and how is this reflected in interlocutors' discourse?

The examples discussed above have illustrated just some of the many different ways of doing leadership in different constellations. Clearly, there are many more ways in which people do leadership and share leadership responsibilities with others. However, the examples chosen provide a good picture of how leadership may be accomplished through talk. Before discussing in more detail the various facets of leadership discourse, I would like to briefly talk about the distinction between two related terms which often cause some confusion, leadership and management.

Leadership and management – is there a difference?

In the leadership literature of the 1980s and 1990s the terms leadership and management were often used synonymously (e.g. Adler and Izraeli 1988; Decker 1991; Ferrario 1994; Maher 1997), and it is only relatively recently that research has begun making a distinction between the two concepts (e.g. Kotter 2001; Rost 1998; Sarros, Butchatsky and Santora 1996; Zaleznik 1998). Some of these recent studies argue that leadership and management are 'different but complementary' concepts (Kotter 2001: 85). According to this view, leaders and managers engage in different activities (Rost 1998): leading comprises setting a direction, aligning, motivating and inspiring people, whereas managing includes planning, budgeting, organising, staffing, controlling and problem solving (Kotter 2001; Northouse 1997; Sarros et al. 1996). Moreover, in order to achieve their goals, leaders draw on influence while managers are said to rely on their authority (Rost 1998). The underlying assumption many of these theories adopt is that '[m]anagers are people who do things right and leaders are people who do the right thing' (Rost 1998: 100). Often the picture of the charismatic leader in comparison to the pragmatic but visionless manager is evoked; and leadership is viewed as an art while management is seen as a necessary practice.

However, some researchers note that differences between leadership and management are not always clear-cut. Rather, in practice 'one cannot function without the other' (Kotter 2001: 85). For example, there is considerable overlap in the activities typically engaged in by leaders and managers (Gardner 1990; Northouse 1997): both leaders and managers deal with 'deciding what needs to be done, creating networks of people and relationships that can accomplish an agenda, and then trying to ensure that people actually do the job' (Kotter 2001: 86). In other words, both managers and leaders aim at achieving their transactional objectives while also considering relational aspects to some extent.

A good illustration of this overlap between leadership and management-type activities is displayed in Sabitha's emails discussed in

Section A (Examples 7.3 to 7.5). The main aim of these emails is to get things done and to ensure her subordinates know what they are expected to do. These activities could thus be described as managing. However, if we place these email exchanges in the bigger picture of what is happening at this workplace, we would have to acknowledge that these predominantly transactional exchanges are just a small part of Sabitha's everyday interactions with her subordinates. In many of her other exchanges (most notably in the one-to-one interactions with her subordinates and clients) Sabitha puts considerably more emphasis on relational aspects and displays a wide range of leadership behaviours, such as creating (and communicating) a vision, as well as inspiring and motivating others (see Schnurr and Mak 2011). In practice, these activities (associated with management and leadership respectively) are often hard to distinguish from each other. For example, in getting things done or solving problems people may at the same time motivate and perhaps even inspire others and set a direction (see Example 7.7). These are just some examples of how leadership and management activities are often intricately interwoven with each other.

Thus, although potential differences between managers and leaders may evolve around the degree to which they perform relational behaviours, the processes and activities associated with leadership and management seem to overlap to such an extent that for our purposes here, potential differences between the two are not considered in much detail. I will thus continue to use the term leader, and acknowledge that some types of leaders may also perform management tasks (see Gardner 1990).

Doing leadership in context

The various discourse examples discussed in Section A have shown that there are different ways of doing leadership, and more specifically of performing relational and transactional behaviours. However, as has been argued throughout this chapter, what exactly constitute effective or most adequate ways of doing leadership very much depends on the specific context in which leadership occurs (as well as, of course, on personal preferences of individuals). Some contextual factors that may have an impact on how leadership is done, and more importantly how leadership is communicated, are discussed below. Among the factors identified in previous leadership literature are the dynamics of the leaders' working groups (including the time they have been working together and the expectations they are facing), the culture of the leaders' workplace, the wider culture in which their workplace is placed, and the ways gender is enacted in the leaders' workplace (see e.g. Dwyer 1993; Schein 1992; Hickman 1998; Ford 2005; Cullen 1999; Guirdham 2005; Schnurr 2009b). I briefly discuss each of these factors in turn.

One of the most crucial factors that have an impact on leadership discourse is the discursive norms that characterise the various working teams in which leaders (and other organisational members) participate on a day-to-day basis (Schnurr 2009b). As was discussed in more detail in Chapter 3, groups that work together for a long time often develop a shared repertoire of behavioural and linguistic norms on which members regularly draw when interacting with each other. These norms are also reflected in the discourse of the leaders of these groups: in particular, since leaders regularly interact with members of their team – whether in larger formal meetings, in spontaneous one-to-one interactions in the corridor, via emails, internal memos, on the phone or via Skype – over time they often develop a repertoire of discursive strategies of what team members consider to be appropriate and normative ways of interacting with each other. (This applies in particular to working groups which have been described as communities of practice.) Due to their special status, then, leaders often play a crucial role in the development and negotiation of the discursive norms that characterise their working groups: through their performance in interactions with other group members they constantly reinforce and shape the norms of acceptable and expected behaviours. These norms may, for example, refer to appropriate ways of enacting power and making decisions (such as who is involved in these processes, how are the outcomes communicated), getting things done (for instance through explicit directives – see Example 7.3–7.5 – or through more implicit and participative ways – see Example 7.7), holding meetings and so on. In other words, these norms of acceptable and expected behaviour apply to all aspects of leadership communication.

These behavioural and discursive norms are also reflected to some extent in the culture of the leaders' workplaces (as was discussed in more detail in Chapter 3). Since organisations or workplaces define notions of what they consider to be appropriate and effective leadership, the ways in which leaders act and talk (and are being talked about) also need to be understood against this background. The following excerpt shows how even the forms and underlying concepts people use to talk about leadership may vary remarkably across workplaces and professions.

Example 7.11

Context: After a presentation (about a certain decision-making model) to a group of medical practitioners at Cleveland Clinic, one of the participants approaches the presenter and makes the following statement:

You know this is all bullshit don't you…. I bet if you counted in both the article and your lecture the number of times the word subordinate was used, it would be close to fifty times .... The problem is that these ideas may be all right for the business world, but they won't do here ... we are a partnership of physicians. I'm not a subordinate. I'm not just an employee here.

Source: Cooperrider, Barrett and Srivatstava
(1995: 185 as cited in Fairhurst 2007: 169).

In analysing this excerpt, Fairhurst (2007: 170) explains that one reason for the participant's strong rejection of the term 'subordinate' may be that 'it lacked the egalitarianism in the group practice democracy that was Cleveland Clinic's culture at the time'. In other words, the terminology used by the presenter, and presumably also the underlying conceptualisations of what leadership is and how it is best accomplished, did not match the ways in which leadership was understood and enacted in this particular workplace. However, the problem brought up by the participant in Example 7.11 illustrates a further issue with talking and thinking about leadership: while this chapter primarily deals with leadership phenomena in corporate environments, conceptualisations and enactments of leadership may be very different in, say, academic or educational contexts. Thus, not only do actual enactments of leadership differ across workplaces, but different sectors may have specific notions of leadership and may consequently use a very different terminology to describe similar activities and processes.

In spite of the close link between leadership and workplace culture, the relationship between the two concepts is multidimensional, and the notion of 'effective' leadership is not only determined by aspects of workplace culture, but leaders in turn also play an important role in the creation, maintenance, and change on all levels of workplace culture (Neuhauser, Bender and Stromberg 2000; Parry and Proctor-Thomson 2003; Schein 1992). Rabey (1997: 410), for instance notes that the culture of a workplace is 'often a reflection of the leadership style': not only do leaders play a crucial role in the constant enactment and reinforcement of the values and assumptions that characterise their workplace, their particular way of doing leadership may also shape the culture of their workplace. For example, their ways of doing leadership may impact on whether members focus on their task or are people-oriented and whether they are more conservative or innovative (Rabey 1997: 41).

As was discussed in Chapter 3, one particularly crucial aspect of workplace culture is the ways in which gender is understood, created and enacted on a day-to-day basis. Among the social factors that impact on leadership, gender is one of the most pervasive ones as it impacts on leadership performance more or less directly through a variety of different channels: not only is the concept of leadership marked by a masculine bias (as was established in Chapter 6), but many of the activities typically associated with leadership are also associated with masculinity (such as displaying power). Thus, because leadership is not a gender-neutral concept, masculine ways of doing leadership are often viewed as normative (Duerst-Lahti and Kelly 1995; Martin Rojo and Esteban 2003; Sinclair 1998; Holmes 2006). This male bias is not only reflected in hegemonic discourses of leadership (Ford 2005), that is, in masculinised perceptions of what makes good leaders and who typically is a leader, but this bias may also impact leaders' everyday workplace interactions.

A final factor mentioned here that has been reported to have an impact on leadership (and, in fact, also impacts on all of the factors mentioned above) is culture. It has been noted that culture seems to be one of the most prominent factors that have an impact on defining 'the array of preferred and acceptable leader behaviours' (Cullen 1999: 527; see also House et al. 2004; Guirdham 2005; Schnurr and Chan 2009). For example, the concept of leadership itself is an Anglophone management concept and most of the existing literature emerged in a Western context (Casimir et al. 2006). The question is thus whether conceptualisations of leadership that have been developed in this specific context also apply to other socio-cultural settings.

It has been argued that notions of 'effective' leadership and specific expectations about appropriate ways of doing leadership may be linked to culture-specific values, and can be explained by drawing on frameworks of cultural dimensions (e.g. Hall 1976; Hofstede 1980). And while there are some issues with such essentialist and often deterministic assumptions that underlie much of this cross-cultural leadership research (see also Chapter 4), a substantial amount of research has been conducted to compare leadership across (national) cultures (e.g. Kim et al. 2004; Dorfman et al. 1997; Casimir et al. 2006). One of the most detailed and comprehensive studies on leadership across cultures is the GLOBE (Global Leadership and Organizational Behavior Effectiveness) cross-cultural leadership project. In this ten-year project 170 researchers across 62 nations have gathered quantitative and qualitative data to explore, conceptualise, test and theorise about the integrated relationship between leadership and culture. Findings indicate that there are some practices and values associated with leadership that are universal (that apply to all cultures under investigation) and there are others that are specific to a few cultures. Among the universal leadership dimensions are, for example, being participative, autonomous and team-oriented (for more information see House et al. 2004).

However, these cross-cultural studies on leadership have also been criticised heavily, for example for their 'deterministic generalizations about national culture and its influence', their over-reliance on measurements of 'cultural factors', and for ignoring the ways in which leadership (and followership) also influence and shape the cultures that supposedly influence them (Guthey and Jackson 2011: 166). Moreover, as Kim (2004: 88) asserts, these studies tend to overlook the wide variation of leadership behaviour that can be found within the same national culture. Based on these and other criticisms of cross-cultural leadership research, Guthey and Jackson (2011: 175) propose that in order to move away from this rather restrictive cross-cultural paradigm, research needs to 'move beyond the quantitative models provided by Hofstede and the GLOBE project' and 'conceive of both leadership and culture in the broad sense, and to look at how different types of leadership interact with culture in different ways'.

In addition to the factors discussed above, it is equally important to consider the specific situational context in which leadership occurs. Factors such as tight deadlines, impending redundancies, budget constraints and individual stylistic preferences also have an impact on how leadership is accomplished in a particular situation. Thus, for example, whether decisions are discussed at length with the entire team or made unilaterally, is not only a matter of workplace culture, group norms and gender, but also reflects the situational constraints and preferences of individuals. Moreover, as the examples in Section A have shown, the medium or channel through which leadership is communicated also has an impact on leadership discourse. Sabitha's style in the internal emails (Examples 7.3–7.5), for example, was very direct and did not include many explicit relationally oriented features, while in the face-to-face and one-to-one meeting between Donald and Ann (Example 7.7), much more emphasis was put on relational aspects while still ensuring that transactional goals were met.

So while channels/media of communication play a role in how leadership is accomplished, the specific norms that govern these different channels/media in turn depend on the culture of the workplace and the norms that characterise specific working teams within a workplace. In other words, not all workplace emails are as direct as the ones sent by Sabitha to her subordinates and not all leaders are as patient and as supportive as Donald in the one-to-one interaction with his subordinate. Moreover, the specific situational demands also have an impact on how leadership is done: if Donald, for example, had been under greater time pressure, he might not have been as relaxed and supportive towards Ann.

Now that we have established that communication does indeed play a crucial role in leadership processes, the next section outlines how leadership can be productively approached through a focus on discourse.

Section C: Approaching leadership discourse

Due to the central role of communication for leadership processes, it has been argued that 'researchers and practitioners require fewer "grand theories" of leadership' but rather need 'a better understanding of the everyday practices of talk that constitute leadership and a deeper knowledge of how leaders use language to craft "reality"' (Clifton 2006: 203). Discourse-analytical approaches seem to be particularly suitable for this kind of endeavour as they provide interesting new perspectives and insights into the complexities of leadership performance. This section briefly introduces discursive leadership, a tradition established in leadership research that is strongly oriented towards leadership discourse. Two specific approaches to discursive leadership are discussed, conversation analysis and interactional sociolinguistics.

Discursive leadership

Discursive leadership draws on tools and methods developed by discourse analytic approaches in order to analyse leadership discourse. Discourse in this context is conceptualised as taking two different forms: discourse (or 'little d' discourse) and Discourse (or 'big D' discourse). In distinguishing between these two forms, Fairhurst (2007: 6) explains that discourse 'refers to the study of talk and text in social practice'. In other words, the actual language used by interlocutors and the interaction processes (Potter and Wetherell 1987 as cited in Fairhurst 2007: 6) are particularly important for this conceptualisation of discourse. The notion of Discourse, on the other hand, is heavily influenced by the work of Foucault. In this conceptualisation of Discourse, 'power and knowledge relations are established in culturally standardized Discourses formed by constellations of talk patterns, ideas, logics, and assumptions that constitute objects and subjects' (Fairhurst 2007: 7). Or, as Foucault (1972: 49) put it, Discourse is viewed as 'practices that systematically form the objects of which they speak'.

'Little d' discourse can be analysed by drawing on a wide range of discourse approaches, such as ethnomethodology, sociolinguistics, conversation analysis and interactions analyses, while 'big D' discourse is often analysed by critical and postmodern discourse analyses that 'heavily focus on systems of thought' (Fairhurst 2007: 7). Crictical discourse analysis (as discussed in Chapter 6), discursive psychology and ethnography of speaking are some of the approaches which aim to analyse both discourse and Discourse. The main advantages of discursive leadership as an approach to understanding leadership processes, in particular in comparison with leadership psychology (another tradition in leadership studies), are elaborated in great detail in Fairhurst (2007) and Chen (2008).

In contrast to leadership psychology which is mainly interested 'in leaders as individuals, their working styles, competencies, persuasive strategies responses, and conditions of such' (Chen 2008: 550), discursive leadership focuses on how leadership is actually enacted in and through discourse. As a consequence, researchers in this tradition analyse the language of leadership, for example in the form of interview discourse, actual dialogue and other discursive formations (see Fairhurst 2007: 7). Discursive leadership conceptualises communication as being at the heart of the leadership processes rather than being a subsidiary aspect which may have effects on other aspects of leadership performance. In other words, the focus is on how people actually do leadership rather than on how they think (and perceive) they do leadership.

Moreover, while leadership psychology views power and influence as traits assigned to leaders that are exercised in a top-down manner, discursive approaches to leadership conceptualise power more dynamically and acknowledge different forms and ways of exercising it (see also Chapter 5). Another important difference between leadership psychology and discursive leadership is the latter's strong focus on how leadership is actually accomplished in specific situations rather than attempting 'to capture the experience of leadership by forming and statistically analyzing a host of cognitive, affective, and conative variables and their casual connections' (Fairhurst 2007: 15).

However, in spite of these significant differences between psychological and discursive traditions, it should be emphasised that each of them offers valuable insights into the complexities of leadership. As Fairhurst (2007: 3) notes, '[t]here is never only one conceptual or paradigmatic framework sufficient for answering all questions about leadership, and I would argue that it is wrong for any perspective to overestimate its influence at the expense of the other'. So, while the focus of this chapter has been on discursive leadership (both in its 'little d' and 'big D' interpretations), it is important to acknowledge that other approaches may be equally suited to meet different aims. Leadership is an enormously complex topic which can only benefit from a combination of approaches and frameworks.

Two specific approaches frequently used by discursive leadership scholars, conversation analysis and interactional sociolinguistics, are briefly introduced below.

Conversation analysis

Conversation analysis (CA) has been used extensively to study institutional talk in a wide range of settings including medical contexts (e.g. Drew and Heritage 1992; Zayts and Schnurr 2011), service encounters (e.g. Lee 2011; Haakana and Sorjonen 2011), and corporate workplaces (e.g. Boden 1994; Deppermann, Schmitt and Mondada 2010). Its main aim is to describe the regularities of sequential patterns and to show how these 'regularities are methodically produced and oriented to by participants' (Liddicoat 2007: 11). This is achieved by analysing natural data, most notably talk (rather than, say, written documents). CA researchers view the subject of their study, or what they refer to as 'talk in interaction' (Schegloff 1986), as a means through which social actions are performed.

Doing CA typically includes the three stages of data recording, data transcription and data analysis. Data typically consists of recordings of authentic, natural interactions, rather than staged or scripted encounters. Interactions are transcribed using very detailed transcription conventions which capture the specifics of talk and which enable the fine-grained analyses that characterise CA research.

Due to its strong focus on the micro-level analysis of an interaction, CA tends to pay less attention to the wider context in which in an interaction takes place. In pure CA, the context of an interaction is only relevant insofar as it is made relevant by the participants. In other words, interlocutors' gender, cultural background and position within their workplace are only relevant insofar as interlocutors orient to these contextual factors in ways that are reflected in their talk. However, more applied versions of CA consider contextual factors to some extent in their interpretations.

Example 7.12 illustrates how CA may be used to analyse leadership talk on the micro-level.

Example 7.12

Context: Meeting at a small cabinet and joinery making company between Nick (managing director), Ray (projects manager), Bob (production manager) and Yann (workshop foreman).

1.	Ray:	we've probably got half a day's work to stitch it
2.	Yann:	( ) cut them cross cut all the pieces match them
3.		[so you'd] so you'd have=
4.	Ray:	[right]
5.	Yann:	=you'd have a good day if not two
6.	Ray:	yeah but I could go that route because our biggest
7.		problem is sheeting it
8.	Yann:	even if you stitch up all those leaves and then ( )
9. →	Nick:	okay alright so Smiths we're happy with apart
10.		from the stick marks
11.	Yann, Ray, Bob:	Yeah

Source: Clifton (2006).[3]

Like the other examples discussed in this chapter, Example 7.12 demonstrates how leadership is accomplished on the micro level of talk. By focusing on how specific action sequences are enacted and which linguistic strategies and devices interlocutors use, CA researchers analyse how leadership is performed. The arrow in line 9 marks the leadership activity of formulating, which in turn can lead to closing discussions, decision making and ensuring consensus among participants. However, a fine-grained CA analysis of this utterance would go beyond such general observations and would, for example, comment on the managing director's use of 'okay alright' to start this utterance and his use of the inclusive pronoun 'we'. Clifton (2006: 211) explains that the 'okay alright' 'is simultaneously responsive to the immediately prior turn, and it projects a formulation that sums up the talk-so-far', while the 'we' 'implicates the other team members in the formulation and presupposes agreement'.

Because of the fine-grained analysis of talk at the micro-level that is typical for CA research, one of the benefits of applying CA to the study of leadership discourse, according to Clifton (2006: 210), is that 'CA is able to provide a description of the machinery for doing leadership'. Such an analysis of how leadership is accomplished in and through talk is based on an analysis of the specific discursive strategies used by interlocutors to construct particular positions, roles, and identities. These strategies for doing leadership may include, in addition to those discussed above, using specific formulations to create organisational reality (as discussed in Clifton 2006) or assigning tasks to people (Svennevig 2008).

However, CA approaches to leadership have also been criticised for primarily focusing on 'understanding the practices of leadership as they unfold in the day-to-day conversations in organizations' (Svennevig 2008: 529) but not sufficiently linking these micro-level observations to the bigger picture of leadership theories. Nevertheless, in spite of this criticism, CA appears to be a valuable tool for making the abstract concept of leadership more tangible and more visible.

Interactional sociolinguistics

Interactional sociolinguistics combines both fine-grained analysis of discourse and information about the context in which an interaction takes place. However, in contrast to CA, interactional sociolinguistics is also concerned about the context in which an interaction takes place.

Interactional sociolinguistics is typically interested in how participants' relationships are constructed and negotiated in and through talk. One of the underlying assumptions of interactional sociolinguistics is that '[s]peakers use language to provide continual indices of who they are and what they want to communicate' (Schiffrin 1994: 133). In other words, through their use of language and through communicating with others, individuals construct and position themselves, for example, as more or less powerful participants, and perhaps even as leaders and subordinates (see also Chapter 5). In analysing leadership discourse through an interactional sociolinguistic lens, then, researchers pay particular attention to a range of 'contextualisation cues' (Gumperz 1999: 461) in order to understand how interlocutors interpret what is going on in an interaction in the specific context in which it occurs. Contextualisation cues may, for example, include prosody (such as intonation, pitch, stress), paralinguistic information (hesitation, pauses), or turn-taking (interrupting, overlapping, selecting the next speaker). An interactional sociolinguistic analysis may involve identifying and describing, for example, the ways in which leaders exercise power through their language use, thereby constructing and reinforcing their more powerful position. Some of these strategies through which power may be enacted include interrupting others, selecting next speakers, summarising progress and discussions, leading through an agenda of a meeting and controlling topics.

The benefits of interactional sociolinguistics for studying leadership are manifold: like CA this approach also provides valuable tools for analysing how people actually do leadership when interacting and communicating with others. In other words, it allows researchers to identify linguistic strategies which are used to enact power and which thus position speakers in powerful positions. And because interactional sociolinguistics puts particular emphasis on the context in which interactions occur, it is very suitable for analysing and understanding different ways of doing leadership in different contexts. Interactional sociolinguistics is thus particularly useful for exploring the close relationship between leadership discourse and the specific context in which it occurs.

Exercise 7.4

Find an authentic example of leadership communication and analyse the ways in which leadership is done by using some of the discourse analytical tools discussed in this (and previous) chapter(s). Your chosen example of leadership communication should be authentic: it could be a clip taken from YouTube of a speech or discussion, a podcast, or a written text such as press release, a blog or a memo. In analysing your chosen example, address the following questions:

- Who is doing leadership? What makes you think so?
- How are they doing leadership, that is, which discursive strategies do they use to achieve their goals?
- Do you think the leadership is 'effective'? Why? What evidence to support your view can you find in the example?

Summary

This chapter has explored a particularly complex aspect of professional communication: leadership performance. A variety of examples of leadership discourse have illustrated the important role of communication for leadership: most of the tasks leaders typically engage in during their normal working day are related to communication. The examples, taken from meetings, emails, one-to-one interactions, and a wiki collaboration, have also demonstrated that there are numerous ways of doing leadership.

Moreover, there exists an array of leadership constellations which differ from typical asymmetrical constellations where the leader is in a more senior or hierarchically higher position. These follower-centred perspectives on leadership, including co-leadership, shared leadership and distributed leadership, are often more suitable to meet the demands of many organisations in the twenty-first century (which are often characterised by, for example, flatter organisational structures). Taking into account the crucial role of communication in leadership processes, leadership was defined as a performance which by influencing others combines both transactional and relational behaviours. However, the specific ways of doing leadership depend on a variety of contextual factors including the working teams of the leaders, the culture of the leaders' workplace, gender, and the medium or channel of communication.

A particularly fruitful approach to understanding leadership communication is discursive leadership. In contrast to other approaches, most notably leadership psychology, discursive leadership conceptualises communication as being at the heart of the leadership process. More specifically, it focuses on how leadership is actually enacted in people's everyday workplace interactions. CA and interactional sociolinguistics are two of the discourse-analytical approaches that are employed in this tradition. Both approaches provide useful tools for analysing leadership discourse and for exploring how leadership is enacted on the micro level of communication.

8 Conclusion

The aim of this final chapter is to bring together some of the arguments provided in the previous chapters, and to outline some avenues for future research in professional communication, in particular for student projects. Since detailed summaries were provided at the end of each chapter highlighting the main points, in this final chapter I will try to avoid repeating myself, and rather attempt to provide a brief synopsis of the overall argument of the book, namely that professional communication is a complex and very fruitful area of academic inquiry which is most productively approached by combining different perspectives, theories, and methodologies – often drawn from different disciplines.

Bringing it all together

It was my aim throughout the various chapters to introduce a range of specific ways of analysing and conceptualising some of the problems and practices that characterise professional communication. However, in doing this I had to face two specific challenges: to decide not only which topics to include and discuss within the limits of space, but also how to present them and how to break down their complexities into manageable units.

With regard to the first challenge of the choice of topics, I have tried to cover traditional (and almost standard) topics such as genre and intercultural communication while also exploring some less well-researched but equally interesting and important aspects of professional communication, such as leadership and gender. And while I have, admittedly, been influenced by my own research interest in choosing these topics, there are clearly other important aspects of professional communication which have not been discussed here. For example, the role of English, Spanish and other lingua francas was only touched upon in Chapter 4, although this is increasingly becoming an issue in the continuously globalised world of work where people with different linguistic backgrounds work and communicate with each other on a daily basis (e.g. Nickerson 2005; Koester 2010). However, while the choice of topics, as reflected in the problems and practices outlined in

Section A of each chapter, was necessarily limited, I hope to have provided at least a glimpse into the intriguing world of professional communication.

Despite these unavoidable limitations, in the discussions of the chosen aspects of professional communication (genres, workplace culture, culture and politeness, identities, gender, and leadership). I hope to have highlighted some of the benefits of approaching the complexities of these topics from the perspective of applied linguistics. As I have argued in the introduction chapter and throughout, such an approach with its focus on language and communication is very suited for exploring some of the practices through which professions and organisations are formed and quite literally talked into being. This central role of communication is not only evident in topics with an explicit focus on language, such as genre (Chapter 2), but, as we have seen, it is also reflected in less obvious topics, such as workplace culture (Chapter 3), culture and politeness at work (Chapter 4), identities (Chapter 5), gender (Chapter 6), and leadership (Chapter 7). In all these aspects of professional communication, as the previous chapters have demonstrated, communication not only plays a crucial part, but approaching the various problems and practices associated with these aspects through a focus on communication offers rewarding and often innovative insights and perspectives into the professional world. Many of these insights are of relevance not only for understanding what is going on in a professional encounter, they also have practical implications for professionals and the (often lay) people they are interacting with.

In addressing the second challenge of presenting the various topics in meaningful ways and breaking down their complexities into manageable units, I have tried to link the arguments presented in the various chapters with each other by referring to discussions and examples across chapters. As these discussions have shown, there is considerable overlap between the topics presented in different chapters, illustrating that any aspect of professional communication is in one way or another embedded or related to others. In this way, the various topics discussed here are intricately linked with each other. For example, the notion of workplace culture (as introduced in Chapter 3) underpins and impacts on probably every aspect of professional communication mentioned throughout the book. Similar importance applies to the role of power which has an impact on (almost) every aspect of workplace reality as has been illustrated, for example, in the chapters on professional identity, gender and leadership. Equally, all the themes discussed in the other chapters are potentially relevant in an intercultural context and thus could have been looked at from this perspective. There are clearly more connections to be drawn between the various chapters linking the diverse aspects of professional communication with each other in meaningful ways, thereby creating new synergies. Exercise 8.1 illustrates this.

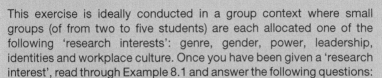

Exercise 8.1

This exercise is ideally conducted in a group context where small groups (of from two to five students) are each allocated one of the following 'research interests': genre, gender, power, leadership, identities and workplace culture. Once you have been given a 'research interest', read through Example 8.1 and answer the following questions:

- Where do you think this exchange took place? What makes you think so?
- Who do you think are the participants? What makes you think so?
- Considering your 'research interest', what would you be particularly interested in finding out about this exchange and what kinds of questions would you ask?
- Based on your 'research interest', how would you answer the question: what is going on here?

Example 8.1

1. A: [softly]: there's another um: + thing that I would like to
2.   ask for
3. B: what's that
4. A: somewhere in delivery suit or at ward 11
5.   er there are those plastic er red containers for ++
6.   for blood tests
7.   I need I need beside the the line there's a plastic end
8.   for this ...
[some discussion between A, B and C of what exactly is needed where and one might be]
9. A: yeah so er we + could you just could we maybe have one
10.   from from er ward 11 oh this stuff er +
11. B: well you go down to ward 11 and get it
12.   cos I don't want to have to

Source: Holmes (2006: 163).

As I mentioned throughout the various chapters, professional communication has received a lot of interest from researchers in many different disciplines, thus making it truly interdisciplinary – which is not only reflected in the theoretical and methodological approaches applied to it but is also shown in the topics and issues that form the focus of research on professional communication in the different disciplines. And although it was only possible to introduce some of these many diverse approaches in the previous chapters, many others exist which may be equally suited to address different issues and topics. The important point, however, is that due to its interdisciplinary nature, any research in professional communication has a lot to gain from drawing on and combining different approaches, perspectives, interests and agendas from different disciplines. Such an exchange of ideas, practices, methodologies and even epistemologies can only be beneficial; and such a cross-fertilisation between different disciplines is often very productive, as for example the discussions of discursive leadership in Chapter 7 have shown. Acknowledging and applying this is particularly important for future research.

Some avenues for future research

Professional communication, I believe, is a particularly fruitful area of academic inquiry – specifically for (postgraduate and advanced undergraduate) students. To put it bluntly, there is still a lot to find out about professional communication. And although there is an increasing amount of research in this area, there are many issues of professional communication that are waiting to be explored further.

There is a potential (and often a practical need) for further research into most, if not all, of the areas of professional communication that have been introduced in the previous chapters. For example, as was shown in Chapter 2, genres of professional communication are constantly changing and new genres are emerging – partly as a consequence of changes in the professional landscape and technological advances (as outlined in Chapter 1). These changes not only lead to the question of how to classify new communicative events but are also highly relevant for the overarching issue of what genre is.

Another fruitful avenue for future research into professional communication, I believe, would be to explore some non-traditional leadership constellations (as outlined in Chapter 7). Such an undertaking could address, for example, ways of enacting power which in turn affect issues of identity construction and negotiation (see Chapter 5).

Another area in dire need of more research studies is culture in professional contexts. Although a lot of research on intercultural communication already exists, I believe there is a need for more studies that draw on authentic recordings of actual intercultural encounters in professional contexts, moving away from often stereotypical perceptions and essentialist interpretations (see Chapter 4) towards exploring how participants construct and negotiate, for example, each other's professional and other identities. These are just a few suggestions for topics for future research. But they show, once again, how the various aspects of professional communication are intertwined with each other, and that exploring one topic inevitably involves also looking at other related topics.

One of the reasons why research into professional communication is not only interesting and relevant but perhaps also particularly appealing is the fact that it often leads to relevant findings with practical implications and applications for practitioners. Some of these implications have been mentioned in previous chapters, such as implementing codes of practice and equal opportunity policies to address gender issues at work (Chapter 6), and devising material that could be used for professional training (Chapter 1). This benefit of research on professional communication is perhaps particularly obvious in research that draws on authentic data involving real people doing real things in real workplaces rather than relying on role-plays, questionnaires and other relatively easily obtainable kinds of data. Thus, although authentic data (for example, in the form of audio and video recordings or written documents) are admittedly harder to obtain, I believe they are vital if we are to understand the complexities of professional communication, and if we are to explore the meaning and implication of our (academic) research in the (professional) real world. The constantly increasing body of research on professional communication that does utilise exactly these kinds of hard to get authentic data illustrates that such an undertaking – even if more challenging than collecting non-authentic data – is well worth the effort (e.g. Holmes and Stubbe 2003b; Holmes 2006; Mullany 2007; Schnurr 2009b; Baxter 2010; Handford 2010).

Although it is beyond the scope of this brief concluding chapter to provide detailed advice and suggestions on how to plan and conduct such research in professional contexts, there are other sources which have addressed these issues comprehensively and which outline some of the processes involved in collecting, processing and analysing authentic professional data (e.g. Mullany 2007, Holmes and Stubbe 2003b; Stubbe 2001, 1998; Marra 2008). One point these researchers agree on is that research on professional communication should ideally produce meaningful outcomes for both academic and practitioner audiences (see also Harris and Bargiela-Chiappini 1997). They advocate a research approach of doing research not only *on* but also *with* and *for* participants (see also Cameron et al. 1992), thereby combining theoretical and applied research interests. Such an attempt 'to give back to practitioners insights which can be applied to their work settings' (Roberts and Sarangi 1999: 389) should play a crucial role in the research agenda on professional communication. And as I have argued above, pursuing a multimethod approach combining insights and practices from different disciplines promises to be a productive way of achieving this.

Regardless of the choice of topic, approach and research agenda, professional communication is clearly an interesting area of study, and one where research findings have potentially important practical applications and implications for the real world. It is thus, I believe, a particularly rewarding field of academic enquiry, and one where many issues remain to be explored. I hope that some of the topics and issues discussed throughout the previous chapters will have created some interest and curiosity among readers to find out more. Professional communication is clearly one of the most intriguing and rewarding topics to engage in.

Task commentaries

Chapter 1

Exercise 1.1

In contrast to the other examples in Chapter 1, this email is not as easily identifiable as professional communication. Without additional contextual information it is hard to infer that it was sent by a professional to her colleagues – it could have equally well been sent to some friends. In particular, the absence of a greeting and the minimal closing ('Anna' – the sender's first name) indicate that the sender and the receivers know each other well, and presumably regularly 'go for coffee (and sandwiches!) outside in the sun'. However, this email was actually sent by Anna to three of her colleagues at an educational institution during lunch time. It is a good illustration of what Fairclough (1992) calls the 'conversationalisation' of discourse. This 'conversationalisation' of workplace (and other public) discourses refers to the observation that markers of power and asymmetry are being increasingly removed from workplace discourse, resulting in more informal types of discourses. As a consequence, many instances of workplace interactions resemble ordinary talk (see also Roberts 2010; Thornborrow 2002; Drew and Heritage 1992; Koester 2010). It is only in one of the replies to Anna's original email that the workplace context in which this interaction occurs is established, as the next example shows.

Example 1.3b[1]

RE: Coffee?
hi my dears,

i am at home, marking my assignments 9today and tomorrow)
emjoy the sun, as much as i do as i am actually sitting in the
garden – have already marked 4!
cheers

Bella

With the reference to 'marking my assignments' Bella's email makes it clear that this exchange is taking place in a workplace context in the widest sense – although Bella is working from home on that day she is still working (by marking her assignments), which is common practice at the institution Bella works. In this email, then, work-related information (about Bella's marking progress) is closely interwoven with information that may initially appear irrelevant, namely the fact that she is 'sitting in the garden' and enjoying the sun while she is going about her work.

Exercise 1.2

Here are some possible answers, but you may also find more similarities.

There is often an asymmetrical role-relationship between interlocutors (as in Example 1.1). The topics of most of the examples are primarily transactionally focused, and relationally oriented behaviours take a back seat (see e.g. Examples 1.1 and 1.2, 1.4, 1.5, 1.6). However, this is challenged to some extent by Example 1.3 (compare with Exercise 1.1). Some of the examples are marked by specialist lexical choices such as jargon and abbreviation (e.g. 'Down Syndrome' in Example 1.4) and others are characterised by a rather generic choice of adjectives (such as 'a rewarding and fulfilling environment' in Example 1.6). The overall organisation/structure of exchanges depends on a wide range of factors including the medium of communication and the type of exchange: often one interlocutor dominates the talking time (and has more discursive rights which is, for example, reflected in their right to ask questions, challenge and interrupt others, select the next speaker, decide when to move on to the next topic (this is exemplified by Clara opening the meeting in Example 1.1)). If you look at other examples throughout this book you may find some of these observations confirmed while others may be challenged (for instance, some exchanges include a substantial amount of relational talk, and in some examples interlocutors do not have an asymmetrical role relationship).

Exercise 1.3

The transactional aspects include the mentioning of the conferences and the reference to the attached paper (which Rebecca has agreed to review for Nina), the reminder of the deadline ('mid September') and the topic of the special issue. Relational aspects, on the other hand, are mainly dealt with in the beginning of the email (such as 'congratulations on the baby' and the talk about FB and the pictures of the children). However, relational and transactional aspects are not strictly separated from each other. Rather, when mentioning the conference that she organises, Nina at the same time does relational work by saying that she would appreciate if Rebecca could attend it. Moreover, Nina's mentioning of the various conferences that she has attended recently and that she is planning to go to next year (which could be described as transactional, work-related information) could also be interpreted as an attempt to reinforce solidarity and to possibly arrange a meeting with Rebecca at one of them.

Exercise 1.4

This issue is described on page 15.

Chapter 2

Exercise 2.1

In the course of the courtroom interaction in Example 2.3 counsel invites the witness to provide her account of 'an incident' (lines 1–4), and he asks a range of questions to clarify or retrieve more information (lines 4, 9–10, 12). The purpose of this exchange is to find out 'what happened' from the perspective of the witness, which will then be used by counsel to establish a version of the reality surrounding that particular event in an attempt to influence the jury in their verdict. The participants in this exchange have different roles (counsel and witness/friend of Ginger Walters, respectively) and thus potentially different aims and motives. Counsel's main aim is presumably to establish a story of the event that is most likely to propitiate the jury with his client, while the witness's aim may be to make her friend Ginger Walters look good in the eyes of the jury. The relationship between witness and counsel is asymmetrical, which is also reflected in their turn-taking rights: for example, only counsel asks questions and thereby plays a major role in the choice of topics that get discussed (and in what detail).

Example 2.4 is a relatively typical example of the examining phase during a doctor–patient interaction. The doctor asks the patient several questions (lines 1, 2, 4, 5) in order to retrieve the information they deem necessary to make an informed assessment of the patient's condition. In contrast to the questions asked by counsel in Example 2.3, however, the GP's questions in this interaction consist of very short incomplete sentences of only a few words each, which is a reflection of the transactionally oriented nature of this exchange. This orientation towards information (rather than establishing relationships) is further reflected in the strong focus on facts (see for instance the GP's responses (after a pause) to the patient's comment that they have cut down cigarette consumption: lines 3, 6, 8). The relationship between the interlocutors in this interaction is asymmetrical with the GP being in a position of the expert or more knowledgeable participant; cooperating with them is in the best interest of the patient if they want to receive the GP's medical help.

Although the exchange in Example 2.5 occurred in a classroom, there are some obvious similarities with the courtroom investigation and the GP consultation: as in the other two instances, the role relationship between participants (teacher and student) is asymmetrical which is, for example, reflected in the observation that the teacher is the one to ask the questions and to assist the student in answering them. In this way, the teacher's role can also be seen as that of a facilitator (similar to that of counsel and the GP – although there are presumably differences in the aims (and perhaps more or less hidden agendas) of participants in each case). Like the previous examples, this interaction is also predominantly transactionally oriented, with the main purpose (presumably) being to go through one of the units in a textbook and get the students to answer the questions about a story that they have just read. However, the form of the questions and the kind of feedback that the teacher provides are different to those uttered by counsel or the GP: the questions not only differ in length and structure, there is much more positive feedback ('good', 'yes') to the student's answer, while there is hardly any acknowledgement by the GP (other than 'hhh', 'erm') and more questions by counsel in responding to the witness' account.

Exercise 2.2

The answer to this question depends on the definition of genre that you use and whether this definition focuses on the communicative purpose of the exchange, its form and function, or the sociocultural context in which it occurs.

Exercise 2.3

This example illustrates some of the problems in identifying and categorising genres. While this exchange might be categorised as collaborative since I and M seem to conjointly negotiate the topics of the interaction and its development and overall purpose, there is more to say about the genre of this exchange. For example, although this excerpt was taken from a meeting between I and M, there are not many indications in the excerpt that it did indeed occur in such a context. Moreover, the interlocutors in this exchange move between discussing non-transactional topics and transactional work-related topics. In fact, the two seem to be intertwined with each other at several points (for example when M recounts her experience of her first day back at work, which includes both transactional and relational elements). However, as the last few lines indicate, the interlocutors seem about to move away from the largely non-transactional nature of the exchange towards establishing more work-related and perhaps even meeting-like genres. This example thus nicely illustrates that it is not always easy to identify and categorise genres, since establishing boundaries between them is not always possible and some exchanges seem to morph from one genre to another.

Exercise 2.4

In addressing this task it is important to move beyond the idea that the main purpose of a company brochure is to promote the company. As Askehave and Swales (2001: 203) maintain, such a description 'remains very general and does not contribute much to the description of the genre as an intentional and purposeful activity'. You should thus try to identify additional purposes of these brochures, taking into account the cultural and situational context in which they are used. For example, you may want to consider the wider context in which they occur (for instance, after the financial crisis), who they are targeted at (perhaps externally: potential or existing clients or potential job applicants; internally: staff members), the status of the company (such as newly founded or well established) and possibly its reputation and/ or any specific issues it was dealing with at the time of the brochure publication (for example, a merger).

Some of the specific features that may be particularly relevant for analysing company brochures, and which may be worth paying attention to, include the interplay between images and text and what potential meaning this creates. For example, you may want to discuss how the images are used to communicate or support the communicative function of the brochures. You may also find some interesting correlations between some of the lexico-grammatical features used across several brochures (for instance are there phrases, lexical items or syntactical patterns that they share?).

Exercise 2.5

Some intertextual links include the reference to an upcoming event, the mentioning of a previous action ('thank you for your registration'), the attachment (invoice), and possibly the reference to 'further information' which may be provided upon request.

Exercise 2.6

This fax is taken from a corpus of sixty-nine business faxes exchanged between a Finnish export company and its international business partners. Louhiala-Salminen (1997: 322) describes the overall purpose of the faxes as 'to achieve the goals of a buying–selling negotiation'; she identifies five subcategories into which the faxes fall. The purpose of the fax displayed in Example 2.11 was categorised as giving specific information, and the following eight moves were identified:

1996-03-26

(1)   Sang San Industrial Co. Ltd
       12-34 Young dang
       Young dang
       Korea

       Fax.123-456-789-123

       Attn. Director John Chang

       Re. Your fax of 26th march

(2)   Dear Mr. John Chang,

(3)   Thank you for your telefax regarding the Fair in march.

(4)   We were glad to hear that the Fair was a success for you.
       Hope that you can get
       orders from ABC products.

       If you need more leaflets, catalogues or information, please
       don't hesitate contacting us again.

(6)   We look forward to hearing from you soon.

(7)   Yours sincerely

       For Vuorio and Co.
       ABC-products

(8)   [signature]

       Teija Tainio
       P.O. Box 12   Tel. +385-12-12121212
       FIN-12345 Vuorio   Fax +385-12-13131313

(5)   PS. Have sent you today Heliseam leaflets and price list.

(1)   recipient's contact data
(2)   salutation
(3)   reference to previous contact
(4)   showing goodwill
(5)   giving information
(6)   pre-closing
(7)   closing
(8)   signature

Chapter 3

Exercise 3.1

The first message (email 1) was written by a member of SCT, and the second (email 2) was written by a member of Revelinu. In interpreting the differences between them, Waldvogel (2007: 465) notes that '[w]hereas both messages are brief and have a transactional purpose, the informal greeting and closing of the second create a greater sense of solidarity than the more detached tone of the first'. This practice is in accordance with the general email style in the two workplaces.

In her study of over 500 emails sent by members of these two workplaces, Waldvogel observed that at Revelinu emails typically contained some form of greeting, most notably Hi + name, while at SCT 59 per cent of the emails contained no form of greeting. The greater use of greetings (and closings) at Revelinu suggests that members put great emphasis on establishing and maintaining good interpersonal relationships, and that there was a relatively strong sense of solidarity among members at this workplace. At SCT, by contrast, the relatively high absence of greetings (and closings) in emails indicates that members put more emphasis on the content of their messages rather than on how it was conveyed. This rather impersonal and often matter-of-fact email style at SCT seems to reflect consequences of the recent restructuring changes which have led to dispersed sections (with members often not knowing members from other sections) and mistrust and uncertainties felt by some (which in turn may have contributed to the relatively high social distance and low solidarity among members).

The styles of both emails thus reflect and at the same time reinforce the atmospheres of the two workplaces: the distant social relationships of members at SCT are also shown in the sparing use of greetings ('Colin' rather than 'Hi Colin'), whereas the high use of more elaborate greetings among members of Revelinu can be interpreted as a reflection of the more friendly and familial atmosphere of a workplace where 'people matter' and 'staff value each other' (Waldvogel 2007: 471).

Exercise 3.2

In answering this question you should explore the content of the mission statements and who they may be specifically targeted at (for example, how are 'customers' or 'clients' addressed?). You could compare, for example, the specific aspects or topics that are mentioned (for instance, what kind of vision is created – such as to become 'the world leader in XY'). You may also want to look at specific expressions, phrases and idioms that occur in the mission statements (like the notions of 'teamwork' and 'excellence'). However, regardless of what types of organisations are chosen for comparison, it is quite likely that there will be some overlap in their mission statements in terms of content and often on the level of lexical choices. Discuss possible reasons for these similarities.

Exercise 3.3

It may be interesting to discuss whether you find Baxter's categories useful for describing the workplaces that you have worked in. One of the more obvious advantages of categorising workplaces as falling into one of three types of gendered corporations lies in the explanations such a categorisation provides for accounting for some of the gendered practices that characterise a particular workplace (such as the low numbers of female senior managers in a particular (presumably male-dominated) workplace). However, these kinds of typologies are necessarily essentialist and thus always run the danger of over-simplifying complex relations. Clearly, the world is not black and white, and as Baxter (2010: 17) admits herself, 'an actual company will incorporate elements of all three types of community'. Whether you may find this typology useful or too restrictive will depend not only on your own experience (and the kinds of workplaces you have worked in), but also on how you perceive gender: that is, for example whether you believe gender can indeed be described in terms of (almost) dichotomous relations (male–female) or whether you think that gender is constructed and dynamically enacted and thus too complex to be captured by such categories. For more discussions of these gender issues see Chapter 6.

Exercise 3.4

Based on knowledge of the workplace culture at the factory where the Power Rangers work described in Section A, we can be relatively confident that the overall challenging and contestive tone of the exchange between Ginette and Peter is interpreted as normal practice among members of this workplace. However, what is particularly interesting about this example is Peter's final response (line 8): in the context of this workplace where members' normal discourse is characterised by 'a generally rough and tough tone, frequent challenging humour and banter, [and] a large amount of swearing', Peter's superficially polite utterance 'thank you very much for your information' can be interpreted as an instance of overly polite and thus inappropriate behaviour (Schnurr, Marra and Holmes 2008: 218). Considering the norms of this workplace culture, the form of the utterance is clearly exaggerated. In fact, rather than genuinely thanking Ginette for the information, Peter's comment seems to be ironic and actually criticises his boss for not having contacted him earlier. This example thus nicely shows that in order to fully understand what is going on in an interaction, it is important to go beyond the form of the utterances and to take into consideration the norms of the wider context (including the cultural norms of a workplace).

Exercise 3.5

For some ideas about what kinds of things to look for and what kinds of data to collect you may want to read Schnurr (2009b) or Holmes, Schnurr and Marra (2007).

Chapter 4

Exercise 4.1

After you have answered this question you may want to read the article in which this (and other similar) example is discussed in detail: Rogerson-Revell (2007).

Exercise 4.2

In describing any 'cultural misunderstandings' that you have experienced yourself, you may find it helpful to use some of the dimensions of cross-cultural differences suggested by House (2005: 21). The five dimensions she proposes to describe the interactional tendencies that the German and English speakers in her study displayed are directness – indirectness, orientation towards self – orientation towards other, orientation towards content – orientation towards addressee, explicitness – implicitness, and ad hoc formulation – verbal routines. It is however, important to note that House conceptualises these dimensions as tendencies rather than as dichotomies.

Exercise 4.3

One of the reasons that his speech was met with silence may be that the audience was expecting a different, perhaps more explicitly enthusiastic speech. More specifically, they might have expected to receive only thanks and congratulations due to their outstanding performance and some acknowledgement of their hard work.

The Vice-President, on the other hand, was most likely surprised and possibly even shocked, offended and perhaps hurt when he heard the response of his American colleague. These experiences and feelings have been described in terms of 'face loss'. This concept is explained in more detail in Sections B and C.

Exercise 4.4

In comparing your definitions of culture, you could for example, look at how culture is conceptualised (for instance, relatively fixed and stable as a trait and attribute, or more dynamically as a performance). It may also be interesting to see what your definition says about how and where culture is reflected on more concrete as well as abstract levels (such as norms, practices, values) (compare with the discussions of workplace culture in Chapter 3).

Exercise 4.5

Answering this question may be particularly interesting in relation to your answer to Exercise 4.4. Does your definition of culture capture the four characteristics identified by Spencer-Oatey and Franklin (2009)? If your definition is substantially different from their list, try to link these differences to underlying conceptualisations of culture (such as culture as a trait versus culture as a performance).

Exercise 4.6

When he first read this email the academic was rather upset and did not want to reply to the student because he considered it to be very rude. Some of the features which gave rise to this impression include the many spelling errors and the txt slang of the email (such as 'u' rather than 'you'), the too informal and intimate opening ('Hi Dear!'), and the demanding closing which could be interpreted as putting pressure on the addressee. These strategies threatened the addressee's positive face (for instance, in the intimate opening) and negative face (in particular the closing and the direct and relatively unmitigated request for sending course material to the sender).

Exercise 4.7

Both speeches may have threatened the face needs and sociality rights of the respective audiences. In particular, the speech of the Japanese

Vice-President of Sales may have threatened the audience's quality face as it did not (in their eyes) emphasise enough their outstanding achievements and hard work. Moreover, by perhaps over-emphasising their 'duty and loyalty to this company' it may have also threatened their identity face. And if the audience felt treated unfairly, this may indicate that their equity rights were threatened too. The speech of the American Director of Sales, in return, is likely to have threatened the identity face of the Japanese Vice-President of Sales by explicitly undermining everything he said in his previous speech ('disregard everything he just said'). And since he challenged a high-ranking senior member of the company in front of others (!) his association rights are also likely to have been threatened.

Chapter 5

Exercise 5.1

The following adjectives nicely summarise how members are portrayed: 'passionate, supportive, collaborative, diverse'. In fact, these adjectives formed the subheading of this rubric and were printed in bold just beneath 'Who we are'. Most of the adjectives used throughout the description seem to fall into the broad categories of being 'passionate', 'supportive', 'collaborative' and 'diverse'. Moreover, members are referred to as 'problem solvers' and 'leaders' who have diverse cultural (and linguistic) backgrounds. While there is clearly more to be said about this example, one important point to make is that most of these descriptions are rather generic. Another interesting issue with these kinds of self-portrayals is the kinds of information that is not provided, for example a requirement to work overtime regularly, to travel a lot, and to be committed to the company (possibly above everything else).

Exercise 5.3

Although there is no overt mention of identity categories in Example 5.3 (for example, none of the participants refer to the others by their title or role), interlocutors nevertheless construct their own as well as each other's identity: as they pursue their goals of the interaction, they at the same time create and enact specific roles and identities which are then responded to by the other interlocutor. For example, they establish that M is leading through this sequence of the interaction which aims at assessing EM's health condition. M is the one to ask questions, while EM's role in this extract is mainly restricted to providing answers to M's inquiries. M also has the right to reformulate EM's contributions (line 12) and to interrupt EM (lines 11 and 12) thereby deciding what topics are to be discussed in how much detail.

Through these linguistics processes, M and EM create and enact certain roles and identities for themselves.

As you probably inferred from interlocutors' contributions, this extract occurred during a routine check-up between a midwife (M) and an expectant mother (EM). In addition to the strategies already mentioned, there are further linguistic indices which reflect the professional nature of this encounter, such as the opening sequence which is not part of a standard greeting–greetings sequence (and which thus already marks this exchange as a form of institutional discourse rather than ordinary conversation), M's use of the term 'foetus' (line 6) (rather than the non-technical term baby), and M's minimal responses to almost everything EM says.

Exercise 5.4

You may find reading Holmes et al. (2007) useful for approaching this task.

Exercise 5.5

This quote is taken from Hall's seminal paper 'Who needs identity?' (1996). It describes identities in the plural rather than singular: individuals do not have one identity but multiple – some of which may not necessarily be in harmony (and could, for example, contradict each other). Identities are constructed in and through 'discourses, practices and positions' which may interact with each other. This quote also acknowledges that identities are dynamic constructs which are constantly changing and transforming themselves.

Exercise 5.6

The processes of identity creation described by Bucholtz and Hall can be applied to the various examples throughout this (and the other chapters). The following are thus just a few examples of possible answers.

Example 5.8 is a prime example of overt mentioning of identity categories but Examples 5.1 and 5.2 also include some, such as 'we are a network of leaders' (5.1); 'the China team' and 'the Australians' (5.2).

The mechanisms underlying implicature and presupposition contribute to constructing Tricia (in Example 5.4) and the inspector (in Example 5.8) as powerful and the one in charge. In both instances, their subordinates' reaction indicates that Tricia's and the inspector's behaviour is normal practice and that they are in a (hierarchically higher) position to do this. Moreover, in both exchanges interlocutors make reference to other people and previous events without explaining them any further (names and titles of people in 5.8 and a meeting in 5.4) thereby constructing themselves and their addressees as people who work together closely and who share these kinds of information.

Examples 5.2 and 5.3 are good illustrations of how evaluative and epistemic orientations of interlocutors contribute to identity construction. For example, Susan's bewilderment and lack of understanding/agreement with the reactions of the Chinese team members (Example 5.2) contribute to portraying Susan as someone who believes in upholding a work–life balance and who does promote employee independence and empowerment (for example by letting people decide when their work is finished and when to go home). Similarly, the midwife's relatively neutral and perhaps even distanced stance throughout the interaction (Example 5.3) contributes to constructing her as a professional (rather than a friend).

The use of linguistic structures and systems that are ideologically associated with specific persons/groups are, for example, reflected in the question–answer sequence in Example 5.3, and the fact that the midwife asks certain questions while the expectant mother provides relevant answers, as well as the midwife's use of the word 'foetus' (rather than baby). Another good illustration is the police officers' behaviour in Example 5.7 and the counsel's performance in Example 5.5: they are the ones to ask questions, interrupt and challenge the complainant. Drawing on these discursive practices they construct themselves as midwife, police officers and counsel respectively.

Chapter 6

Exercise 6.1

If you are doing this exercise in a classroom context, compare your results with those of your classmates. Note some of the similarities and differences in people's answers why they chose feminine or masculine names for particular speakers.

Looking at Example 6.1, C's way of dealing with H's request can be described as direct and perhaps even confrontational: C refuses the request rather bluntly without providing any information initially, and repeating the unmitigated refusal (lines 5 and 7) is rather face-threatening to the other interlocutors and leaves little doubt that C is the one in charge. Some of the behaviours C displays in this extract, such as being direct, confrontational and autonomous, have traditionally been associated with masculine ways of talking (Holmes 2000c). And by displaying these behaviours, C is often perceived as 'talking like a man', although C is actually a woman – a very successful leader in her workplace. The linguistic performance of C, or Clara (her actual first name) has been researched intensively: see for example Marra, Schnurr and Holmes (2006) and Holmes (2006).

Similar to Clara's behaviours, which are often associated with masculinity, some of the behaviours displayed by the other team members are typically ascribed to feminine ways of doing things: hedging a request (for example by using a passive construction and indirect ways of asking, as H does in lines 1–4) and M's conciliatory attempt to facilitate the discussion and to support H's request (lines 6 and 10–11) are discursive behaviours often associated with femininity. Hence, H and M display speech elements that tend to be referred to as 'feminine' although both H and M are actually men.

Exercise 6.2

This exercise demonstrates some of the problems associated with ascribing certain speech behaviours to masculine and feminine styles. In particular, some utterances may contain elements of both masculine and feminine speech styles (such as line 27).

In this example Sabitha, the CEO and chair of the meeting, employs both masculine and feminine speech styles in order to achieve her goals. In the first part of the example she primarily draws on elements ascribed to feminine ways of talking: the overall discussion seems collaborative with various people making contributions (as in lines 2–5). Sabitha also includes her subordinates in the process of making a decision by providing explanations for her choices and suggestions (as in lines 6–10, line 26), she produces minimal supportive feedback (line 17), and she overtly utters her agreement (line 23).

However, from about line 27 onwards we can observe a change in Sabitha's behaviour towards a more authoritarian and decisive style. The initial 'okay' utterance (line 27) functions as a boundary marker here which brings the previous discussion to an end, signalling the beginning of a new stage in the decision-reaching process (Fung and Carter 2007). Sabitha's utterances are more direct (as in lines 27–29) and sometimes almost confrontational (such as her interruption of ?? in line 32). These behaviours are indexed for masculinity, as is her swearing in line 25. But as the example shows, Sabitha does not only rely on masculine or feminine speech elements but instead skilfully combines both aspects in her talk. In lines 32–33, for example, after interrupting an unidentified speaker (??), she produces some hedges ('I would like to recommend if possible') thereby minimising the potential impact of her previous interruption. And in line 15 she utters an unmitigated directive towards Beth asking her to 'repeat' her previous point, which albeit being direct (and hence indexed for masculinity) could also be viewed as an attempt to facilitate her subordinate's contribution and to ensure that it gets heard (these behaviours, in turn, would be indexed for femininity).

Thus, on the macro level the decision-making style displayed in Example 6.5 appears to be indexed for femininity: the issue is collaboratively discussed and everybody gets their say. But on the micro level this feminine way of making decisions is instantiated by drawing on features typically ascribed to feminine and masculine speech styles (for example, Sabitha dominates the talking time but also allows others to contribute; she is sometimes direct while facilitative at other times). The decision-reaching process is thus characterised by collaborative and conjoint efforts, as well as by autonomous, direct and perhaps even confrontational behaviours (see also Schnurr 2010).

Exercise 6.3

In analysing this example, Mullany (2007: 187) notes that 'Martin here overtly espouses the sexist, stereotypical view that for a "week" of every month, women are incapable of making rational decisions due to their hormones, thus placing all women managers in direct opposition with the rationality, effectiveness and efficiency associated with the discourse of scientific modernism'. He thus draws on discourses of gender difference (women as hormonal and irrational, men as stable and rational) and on discourses of female emotionality/irrationality.

Exercise 6.4

In addressing this task you may find it helpful to refer back to some of the discussions and exercises in previous chapters (such as the task commentaries to Exercises 2.4 and 3.2).

Chapter 7

Exercise 7.2

This extract occurred during an interaction between Donald, the CEO of an IT company, and Ann, a junior project manager. In this example Donald talks Ann through the process of writing a letter of offer to the successful candidate of a job interview. He thus makes sure things are getting done by providing guidance (such as referring Ann to 'standard templates', line 9) and giving specific explanations of what to do (lines 13–16, 18–20). In achieving this, Donald draws on a range of strategies, such as formulating the directive as a (rhetorical) question: 'do you wanna write do up a letter of offer' (line 2). He also employs laughter (lines 4, 6, 8, 16, 23, 28) and humour (as when he humorously asks

Ann whether she is the project manager (line 5) or when he jokingly suggests giving Beverley the title of 'chief coffee maker' (line 25). In using these strategies Donald successfully downplays the importance of the task and facilitates Ann's learning how to write the letter of offer. And he uses the inclusive pronoun 'we' (lines 16, 27), thereby taking over some responsibility for finding a suitable job title. Thus, instead of simply telling Ann to write that letter and referring her to the guidelines, Donald encourages her and builds her confidence so that in the end she agrees to perform the task.

Exercise 7.3

In going back to the examples in Section A, you will see that not all of the people who do leadership in these excerpts actually bear the title of 'leader'.

Examples 7.1 and 7.2, which are both taken from the same working team, illustrate how Clara (the team leader and most senior person in the meeting) and Smithy (the section head and second-in-command) share leadership responsibilities: while Clara motivates her team and thereby performs relational aspects of leadership (Example 7.1), Smithy focuses on transactional goals by checking people are on track (Example 7.2). This way of collaborating with each other and sharing leadership responsibilities is typical for co-leadership constellations (see also Vine et al. 2008 for a more detailed discussion of Clara and Smithy's co-leadership performance, and Schnurr and Chan 2011 for further examples of co-leadership).

In Examples 7.3 to 7.5 it is Sabitha, the CEO and most senior person in the organisation, who is doing leadership by making sure her subordinates know what they are supposed to be doing. Similar observations apply to Example 7.7 where Donald, the CEO of the company, is the one in charge: he gives advice and guidance to his subordinate, combining transactional and relational behaviours. Example 7.8 is a good illustration of distributed leadership, that is, teams without an officially appointed leader. In this group, participants share and collaboratively perform leadership responsibilities: they provide feedback on each others' suggestions and make decisions collaboratively, thereby advancing the project.

Chapter 8

Exercise 8.1

This exercise nicely shows some of the overlaps that exist between different topics (as discussed throughout the book) and highlights some of the benefits of approaching data from different perspectives.

The extract occurred during an interaction between a young doctor (A) and a senior nurse (B) at the nurse's station of a hospital ward. Several interesting observations can be made by approaching this short excerpt from different 'research interests'. For example, in identifying the context of this exchange, you will have to draw on what you have learned in Chapter 1 but your specific answer may be different based on your 'research interest'.

Question 2 requires you to think about the notions of (professional and perhaps also gender) identities and roles as discussed in Chapter 5. You may find revisiting the framework for studying identity construction (Bucholtz and Hall) as discussed in Chapter 5 helpful for addressing this question. It might be particularly interesting to talk about why you thought A and B are specific kinds of professionals, and to link these identities and roles to power relations. A discussion may emerge then between those who have approached the extract from a 'gender', a 'leadership', a 'power' and an 'identity' angle, and it could be very interesting to explore differences and overlaps.

You may also be surprised to find out that A is a male doctor and that B is a female nurse – which is often in contrast to people's intuitive (gendered) expectations. An analysis of how interlocutors draw on elements of feminine and masculine speech styles (and to what effect) could usefully be linked back to the discussions in Chapter 6 – and it is likely that there will be overlaps with the research interests on workplace culture and power. In terms of identifying the genre of this exchange and to explore workplace culture, it would be particularly interesting to explore the third question and to discuss what specific aspects you would be particularly interested in finding out about this exchange and what kinds of questions you would ask.

Appendix A

Transcription conventions

[laughs]	Paralinguistic features in square brackets
+	Pause up to one second
...//...\	
.../...\\	Simultaneous speech
(hello)	Transcriber's best guess at unclear utterance
{it was}	Words added in English translation to help comprehension
?	Rising or question intonation
VERY	Capitals indicate emphatic stress
[...]	Section of transcript omitted
ke-	Incomplete word
[drawls] :...:	Word between colons is drawled

All names are pseudonyms.

The transcription conventions are adapted from the Language in the Workplace Project.
For more information please visit www.vuw.ac.nz/lals/research/lwp.aspx.

Appendix B

Example 7.2

Dear all
we're meeting as announced on [date and time] (thanks to Philippe
for checking that the room – distributed by paper/pencil;) – is
available) ...
in order to hear about the thesis project of a new PhD student
(2–2:45pm) and to discuss the readings (we have) done (MAKE
SURE YOU READ TO OF THE ARTICLES _PRIOR_ to the
session.

Message from Prof. [name]: The articles for the reading session on
systems are accessible via the blog. http://xxx password: xxx

NOTE – ALL active [name of system] useers (especially [other
name] system) are invited to come at 13h as [name] will be
available for discussing (the urgent) essentials! DONT FORGET!

Happy Kleeschen!

Notes

1 What is professional communication?

1 The names of people and workplaces are pseudonyms in all examples throughout the book. For some examples the transcripts have been slightly modified to ensure all examples conform to the same transcription conventions.

2 The exchange occurred in French and has been translated into English; see the original text for the French version.

3 In line with general practice at the hospital where the data was recorded, the term *patient* is used to refer to the pregnant women who make use of the hospital's services (see Zayts and Schnurr 2011).

4 An ongoing debate exists among scholars as to whether sociolinguistics and applied linguistics constitute distinct or overlapping fields. I tend to follow Boxer, who maintains that "[a]ny time we make a study of how language is used by it speakers or learners in interaction, we are doing applied sociolinguistics' (2002: 1). According to this line of argument, then, any investigation of how people at work use language and communication almost necessarily means applying linguistics. It thus seems logical to include these kinds of sociolinguistic endeavours within the field of applied linguistics. The term 'applied linguistics' is thus used in this wider meaning throughout the book.

3 Workplace culture

1 Although strictly speaking, organisational culture and workplace culture are not exactly the same, the terms are used interchangeably here as the models of organisational culture outlined in the next section can usefully be utilised to explore the culture of a workplace.

2 Note that you may need to obtain ethics approval from your department or university before collecting data.

4 Culture and politeness at work

1 I am very grateful for Julia deBres for drawing my attention to this example and for sharing it with me. A translated version of the email can be found in Appendix B.

2 Although the terms intercultural and cross-cultural are often used interchangeably in the literature, they are used here in the following

meaning: intercultural studies are those studies which look at how members from different countries interact with each other, whereas cross-cultural studies compare the behaviour of members of one country with the behaviour of members from another.

3 I am very grateful to Hans-Georg Wolf for sharing this example with me.

5 Identities at work

1 The observation that people often construct and enact several identities – and the potential conflicts that may arise from this – is further discussed in Chapter 6, which takes a closer look at how two specific types identities, namely professional and gender identities, are often intertwined with each other in complex ways.

6 Gender

1   I am very grateful for Bernie Mak for sharing this example with me. It was originally in Cantonese and has been translated into English.

7 Leadership

1 A wiki is 'a particular form of user generated website that has become popular through sites such as wikipedia.org or wikitravel.org' (Schroeder, Minocha and Schneider 2010: 550).

2 This exchange is taken from OpenWetWare which describes itself as 'an effort to promote the sharing of information, know-how, and wisdom among researchers and groups who are working in biology & biological engineering'. See also http://openwetware.org/wiki/Main_Page.

3 The transcription conventions for this example are not in line with the transcription conventions used for the other examples in this book but reflect the CA conventions used in Clifton (2006):

[But]	Overlapping utterances
( )	Inaudible
=	Latched utterances

Task commentaries

1 The email has not been altered except where names have been replaced with pseudonyms. Spelling and capitalisation is left as in the original.

Glossary

aggravator
word or phrase that increases the illocutionary force of an utterance, for example *this was really very good*. Also called an intensifier in some grammars.

blue-collar workplace
workplaces where manual labour is performed (for example in manufacturing, building and construction).

booster
intensifier. Increases the illocutionary force of an utterance. See also **aggravator**.

channel
transmits messages. The term is often used in a similar sense as medium.

community of practice (CofP)
term coined by Lave and Wenger (1991) and further developed by Wenger (1998) to describe groups of people who come together regularly to engage in a particular practice. Members of CofPs have developed a shared repertoire of doing things and of communicating which, in turn, characterise this particular CofP (see also Chapter 3). Examples of CofPs include working teams, book clubs and antenatal classes.

conventionalised politeness markers
conventional or routinised ways of expressing politeness, for example the use of *please* and *thank you* in English.

corporate workplace
used here to refer to business workplace environments (as opposed to, for example, government organisations).

deixis
words that refer to something in relation to the speaker or the context of the utterance, for example: *here, there, this report*.

discourse
used here in a dual meaning (see also Chapter 7): i) as 'language above the sentence' (Cameron 2001: 10), and ii) on a more abstract level as 'the practices that

systematically form the objects of which they speak' (Foucault 1972: 49). See Chapter 6 for some examples.

epistemic orientation
refers to a speaker's degree of certainty that their utterance is true. For example, compare *He is coming tomorrow* versus *He might be coming tomorrow*. See also **modal**.

epistemological stance
reflects the researcher's beliefs about the nature of knowledge. Depending on the epistemological stance a researcher takes, they will ask different kinds of questions and will be interested in exploring different aspects of a specific topic.

ethnographic data
data obtained through ethnographic methods including participant observation and interviews. Ethnographic research usually studies subjects in their natural environment (such as a workplace) and involves researchers who try to get an insider's perspective on what is going on.

expletive
swear word.

face-threatening act (FTA)
term coined by Brown and Levinson (1987) to describe speech acts that threaten the hearer's and/or the speaker's face (see also Chapter 4).

floor
a speaker currently holds the floor if they have the right to speak at a certain point in a conversation.

formulaic language
sequence of words which appears to be prefabricated rather than made up on the spot. Examples include idioms, proverbs and linguistic routines. For example, *nice to meet you, I've heard so much about you.*

hedge
word or phrase that mitigates the illocutionary force of an utterance: for example, *kind of, sort of.*

hesitation marker
expression that signals hesitation: for example, *erm.*

honorific
expression of respect and deference: for example, in English the use of titles such as *Dr French.*

illocutionary force
the force an utterance has: for example, whether something is meant and interpreted as a compliment or a criticism.

implicature
term coined by Grice to describe an additional meaning conveyed by an utterance which is not explicitly expressed. For example, *A: Have you done the report and the letter? B: I've done the letter. Implicature: B has not done the report.*

interactional footing
term coined by Goffman to describe interlocutors' alignment or stance towards each other and the situational context. Footings regularly change throughout an interaction, which is reflected in interlocutors' language use. For example, the shift from small talk towards more formal, transactional talk during the opening stages of a meeting is not only reflected in a change towards (presumably more formal) language use but is also indicated in a change in interlocutors' alignment and stance towards each other.

interrogative
question.

lexis
vocabulary of a language.

lingua franca
variety used between speakers of different languages as a means of communication. For example, if a native German speaker and a native Cantonese speaker want to negotiate a business deal they may use English as a lingua franca.

marked
describes forms that are not neutral (unmarked) but that are clearly distinct and noticeable in some respect. For example, the use of swearing is marked and inappropriate in some workplaces while it may be unmarked (and thus normal and appropriate) in others (see Chapter 3).

medium
means through which communication takes place: for example, email.

metaphor
literary figure of speech in which a term or phrase is replaced by another, often more tangible one, thereby suggesting likeness between them. For example, *The meeting was such a breeze.*

mitigation
process to minimise the illocutionary force of an utterance: for example, by using hedges.

modal
expression (often verbs) that assists speakers/writers in expressing how certain they are about the truth of their utterance. For example, *The deadline may be 1st of May.*

move
in genre analysis a move refers to the different steps or building blocks that characterise a particular genre (see Chapter 2 for some examples).

nominalisation
describes the process of converting a word (such as an adjective or verb) into a noun. For example *to manage staff* becomes *the management of staff, increasing numbers* becomes *an increase in numbers*.

non-profit workplace
describes those workplaces whose main aim is not necessarily to create monetary profits but to pursue other goals (for example, fund cancer research).

overlap
a CA term which describes those situations in which a speaker starts speaking before the other one has completed his/her turn.

paradigm
a comprehensive (and often quoted) definition of this complex concept is provided by Guba and Lincoln (1994: 107):

> A paradigm may be viewed as a set of basic beliefs (or metaphysics) that deals with ultimates or first principles. It represents a world view that defines, for its holder, the nature of the 'world', the individual's place in it, and the range of possible relationships to that world and its parts, as, for example, cosmologies and theologies do. The beliefs are basic in the sense that they must be accepted simply on faith (however well argued); there is no way to establish their ultimate truthfulness.

One aspect of a paradigm is the **epistemological stance** a researcher takes (whose work can be placed in a certain paradigm).

presupposition
refers to the speaker's assumptions prior to making an utterance.

register
people use language differently in different contexts: for example, different registers are used in job interviews than during lunch breaks. Examples of professional registers include legal language and medical language.

small talk
term frequently used to refer to talk that is often negatively perceived as purposeless and thus superfluous, in particular in professional contexts. Typical small talk topics (in many Western countries) include the weather and sports. However, see Holmes (2000b) for a discussion of the various functions of small talk in workplace environments.

speech act

the act performed by an utterance. Examples of speech acts include compliments, complaints, apologies and many more.

tag question

a question that is attached at the end of an utterance. For example, *Nice weather, isn't it?*

text-patterning

term used by Bhatia (1993) to describe information about the syntactic and grammatical features of a particular genre which have become part of the conventions of that genre. According to Bhatia (1993: 26), the term *textualization* is used by Widdowson (1979) to describe the same phenomenon.

vernacular

a language variety which has not been standardised and which does not have official status in a particular context.

white-collar workplace

often used to describe office environments and similar types of workplace. Examples of white-collar workplaces are the service sector and commercial organisations.

Further reading

Although the previous chapters have attempted to provide a comprehensive overview of the various topics of professional communication, you may find some of the following references useful in finding out more about specific aspects. Most of the sources provided below are monographs or collections of papers. With a few exceptions, I have not included individual journal articles or book chapters here that report on research studies, but I have mentioned several studies in the respective chapters.

Chapter 1 What is professional communication?

Sarangi, Srikant and Celia Roberts (eds) (1999). *Talk, Work and Institutional Order. Discourse in Medical, Mediation and Management Settings*. Berlin: De Gruyter.
A collection of research papers that take an interdisciplinary approach to spoken interactions in a range of different professional contexts. The introductory chapter is particularly useful as it addresses many of the issues discussed in Chapter 1.

Sarangi, Srikant and Christopher Candlin (2011). Professional and organisational practice: A discourse/communication perspective. In Christopher Candlin and Srikant Sarangi (eds), *Handbook of Communication in Professions and Organisations*. Berlin: Mouton de Gruyter. 1–49.
Provides a good overview of the developments of professional communication and discusses recent trends in applied linguistics research on professional communication.

Drew, Paul and John Heritage (eds) (1992). *Talk at Work: Interaction in Institutional Settings*. Cambridge: Cambridge University Press.
This is a seminal collection of research on professional communication from a CA perspective. It contains numerous research studies that explore interactions between professionals and clients in a range of different professional contexts.

Other monographs and collected editions which deal with communication in professional contexts and which you may find useful include:

Gunnarsson, Britt-Louise (2009). *Professional Discourse*. London: Continuum.
Provides an overview of discourse in specific professional domains, including law, business, medicine, science and academia. It makes extensive reference to research conducted in Scandinavia.

Bargiela-Chiappini, Francesca, Catherine Nickerson and Brigitte Planken (2007). *Business Discourse*. Basingstoke: Palgrave Macmillan.
Provides a comprehensive introduction to business communication and outline of seminal research in this area. It also includes discussions on various topics discussed in this book, including gender, identity and workplace culture, and a very useful guide to resources for research on business discourse.

Holmes, Janet and Maria Stubbe (2003). *Power and Politeness in the Workplace: A Sociolinguistic Analysis of Talk at Work*. London: Longman.
Explores issues of power and politeness through an analysis of workplace talk recorded in a range of New Zealand workplaces.

Koester, Almut (2010). *Workplace Discourse*. London: Continuum.
Investigates spoken and written discourse in some workplaces in the United Kingdom.

Chapter 2 Genres of professional communication

Bargiela-Chiappini, Francesca and Catherine Nickerson (eds) (1999). *Writing Business: Genres, Media and Discourses*. London: Longman.
Provides a collection of research papers on written genres in a range of professional contexts.

Koester, Almut (2006). *Investigating Workplace Discourse*. London: Routledge.
Discusses various genres of spoken interaction by drawing on authentic data collected in UK and US workplaces.

Handford, Michael (2010). *The Language of Business Meetings*. Cambridge: Cambridge University Press.
An in-depth analysis of business meetings from a genre perspective.

Gillaerts, Paul and Maurizio Gotti (eds) (2005). *Genre Variation in Business Letters*. Bern: Peter Lang.
A collection of research papers exploring the genre of business letters.

Swales, John (1990). *Genre Analysis: English in Academic and Research Settings*. Cambridge: Cambridge University Press.
Seminal work on genre analysis from an ESP perspective.

Research papers and theoretical discussions of genre from an ESP perspective can be found in the *Journal of English for Specific Purposes*: http://www.sciencedirect.com/science/journal/08894906

Chapter 3 Workplace culture

Brown, Andrew (1995). *Organisational Culture*. London: Pitman.
  A useful and easily accessible introduction to organisational culture which
  includes some case studies and examples for illustration.

Wenger, Etienne (1998). *Communities of Practice: Learning, Meaning, and
  Identity*. Cambridge: Cambridge University Press.
  For more information about the concept of CofP.

Useful applications of the concept of workplace culture in applied
linguistic research on professional communication are the following:

Holmes, Janet and Meredith Marra (2002). Having a laugh at work: how
  humour contributes to workplace culture. *Journal of Pragmatics*, 34:
  1683–710.
Holmes, Janet, Stephanie Schnurr and Meredith Marra (2007). Leadership
  communication: discursive evidence of a workplace culture change.
  Discourse and Communication, 1.4: 433–51.

Chapter 4 Culture and politeness at work

A number of introductions to intercultural communication exist, but I
found the following particularly useful as they specifically address
some issues that are relevant in professional contexts:

Scollon, Ron and Suzanne Wong Scollon (2001). *Intercultural Communication:
  A Discourse Approach*. Malden, Mass.: Blackwell.
  Approaches intercultural communication from the perspective of interactional
  sociolinguistics. It specifically discusses issues of face and politeness in
  intercultural contexts and has a chapter on professional discourse.

Piller, Ingrid (2011). *Intercultural Communication: A Critical Introduction*.
  Edinburgh: Edinburgh University Press.
  This introduction to intercultural communication provides a critical
  overview of the field. The chapter on intercultural communication at work
  is particularly relevant.

Meyer, Bernd and Birgit Apfelbaum (2010). *Multilingualism at Work: From
  Policies to Practices in Public, Medical and Business Settings*. Amsterdam:
  Benjamins.
  A collection of research papers on case studies of multilingualism at work
  in different socio-cultural contexts.

Bührig, Kristin and Jan ten Thije (eds) (2006). *Beyond Misunderstanding:
  Linguistic Analyses of Intercultural Communication*. Amsterdam: Benjamins.
  A collection of research studies that challenge the assumptions that
  misunderstandings frequently occur in intercultural contexts and that
  question the role of culture.

Sarangi, Srikant (1994). Intercultural or not? Beyond celebration of cultural differences in miscommunication analysis. *Pragmatics*, 4.3: 409–27.
Seminal paper that challenges essentialist views of culture and critically discusses the purpose of research on intercultural encounters.

Spencer-Oatey, Helen (ed.) (2008). *Culturally Speaking: Communication and Politeness Theory*, 2nd edn. London: Continuum.
Edited volume which contains an introductory chapter to rapport management as well as several empirical studies that apply rapport management to different kinds of data in different socio-cultural contexts.

Fraser, Bruce (2005). Whither politeness. In Robin Tolmach Lakoff and Sachiko Ide (eds), *Broadening the Horizon of Linguistic Politeness*. Amsterdam: Benjamins. 65–83.
Provides a comprehensive criticism of politeness theory.

Chapter 5 Identities at work

Bucholtz, Mary and Kira Hall (2005). Identity and interaction: a sociocultural linguistic approach. *Discourse Studies*, 7.4-5: 585–614.
This is a seminal paper which outlines a framework for studying identity construction by drawing on a wide range of literature in linguistics and anthropology.

Burr, Vivien (2003). *Social Constructionism*, 2nd edn. London: Routledge.
Provides a general overview of social constructionism.

The following two introductions of identity are particularly accessible:

Benwell, Bethan and Elizabeth Stokoe (2006). *Discourse and Identity*. Edinburgh: Edinburgh University Press.
The introduction chapter provides a comprehensive overview of the complexities of identity, and the book also includes a useful chapter on institutional identities.

Jenkins, Richard (2008). *Social Identity*, 3rd edn. London: Routledge.

The following two references are collections of research papers that explore various issues of identity construction in professional contexts.

Angouri, Jo and Meredith Marra (2011). *Constructing Identities at Work*. Basingstoke: Palgrave Macmillan.

Van de Mieroop, Dorien and Jonathan Clifton (2012fc). *Pragmatics. Special Issue on the Interplay between Professional Identities and Age, Gender and Ethnicity*.

Chapter 6 Gender

Holmes, Janet (2006). *Gendered Talk at Work: Constructing Social Identity through Workplace Interaction*. Oxford: Blackwell.
Explores various issues of gendered discourse in the workplace, including leadership. Particularly useful for an understanding of identity construction.

Mullany, Louise (2006). *Gendered Discourse in the Professional Workplace*. Basingstoke: Palgrave Macmillan.
Explores the central role of gendered discourses in perpetuating gender inequalities in professional workplaces.

Litosseliti, Lia (2006). *Gender and Language: Theory and Practice*. London: Hodder Arnold.
Provides a comprehensive overview of various topics of language and gender research and includes a chapter on gender and language in the workplace.

Eckert, Penelope and Sally McConnell-Ginet (2003). *Language and Gender*. Cambridge: Cambridge University Press.
Although the book does not include a chapter specifically on gender at work, this is a comprehensive introduction of language and gender which makes references to a variety of gender issues in the professional domain.

Mullany, Louise (ed.) (2011). *Gender and Language. Special Issue on Gender, Language, and Leadership in the Workplace*.
This special issue of Gender and Language features a collection of research articles on gender and leadership in a range of different workplaces in different socio-cultural contexts.

Chapter 7 Leadership

Jackson, Brad and Ken Parry (2008). *A Very Short, Fairly Interesting and Reasonably Cheap Book about Studying Leadership*. London: Sage.
The title is programmatic: this book is a very readable introduction to the complex topic of leadership from a non-linguistic perspective.

Schnurr, Stephanie (2009). *Leadership Discourse at Work. Interactions of Humour, Gender and Workplace Culture*. Basingstoke: Palgrave Macmillan.
Approaches the topic of leadership discourse by focusing on humour.

Tourish, Dennis and Brad Jackson (eds) (2008). *Leadership. Special Issue on Communication and Leadership*.
This special issue of *Leadership* contains various research papers which approach leadership from a communication perspective.

Fairhurst, Gail (2007). *Discursive Leadership: In Conversation with Leadership Psychology*. Los Angeles, Calif.: Sage.
Explores communicative aspects of leadership and introduces the notion of discursive leadership.

References

Aaltio, Iris and Albert Mills (2002). Organizational culture and gendered identities in context. In Iris Aaltio and Albert Mills (eds), *Gender, Identity and the Culture of Organizations*. London: Routledge. 3–18.

Adler, Nancy and Dafna Izraeli (eds) (1988). *Women in Management Worldwide*. London: M.E. Sharpe.

Akar, Didar (2002). The macro contextual factors shaping business discourse: the Turkish case. *International Review of Applied Linguistics*, 40: 305–22.

Akar, Didar and Leena Louhiala-Salminen (1999). Towards a new genre: a comparative study of business faxes. In Francesca Bargiela-Chiappin and Catherine Nickerson (eds), *Writing Business: Genres, Media and Discourses*. London: Longman. 207–26.

Alvarez, Jose Luis and Silviya Svejenova (2005). *Sharing Executive Power: Roles and Relationships at the Top*. Cambridge: Cambridge University Press.

Alvesson, Mats and Yvonne Due Billing (1997). *Understanding Gender and Organizations*. London: Sage.

Alvesson, Mats and Yvonne Due Billing (2002). Beyond body counting. A discussion of the social construction of gender at work. In Iris Aaltion and Albert Mills (eds), *Gender, Identity and the Culture of Organizations*. London: Routledge. 72–91.

Alvesson, Mats and Andre Spicer (2012). Critical leadership studies: the case for critical performativity. *Human Relations*, 65: 367–90.

Angouri, Jo and Meredith Marra (2010). Corporate meetings as genre: a study of the role of the chair in corporate meeting talk. *Text and Talk*, 30.6: 615–36.

Angouri, Jo and Meredith Marra (eds) (2011). *Constructing Identities at Work*. Basingstoke: Palgrave Macmillan.

Antaki, Charles and Sue Widdicombe (1998). Identity as an achievement and as a tool. In Charles Antaki and Sue Widdicombe (eds), *Identities in Talk*. London: Sage. 1–14.

Askehave, Inger and John Swales (2001). Genre identification and communicative purpose: a problem and a possible solution. *Applied Linguistics*, 22.2: 195–212.

Balmer, John (2001). Corporate identity, corporate branding and corporate marketing: seeing through the fog. *European Journal of Marketing*, 35: 248–92.

Balmer, John and Alan Wilson (1998). Corporate identity. There is more to it than meets the eye. *International Studies of Management and Organisation*, 28.3: 12–31.

Bargiela-Chiappini, Francesca and Sandra Harris (1996). Requests and status in business correspondence. *Journal of Pragmatics*, 28: 635–62.

Bargiela-Chiappini, Francesca and Sandra Harris (1997a). *The Language of Business: An International Perspective*. Edinburgh: Edinburgh University Press.

Bargiela-Chiappini, Francesca and Sandra Harris (1997b). *Managing Language. The Discourse of Corporate Meetings*. Amsterdam: Benjamins.

Bargiela-Chiappini, Francesca and Catherine Nickerson (1999). Business writing as social action. In Francesca Bargiela-Chiappini and Catherine Nickerson (eds), *Writing Business: Genres, Media and Discourses*. London: Longman. 1–32.

Bargiela-Chiappini, Francesca and Catherine Nickerson (2002). Business discourse: Old debates, new horizons. *International Review of Applied Linguistics*, 40: 273–86.

Bargiela-Chiappini, Francesca, Catherine Nickerson and Brigitte Planken (2007). *Business Discourse*. Basingstoke: Palgrave Macmillan.

Bass, Bernard (1981). *Stogdill's Handbook of Leadership. A Survey of Theory and Research*. New York: Free Press.

Bass, Bernard (1998). *Transformational Leadership: Industrial, Military, and Educational Impact*. Mahawah, N.J.: Erlbaum.

Baxter, Judith (ed.) (2006). *Speaking Out: The Female Voice in Public Contexts*. Basingstoke: Palgrave.

Baxter, Judith (2010). *The Language of Female Leadership*. Basingstoke: Palgrave.

Baxter, Judith and Kieran Wallace (2009). Outside in-group and out-group identities? Constructing male solidarity and female exclusion in UK builders' talk. *Discourse and Society*, 20.4: 411–29.

Beck, Dominique (1999). *Managing Discourse, Self and Others: Women in Senior Management Positions*. Unpublished PhD thesis, University of Western Sydney, Nepean.

Benwell, Bethan and Elizabeth Stokoe (2006). *Discourse and Identity*. Edinburgh: Edinburgh University Press.

Bergvall, Victoria (1999). Toward a comprehensive theory of language and gender. *Language in Society*, 28.2: 273–93.

Berryman-Fink, Cynthia (1997). Gender issues: management style, mobility, and harassment. In Peggy Yuhas Byers (ed.), *Organizational Communication: Theory and Behavior*. Needham Heights, Mass.: Allyn & Bacon. 259–83.

Bhatia, Vijay (1993). *Analysing Genre: Language Use in Professional Settings*. London: Longman.

Bhatia, Vijay (2008). Genre analysis, ESP and professional practice. *English for Specific Purposes*, 27: 161–74.

Bilbow, Grahame (2002). Commissive speech act use intercultural business meetings. *International Review of Applied Linguistics*, 40: 287–303.

Blundel, Richard (2004). *Effective Organisational Communication: Perspectives, Principles and Practices,* 2nd edn. Harlow: Prentice Hall.

Boden, Deirdre (1994). *The Business of Talk. Organization in Action*. Cambridge: Polity Press.

Bond, Michael Harris (1991). *Beyond the Chinese Face. Insights from Psychology*. Hong Kong: Oxford University Press.

Boxer, Diana (2002). *Applying Sociolinguistics: Domains and Face-to-Face Interaction*. Amsterdam: Benjamins.

Boxer, Diana and Florencia Cortes-Conde (1997). From boxing to nipping to biting: conversational joking and identity display. *Journal of Pragmatics*, 27: 275–94.

Bredmar, Margareta and Per Linell (1999). Reconfirming normality: the constitution of reassurance in talks between midwives and expectant mothers. In Srikant Sarangi and Celia Roberts (eds), *Talk, Work and Institutional Order. Discourse in Medical, Mediation and Management Settings*. Berlin: De Gruyter. 237–70.

Brewis, Joanna (2001). Telling it like it is? Gender, language and organizational theory. In Robert Westwood and Stephen Linstead (eds), *The Language of Organization*. London: Sage. 47–70.

Brown, Andrew (1995). *Organisational Culture*. London: Pitman Publishing.

Brown, Penelope and Steven Levinson (1987). *Politeness Theory. Some Universals in Language Use,* rev. edn (first pub. 1978). Cambridge: Cambridge University Press.

Brumfit, Christopher J. (1995). Teacher professionalism and research. In Guy Cook and Barbara Seidlhofer (eds), *Principle and Practice in Applied Linguistics*. Oxford: Oxford University Press. 27–42.

Bubel, Claudia (2006). 'How are you?' 'I'm hot.' An interactive analysis of small talk sequences in British–German telephone sales. In Kristin Bühring and Jan ten Thije (eds), *Beyond Misunderstanding: Linguistic Analyses of Intercultural Communication*. Amsterdam: Benjamins. 245–59.

Bucholtz, Mary and Kira Hall (2004). Language and identity. In Allesandro Duranti (ed.), *A Companion to Linguistic Anthropology*. Malden, Mass.: Blackwell. 369–94.

Bucholtz, Mary and Kira Hall (2005). Identity and interaction: a sociocultural linguistic approach. *Discourse Studies*, 7.4–5: 585–614.

Burke, Ronald and Marilyn Davidson (1994). Women in management: current research issues. In Marilyn Davidson and Ronald Burke (eds), *Women in Management. Current Research Issues*. London: Paul Chapman. 1–8.

Burr, Vivien (1995). *An Introduction to Social Constructionism*. London: Routledge.

Butler, Judith (1990). *Gender Trouble. Feminism and the Subversion of Identity*. New York: Routledge.

Calás, Marta and Linda Smircich (1999) From 'the woman's' point of view: feminist approaches to organization studies. In Stewart Clegg and Cynthia Hardy (eds), *Studying Organization. Theory and Method*. London: Sage. 212–51.

Cameron, Deborah (2000). *Good to Talk? Living and Working in a Communication Culture*. London: Sage.

Cameron, Deborah (2001). *Working with Spoken Discourse*. London: Sage.

Cameron, Deborah, Elizabeth Fraser, Penelope Harvey, M. B. H. Rampton and Kay Richardson (1992). *Researching Language. Issues of Power and Method*. London: Routledge.

Campbell, Sarah and Celia Roberts (2007). Migration, ethnicity and competing discourse in the job interview: synthesizing the institutional and personal. *Discourse and Society*, 18: 243–71.

Candlin, Christopher and Srikant Sarangi (2004). Making applied linguistics matter. *Journal of Applied Linguistics*, 1.1: 1–8.

Case, Schick Susan (1988). Cultural differences, not deficiencies: an analysis of managerial women's language. In Suzanna Rose and Laurie Larwood (eds), *Women's Careers: Pathways and Pitfalls*. New York: Praeger. 41–63.

Casimir, Gian, David Waldman, Timothy Bartram and Sarah Yang (2006). Trust and the relationship between leadership and follower performance: opening the black box in Australia and China. *Journal of Leadership and Organizational Studies*, 12.3: 68–84.

Chambers, J. K., Peter Trudgill and Natalie Schilling-Estes (eds) (2011). *The Handbook of Language Variation and Change*. Oxford: Blackwell.

Chan, Angela (2005). Managing business meetings in different workplace cultures. Unpublished PhD thesis, University of Wellington, New Zealand.

Chen, Ling (2008). Leaders or leadership: alternative approaches to leadership studies. *Management Communication Quarterly*, 21.4: 547–55.

Cheng, Winnie (2003). *Intercultural Conversation*. Amsterdam: Benjamins.

Chouliaraki, Lilie and Norman Fairclough (1999). *Discourse in Late Modernity*. Edinburgh: Edinburgh University Press.

Clarke, Clifford and G. Douglas Lipp (1998). *Danger and Opportunity: Resolving Conflict in U.S.-Based Japanese Subsidiaries*. Yarmouth: Intercultural Press.

Clegg, Stewart and Cynthia Hardy (eds) (1999). *Studying Organization. Theory and Method*. London: Sage.

Clifton, Jonathon (2006). A conversation analytical approach to business communication. *Journal of Business Communication*, 43.3: 202–19.

Clyne, Michael (2009). Address in intercultural communication across languages. *Intercultural Pragmatics*, 6.3: 395–409.

Coates, Jennifer (1993). *Women, Men and Language. A Sociolinguistic Account of Gender Differences in Language*, 2nd edn. London: Longman.

Coates, Jennifer (1994). The language of the professions: Discourse and career. In Julia Evetts (ed.), *Women and Career: Themes and Issues in Advanced Industrial Societies*. London: Longman. 72–86.

Coates, Jennifer (1996). *Women Talk: Conversations Between Women Friends*. Oxford: Blackwell.

Coates, Jennifer (1997). One-at-a-time: the organization of men's talk. In Sally Johnson and Ulrike Hanna Meinhof (eds), *Language and Masculinity*. Oxford: Blackwell. 107–30.

Coates, Jennifer (2003). *Men Talk: Stories in the Making of Masculinities*. Oxford: Oxford University Press.

Collinson, David (1988). 'Engineering humour': masculinity, joking and conflict in shop-floor relations. *Organization Studies*, 9.2: 181–99.

Connell, Robert (1987). *Gender and Power: Society, the Person and Sexual Politics*. Stanford, Calif.: Stanford University Press.

Connell, Robert (1995). *Masculinities*. Berkeley, Calif.: University of California Press.

Cook-Gumperz, Jenny and Lawrence Messerman (1999). Local identities and institutional practices: constructing the record of professional collaboration. In Srikant Sarangi and Celia Roberts (eds), *Talk, Work and Institutional Order: Discourse in Medical, Mediation and Management Settings*. Berlin: De Gruyter. 146–181.

Cooperrider, David, Frank Barrett and Suresh Srivatstva (1995). Social construction and appreciative inquiry: a journey in organizational theory. In Dian Hosking, Peter Dachler and Kenneth Gergen (eds), *Management and Organization: Relational Alternatives to Individualism*. Aldershot: Avebury Press. 157–200.

Cotterill, Janet (2003). *Language and Power in Court. A Linguistic Analysis of the O.J Simpson Trial*. Basingstoke: Palgrave Macmillan.

Coupland, Justine (ed.) (2000). *Small Talk*. London: Longman.

Crawford, Mary (1995). *Talking Difference: On Gender and Language*. London: Sage.

Cullen, John (1999). *Multinational Management. A Strategic Approach*. Cincinnati, Oh.: South-Western Publishing.

Daly, Nicola, Janet Holmes, Jonathan Newton and Maria Stubbe (2004). Expletives as solidarity signals in FTAs on the factory floor. *Journal of Pragmatics*, 36.5: 945–64.

Day, David, Peter Gronn and Eduardo Salas (2004). Leadership capacity in teams. *Leadership Quarterly*, 15: 857–880.

De Fina, Anna (2010). The negotiation of identities. In Miriam Locher and Sage Graham (eds), *Interpersonal Pragmatics*. Berlin: de Gruyter. 205–24.

Decker, Wayne (1991). Style, gender, and humor effects in evaluating leaders. *Mid-Atlantic Journal of Business* 27.2: 117–28.

Decker, Wayne and Denise Rotondo (2001). Relationships among gender, type of humor, and perceived leader effectiveness. *Journal of Managerial Issues* 13.4: 451–65.

Deppermann, Arnulf, Reinhold Schmitt and Lorenza Mondada (2010). Agenda and emergence: contingent and planned activities in a meeting. *Journal of Pragmatics* 42: 1700–18.

Deschamps, Jean-Claude and Thierry Devos (1998). Regarding the relationship between social identity and personal identity. In Stephen Worchel, Francisco Morales, Dario Paez and Jean-Claude Deschamps (eds), *Social Identity*. London: Sage. 1–12.

Devitt, Amy (1991). Intertextuality in tax accounting: Genre, referential, and functional. In Charles Bazerman and James Paradis (eds), *Textual Dynamics of the Professions*. Madison, Wisc.: University of Wisconsin Press. 336–57.

Devitt, Amy (2004). *Writing Genres*. Carbondale, Ill.: Southern Illinois University Press.

Dorfman, Peter, Jon Howell, Shozo Hibino, Jin Lee, Uday Tate and Arnoldo Bautista (1997). Leadership in Western and Asian countries: Commonalities and differences in effective leadership processes across cultures. *Leadership Quarterly* 8.3: 233–274.

dos Santos, Valeria B. M. Pinto (2002). Genre analysis of business letters of negotiation. *English for Specific Purposes*, 21: 167–99.

Drew, Paul and John Heritage (eds) (1992). *Talk at Work: Interaction in Institutional Settings*. Cambridge: Cambridge University Press.

Duerst-Lahti, Georgina and Rita Mae Kelly (1995). Introduction. In Georgina Duerst-Lahti and Rita Mae Kelly (eds), *Gender Power, Leadership, and Governance*. Ann Arbor, Mich.: University of Michigan Press. 1–7.

Dwyer, Judith (1993). *The Business Communication Handbook*. New York: Prentice Hall.

Eagly, Alice and Linda Carli (2003). The female advantage: an evaluation of the evidence. *Leadership Quarterly*, 14.14.: 807–34.

Eagly, Alice and Jean Lau Chin (2010). Diversity and leadership in a changing world. *American Psychologist*, 65.3: 216–24.

Eckert, Penelope and Sally McConnell-Ginet (1992). Communities of practice: where language, gender, and power all live. In Kira Hall, Mary Bucholtz and Birch Moonwomon (eds), *Locating Power. Proceedings of the Second Berkeley Women and Language Conference*. Berkeley, Calif.: Berkeley Women and Language Group, University of California. 89–99.

Eckert, Penelope and Sally McConnell-Ginet (2003). *Language and Gender.* Cambridge: Cambridge University Press.

Eelen, Gino (2001). *A Critique of Politeness Theories.* Manchester: St. Jerome.

Ellemers, Naomi, Alexander Haslam, Michael Platow and Daan van Knippenberg (2003). Social identity at work: developments, debates, directions. In Alexander Haslam, Daan van Knippenberg, Michael Platow and Naomi Ellemers (eds), *Social Identity at Work: Developing Theory for Organizational Practice*. New York: Psychology Press. 3–28.

Fairclough, Norman (1989). *Language and Power.* London: Longman.

Fairclough, Norman (1992). *Discourse and Social Change.* Cambridge: Polity Press.

Fairclough, Norman (1995). *Critical Discourse Analysis: The Critical Study of Language*. London: Longman.

Fairclough, Norman and Ruth Wodak (1997). Critical discourse analysis. In Teun van Dijk (ed.), *Discourse as Social Interaction*. London: Sage. 258–84.

Fairhurst, Gail (2007). *Discursive Leadership: In Conversation with Leadership Psychology*. London: Sage.

Fasulo, Alessandra and Cristina Zucchermaglio (2002). My selves and I: identity markers in work meeting talk. *Journal of Pragmatics* 34: 1119–44.

Fenstermaker, Susan and Candace West (eds) (2002). *Doing Gender, Doing Difference: Inequality, Power and Institutional Change*. New York: Routledge.

Ferch, Shann and Matthew Mitchell (2001). Intentional forgiveness in relational leadership: a technique for enhancing effective leadership. *Journal of Leadership Studies*, 7.4: 70–83.

Ferrario, Margaret (1994). Women as managerial leaders. In Marilyn Davidson and Ronald Burke (eds), *Women in Management: Current Research Issues*. London: Paul Chapman. 110–25.

Fletcher, Joyce (1999). *Disappearing Acts. Gender, Power, and Relational Practice at Work*. Cambridge, Mass.: MIT Press.

Fletcher, Joyce (2004). The paradox of postheroic leadership: an essay on gender, power, and transformational change. *Leadership Quarterly*, 15: 647–61.

Flowerdew, John and Alina Wan (2006). Genre analysis of tax computation letters: how and why tax accountants write the way they do. *English for Specific Purposes*, 25: 133–53.

Ford, Jackie (2005). Examining leadership through critical feminist readings. *Journal of Health Organization and Management*, 19.3: 236–51.

Foucault, Michel (1972). *The Archeology of Knowledge and the Discourse on Language*. New York: Pantheon.

Foucault, Michel (1980). *Power/Knowledge*. New York: Pantheon.

Fraser, Bruce (2005). Whither politeness. In Robin Tolmach Lakoff and Sachiko Ide (eds), *Broadening the Horizon of Linguistic Politeness*. Amsterdam: Benjamins. 65–83.

French, John and Bertram Raven (1959). The bases of social power. In Dorwin Cartwright (ed.), *Studies in Social Power*. Ann Arbor, Mich.: University of Michigan Press.

Frost, Peter, Larry Moore, Merrly Louis, Craig Lundberg and Joanne Martin (eds) (1991). *Reframing Organisational Culture*. Beverly Hills, Calif.: Sage.

Fung, Loretta and Ron Carter (2007). Discourse markers and spoken English: Native and learner use in pedagogic settings. *Applied Linguistics*, 28.3: 410–39.

Gardner, John (1990). *On Leadership*. New York: Free Press.

Gee, James Paul, Glynda Hull and Colin Lankshear (1996). *The New Work Order: Behind the Language of the New Capitalism*. St Leonards: Allen & Unwin.

Geis, Florence, Virgina Brown and Carolyn Wolfe (1990). Legitimizing the leader: endorsement by male versus female authority figures. *Journal of Applied Psychology*, 20.12: 943–70.

Gherardi, Silvia (1995). *Gender, Symbolism and Organizational Cultures*. London: Sage.

Gimenez, Julio (2000). Business e-mail communication: Some emerging tendencies in register. *English for Specific Purposes*, 19: 237–51.

Gimenez, Julio (2002). New media and conflicting realities in multinational corporate communication: A case study. *International Review of Applied Linguistics*, 40: 323–43.

Gimenez, Julio (2006). Embedded business emails: Meeting new demands in international business communication. *English for Specific Purposes*, 25: 154–72.

Goffman, Erving (1969). *The Representation of Self in Everyday Life*. London: Penguin.

Grace, Gerald Rupert (1995). *School Leadership: Beyond Education Management. An Essay in Policy Scholarship*. London: Falmer.

Greatbatch, David and Robert Dingwall (1999). Professional neutralism in family mediation. In Srikant Sarangi and Celia Roberts (eds), *Talk, Work and Institutional Order: Discourse in Medical, Mediation and Management Settings*. Berlin: De Gruyter. 271–92.

Grint, Keith (2005). *Leadership: Limits and Possibilities*. Basingstoke: Palgrave.

Gronn, Peter (2002). Distributed leadership as a unit of analysis. *Leadership Quarterly*, 13: 423–51.

Gu, Yuego (1990). Politeness phenomena in modern Chinese. *Journal of Pragmatics*, 14: 237–57.

Guba, Egon and Yvonna Lincoln (1994). Competing paradigms in qualitative research. In Norman Denzin and Yvonna Lincoln (eds), *Handbook of Qualitative Research*. Thousand Oaks, Calif.: Sage. 105–17.

Guirdham, Maureen (2005). *Communicating across Cultures at Work*. Basingstoke: Palgrave Macmillan.

Gumperz, John (1999). On interactional sociolinguistic method. In Srikant Sarangi and Celia Roberts (eds), *Talk, Work and Institutional Order: Discourse in Medical, Mediation and Management Settings*. Berlin: de Gruyter. 453–71.

Gumperz, John, Thomas Cyprian Jupp and Celia Roberts (2007). *Crosstalk: A Study of Cross-Cultural Communication*. London: National Centre for Industrial Language Training.

Gunnarsson, Britt-Louise (1997). The writing process from a sociolinguistic viewpoint. *Written Communication*, 4.3: 139–88.

Gunnarsson, Britt-Louise (2009). *Professional Discourse*. London: Continuum.

Gunnarsson, Britt-Louise, Per Linell and Bengt Nordberg (1997). Introduction. In Britt-Louise Gunnarsson, Per Linell and Bengt Nordberg (eds), *The Construction of Professional Discourse*. London: Longman. 1–12.

Guthey, Eric and Brad Jackson (2011). Cross-cultural leadership revisited. In Alan Bryman, David Collinson, Keith Grint, Brad Jackson and Mary Uhl-Biehl (eds), *The SAGE Handbook of Leadership*. London: Sage. 165–494.

Haakana, Markku and Marja-Leena Sorjonen (2011). Invoking another context: playfulness in buying lottery tickets at convenience stores. *Journal of Pragmatics*, 42: 1288–302.

Hagner, David and Dale DiLeo (1993). *Working Together: Workplace Culture, Supported Employment, and Persons with Disabilities*. Cambridge, Mass.: Brooklyn Books.

Hall, Christopher, Srikant Sarangi and Stefaan Slembrouck (1999). The legitimation of the client and the profession: Identities and roles in social work discourse. In Srikant Sarangi and Celia Roberts (eds), *Talk, Work and Institutional Order: Discourse in Medical, Mediation and Management Settings*. Berlin: De Gruyter. 293–322.

Hall, Edward Twitchell (1976) *Beyond Culture*. Garden City, N.Y.: Anchor Press.

Hall, Stuart (1996). Introduction: Who needs 'identity'? In Stuart Hall and Paul du Gay (eds), *Questions of Cultural Identity*. London: Sage. 1–17.

Halliday, M. A. K. (1994). *An Introduction to Functional Grammar*, 2nd edn. London: Arnold.

Handford, Michael (2010). *The Language of Business Meetings*. Cambridge: Cambridge University Press.

Harris, Sandra and Francesca Bargiela-Chiappini (1997). The languages of business: introduction and overview. In Francesca Bargiela-Chiappini and Sandra Harris (eds), *The Languages of Business: An International Perspective*. Edinburgh: Edinburgh University Press. 1–18.

Hartog, Jennifer (2006). Beyond 'misunderstandings' and 'cultural stereotypes': Analysing intercultural communication. In Kristin Bühring and Jan ten Thije (eds), *Beyond Misunderstanding: Linguistic Analyses of Intercultural Communication*. Amsterdam: Benjamins. 175–88.

Hatch, Jo Mary (1997). *Organization Theory. Modern, Symbolic, and Postmodern Perspectives*. Oxford: Oxford University Press.

Haugh, Michael (2004). Revisiting the conceptualisation of politeness in English and Japanese. *Multilingua*, 23.1–2: 85–110.

Haugh, Michael and Carl Hinze (2003) A metalinguistic approach to deconstructing the concepts of 'face' and 'politeness' in Chinese, English and Japanese. *Journal of Pragmatics*, 35: 1581–611.

Heath, Christian (1992). The delivery and reception of diagnosis in the general-practice consultation. In Paul Drew and John Heritage (eds), *Talk at Work: Interaction in Institutional Settings*. Cambridge: Cambridge University Press. 235–67.

Heenan, David and Warren Bennis (1999). *Co-Leaders: The Power of Great Partnerships*. New York: John Wiley & Sons.

Heffer, Chris (2005). *The Language of the Jury Trial: A Corpus-Aided Analysis of Legal-Lay Discourse*. Basingstoke: Palgrave Macmillan.

Heifertz, Ronald (1998). Values in leadership. In Gill Robinson Hickman (ed.), *Leading Organizations: Perspectives for a New Era*. London: Sage. 343–56.

Hickman, Gill Robinson (ed.) (1998). *Leading Organizations: Perspectives for a New Era*. London: Sage.

Hofstede, Geert (1980). *Culture's Consequences. International Differences in Work-Related Values*. Beverly Hills and London: Sage.

Hofstede, Geert (1997). *Cultures and Organizations: Software of the Mind*. New York: McGraw-Hill.

Hofstede, Geert (2001). *Culture's Consequences: Comparing Values, Behaviors, Institutions, and Organization Across Nations*, 2nd edn. London: Sage.

Hofstede, Geert, Bra Neuijen, Denise Daval Ohayv and Geert Sanders (1990). Measuring organizational cultures: A qualitative and quantitative study across twenty cases. *Administrative Science Quarterly*, 35.2: 286–316.

Holmes, Janet (1998). Women's talk: The question of sociolinguistic universals. In Jennifer Coates (ed.), *Language and Gender: A Reader*. Oxford: Blackwell. 461–83.

Holmes, Janet (2000a). Doing collegiality and keeping control at work: Small talk in government departments. In Justine Coupland (ed.), *Small Talk*. London: Longman. 32–61.

Holmes, Janet (2000b). Women at work: Analysing women's talk in New Zealand workplaces. *Australian Review of Applied Linguistics*, 22.2: 1–17.

Holmes, Janet (2003). Social constructionism. In Frawley William (ed.), *International Encyclopedia of Linguistics*, vol. 4. Oxford: Oxford University Press. 88–91.

Holmes, Janet (2006). *Gendered Talk at Work*. Oxford: Blackwell.

Holmes, Janet and Meredith Marra (2002a). Over the edge? Subversive humour between colleagues and friends. *Humor*, 15.1: 1–23.

Holmes, Janet and Meredith Marra (2002b). Humour as a discursive boundary marker in social interaction. In Anna Duszak (ed.), *Us and Others: Social Identities Across Languages, Discourse and Cultures*. Amsterdam: Benjamins. 377–99.

Holmes, Janet and Meredith Marra (2002c). Having a laugh at work: How humour contributes to workplace culture. *Journal of Pragmatics*, 34: 1683–710.

Holmes, Janet and Meredith Marra (2004). Relational practice in the workplace: women's talk or gendered discourse? *Language in Society*, 33: 337–98.

Holmes, Janet, Meredith Marra and Bernadette Vine (2011). *Leadership, Discourse and Ethnicity*. Oxford: Oxford University Press.

Holmes, Janet and Miriam Meyerhoff (1999). The community of practice: Theories and methodologies in language and gender research. *Language in Society*, 28.2: 173–83.

Holmes, Janet and Stephanie Schnurr (2005). Politeness, humor and gender in the workplace: Negotiating norms and identifying contestation. *Journal of Politeness Research*, 1: 121–49.

Holmes, Janet, Stephanie Schnurr and Meredith Marra (2007). Leadership and communication: Discursive evidence of a workplace culture change. *Discourse and Communication*, 1.4: 433–51.

Holmes, Janet and Maria Stubbe (2003a). 'Feminine' workplaces: Stereotypes and reality. In Janet Holmes and Miriam Meyerhoff (eds), *Handbook of Language and Gender*. Oxford: Blackwell. 573–99.

Holmes, Janet and Maria Stubbe (2003b). *Power and Politeness in the Workplace: A Sociolinguistic Analysis of Talk at Work*. London: Longman.

Holmes, Janet, Maria Stubbe and Bernadette Vine (1999). Constructing professional identity: 'Doing power' in policy units. In Srikant Sarangi and Celia Roberts (eds), *Talk, Work and Institutional Order: Discourse in Medical, Mediation and Management Settings*. Berlin: De Gruyter. 351–85.

Hosking, Dian Marie (1997). Organizing, leadership, and skilful process. In Keith Grint (ed.), *Leadership: Classical, Contemporary, and Critical Approaches*. Oxford: Oxford University Press. 293–318.

House, Juliane (2005). Politeness in Germany: Politeness in *Germany*? In Leo Hickey and Miranda Stewart (eds), *Politeness in Europe*. Clevedon: Multilingual Matters. 13–28.

House, Robert, Paul Hanges, Mansour Javidan, Peter Dorfman and Vipin Gupta (2004). *Culture, Leadership, and Organizations: The GLOBE study of 62 Societies*. Thousand Oaks, Calif.: Sage.

Howard, Ann (1998). The empowering leader: Unrealized opportunities. In Gill Robinson Hickman (ed.), *Leading Organizations: Perspectives for a New Era*. London: Sage. 202–13.

Huckin, Thomas N. (1997). Critical discourse analysis. In Tom Miller (ed.), *Functional Approaches to Written Text: Classroom Applications*. Washington DC: United States Information Agency. 78–92.

Humphries, Maria and Bev Gatenby (1996). Career development: leadership through networking. In Su Olsson and Nicole Stirton (eds), *Women and Leadership: Power and Practice*. Palmerston North, New Zealand: Massey University Press. 221–35.

Hyland, Ken (2003). Genre-based pedagogies: A social response to process. *Journal of Second Language Writing*, 12: 17–29.

Hyon, Sunny (1996). Genres in three traditions: Implications for ESL. *TESOL Quarterly*, 30.4: 693–722.

Iedema, Rick and Hermine Scheeres (2003). From doing work to talking work: Renegotiating knowing, doing, and identity. *Applied Linguistics*, 24.3: 316–37.

Iedema, Rick and Ruth Wodak (1999). Introduction: Organizational discourses and practices. *Discourse and Society*, 10.1: 5–19.

Jackson, Brad and Ken Parry (2008). *A Very Short, Fairly Interesting and Reasonably Cheap Book About Studying Leadership*. Los Angeles, Calif.: Sage.

Jenkins, Richard (1996). *Social Identity*. London: Routledge.

Jenkins, Richard (2008). *Social Identity*, 3rd edn. Abingdon: Routledge.

Jensen, Astrid (2009). Discourse strategies in professional e-mail negotiation: A case study. *English for Specific Purposes*, 28: 4–18.

Kaur, Jagdisch (2011). Intercultural communication as a lingua franca: Some sources of misunderstanding. *Intercultural Pragmatics*, 8.1: 93–116.

Kerbrat-Orecchioni, Catherine (2006). Politeness in small shops in France. *Journal of Politeness Research* 2: 79–103.

Kets de Vries, Manfred (1994). The leadership mystique. *Academy of Management Executive*, 8.3: 73–93.

Kidd, Warren (2002). *Culture and Identity*. Basingstoke: Palgrave.

Kim, Kyoungsu (2004). In Sook Kim and Kong Sook Kim, A multiple-level theory of leadership: The impact of culture as a moderator. *Journal of Leadership and Organizational Studies*, 11.1: 78–92.

Kirkbride, Paul and Shae Wan Chaw (1987). The cross-cultural transfer of organizational cultures: Two case studies of corporate mission statements. *Asia-Pacific Journal of Management*, 5.1: 55–66.

Kjaerbeck, Susanne (2008). Narratives as resource to manage disagreement: Examples from a parents' meeting in an extracurricular activity centre. *Text and Talk*, 28: 307–26.

Koester, Almut (2006). *Investigating Workplace Discourse*. London: Routledge.

Koester, Almut (2010). *Workplace Discourse*. London: Continuum.

Koller, Veronika (2004). Business women and war metaphors: 'Possessive, jealous and pugnacious'? *Journal of Sociolinguistics*, 8.1: 3–22.

Koller, Veronika (2007). 'The world's local bank': Glocalisation as a strategy in corporate branding discourse. *Social Semiotics*, 17.1: 111–31.

Koller, Veronika (2011). 'Hard-working, team-oriented individuals': Constructing professional identities in corporate mission statements. In Jo Angouri and Meredith Marra (eds), *Constructing Identities at Work*. Basingstoke: Palgrave Macmillan. 105–28.

Kotter, John (2001). What leaders really do. *Harvard Business Review. Special Issue on Leadership*, 79.11: 85–96.

Kress, Guenther and Theo van Leeuwen (2001). *Multimodal Discourse. The Modes and Media of Contemporary Communication*. London: Arnold.

Kress, Guenther and Theo van Leeuwen (2006). *Reading Images: The Grammar of Visual Design*, 2nd edn. London: Routledge.

Laforest, Marty (2002). Scenes of family life: Complaining in everyday conversation. *Journal of Pragmatics*, 34.10–11: 1595–620.

Lave, Jean and Etienne Wenger (1991). *Situated Learning: Legitimate Peripheral Participation*. Cambridge: Cambridge University Press.

Lee, Seung-Hee (2011). Managing nongranting of customers' requests in commercial service encounters. *Research on Language and Social Interaction*, 44.2: 109–34.

Leech, Geoffrey (1983). *Principles of Pragmatics*. London: Longman.

Lewis, Richard (2006). *When Cultures Collide: Leading Across Cultures*. Boston, Mass.: Nicholas Brealey International.

Liddicoat, Anthony (2007). *An Introduction to Conversation Analysis*. London: Continuum.

Litosseliti, Lia (2006). *Gender and Language: Theory and Practice*. London: Hodder Arnold.

Locher, Miriam (2008). Relational work, politeness, and identity construction. In Gerd Antos and Eija Ventola (eds) in cooperation with Tilo Weber, *Handbook of Interpersonal Communication*. Berlin: de Gruyter. 509–40.

Loos, Eugene (1999). Intertextual networks in organisations: The use of written and oral business discourse in relation to context. In Francesca Bargiela-Chiappini and Catherine Nickerson (eds), *Writing Business: Genres, Media and Discourses*. London: Longman. 315–32.

Louhiala-Salminen, Leena (1997). Investigating the genre of a business fax: A Finnish case study. *Journal of Business Communication*, 34.3: 316–33.

Louhiala-Salminen, Leena (2002). The fly's perspective: Discourse in the daily routine of a business manager. *English for Specific Purposes*, 21: 211–31.

Lüdi, Georges, Katharina Höchle and Patchareerat Yanaprasart (2010). Plurilingual practices at multilingual workplaces. In Bernd Meyer and Birgit Apfelbaum (eds), *Multilingualism at Work: From Policies to Practices in Public, Medical and Business Settings*. Amsterdam: Benjamins.

Luthans, Fred (1989). *Organizational Behavior*, 5th edn. New York: McGraw-Hill.

Luyendijk, Joris (2011). Women in finance. *Guardian*, 3 November. Accessed online at: www.guardian.co.uk/commentisfree/2011/nov/03/voices-of-finance-women (7 November 2011).

Maher, Karen (1997). Gender-related stereotypes of transformational and transactional leadership. *Sex Roles*, 37.3–4: 209–26.

Mahtani, Shalini, Kate Vernon and Ruth Sealy (2009). *Women on Boards: Hang Send Index 2009*. Hong Kong: Community Business.

Manian, Ranjini (2007). *Doing Business in India for Dummies*. Hoboken, N.J.: Wiley.

Marra, Meredith (2008) Recording and analysing talk across cultures. In Helen Spencer-Oatey (ed.), *Culturally Speaking: Managing Rapport Across Cultures*, 2nd edn. London: Continuum. 304–21.

Marra, Meredith and Janet Holmes (2008). Constructing ethnicity in New Zealand workplace stories. *Text and Talk*, 28.3: 397–419.

Marra, Meredith, Stephanie Schnurr and Janet Holmes (2006). Effective leadership in New Zealand workplaces: Balancing gender and role. In Judith Baxter (ed.), *Speaking Out: The Female Voice in Public Contexts*. Basingstoke: Palgrave. 240–60.

Marsh, Emily and Marilyn Domas White (2003). A taxonomy of relationships between images and text. *Journal of Documentation*, 59.6: 647–72.

Martin, J. R. (1997) Analysing genre: Functional parameters. In Frances Christie and Jim R. Martin (eds), *Genre and Institutions. Social Processes in the Workplace and School*. London: Cassell. 3–39.

Martin, Patricia Yancey (1993). Feminist practice in organizations: Implications for management. In Ellen Fagenson (ed.), *Women in Management: Trends, Issues, and Challenges in Managerial Diversity*. London: Sage. 274–96.

Martin Rojo, Luisa and Conception Gomez Esteban (2003). Discourse at work: Take on the role of manager. In Gilbert Weiss and Ruth Wodak (eds), *Critical Discourse Analysis: Theory and Interdisciplinarity*. New York: Palgrave Macmillan. 241–71.

Matsumoto, Yoshiko (1988). Reexamination of the universality of face: Politeness phenomena in Japanese. *Journal of Pragmatics*, 12: 403–26.

Melewar, T. C. (2003). Determinants of the corporate identity construct: A review of the literature. *Journal of Marketing Communications*, 9.4: 195–220.

Melewar, T. C. and Elizabeth Jenkins (2002). Defining the corporate identity construct. *Corporate Reputation Review*, 5.1: 76–90.

Meyer, Michael (2001). Between theory, method, and politics: Positioning of the approaches to CDA. In Ruth Wodak and Michael Meyer (eds), *Methods of Critical Discourse Analysis*. London: Sage. 14–31.

Meyerhoff, Miriam (2001). Communities of practice. In J. K. Chambers, Peter Trudgill and Natalie Schilling-Estes (eds), *The Handbook of Language Variation and Change*. Oxford: Blackwell. 526–48.

Meyerhoff, Miriam and Nancy Niedzielski (1994). Resistance to creolization: An intergroup account. *Language and Communication*, 14.4: 313–30.

Miller, Carolyn (1984). Genre as social action. *Quarterly Journal of Speech*, 70: 151–67.

Miller, Katherine (1999). *Organizational Communication: Approaches and Processes*, 2nd edn. Belmont, Calif.: Wadsworth.

Miller, Laura (1994). Japanese and American meetings and what goes on before them: A case study of co-worker misunderstanding. *Pragmatics*, 4.2: 221–38.

Mills, Sara (2003). *Gender and Politeness*. Cambridge: Cambridge University Press.

Modaff, Daniel and Sue DeWine (2002). *Organizational Communication: Foundations, Challenges, Misunderstandings*. Los Angeles, Calif.: Roxbury.

Morgan, Gareth (1997). *Images of Organization*, 2nd edn. London: Sage.

Mulholland, Joan (1999) E-mail: Uses, issues and problems in an institutional setting. In Francesca Bargiela-Chiappini and Catherine Nickerson (eds), *Writing Business: Genres, Media and Discourses*. London: Longman. 57–84.

Mullany, Louise (2006). 'Girls on tour': Politeness, small talk, and gender in managerial business meetings. *Journal of Politeness Research*, 2: 55–77.

Mullany, Louise (2007). *Gendered Discourse in the Professional Workplace*. Basingstoke: Palgrave Macmillan.

Mullany, Louise and Lia Litosseliti (2006). Gender and language in the workplace. In Lia Litosseliti (ed.), *Gender and Language: Theory and Practice*. London: Hodder Arnold. 123–47.

Nair-Venugopal, Shanta (2009). Interculturalities: Reframing identities in intercultural communication. *Language and Intercultural Communication*, 9.2: 76–90.

Neuhauser, Peg, Ray Bender and Kirk Stromberg (2000). *Culture.com: Building Corporate Culture in the Connected Workplace*. Toronto: John Wiley & Sons.

Nickerson, Catherine (1999). The use of English in electronic mail in a multinational corporation. In Francesca Bargiela-Chiappini and Catherine Nickerson (eds), *Writing Business: Genres, Media and Discourses*. London: Longman. 35–56.

Nickerson, Catherine (2005). English as a lingua franca in international business contexts. *English for Specific Purposes,* 24.4: 367–80.

Nielsen, Jeffrey (2004). *The Myth of Leadership: Creating Leaderless Organizations.* Palo Alto, Calif.: Davies-Black.

Northouse, Peter (1997). *Leadership: Theory and Practice.* London: Sage.

O'Toole, James, Jay Galbraith and Edward Lawler (2002). When two (or more) heads are better than one: The promise and pitfalls of shared leadership. *California Management Review,* 44.4: 65–83.

Ochs, Elinor (1992). Indexing gender. In Allessandro Duranti and Charles Goodwin (eds), *Rethinking Context: Language as an Interactive Phenomenon.* Cambridge: Cambridge University Press. 335–58.

Ochs, Elinor (1993). Constructing social identity: A language and socialization perspective. *Research on Language and Social Interaction,* 26.3: 287–306.

Offermann, Lynn (1998). Leading and empowering diverse followers. In Gill Robinson Hickman (ed.), *Leading Organizations: Perspectives for a New Era.* London: Sage. 397–403.

Olsson, Su (1996). A takeover? Competencies, gender and the evolving discourses of management. In Su Olsson and Nicole Stirton (eds), *Women and Leadership: Power and Practice.* Palmerston North, New Zealand: Massey University Press. 359–78.

Orlikowski, Wanda and Jo Anne Yates (1994). Genre repertoire: The structuring of communicative practices in organizations. *Administrative Science Quarterly,* 39: 541–74.

Pan, Yuling, Suzanne Wong Scollon and Ron Scollon (2002). *Professional Communication in International Settings.* Malden, Mass.: Blackwell.

Parry, Ken and Sarah Proctor-Thomson (2000). Leadership, culture and performance: The case of New Zealand public sector. *Journal of Change Management,* 3.4: 376–99.

Pauwels, Anne (2000). Inclusive language is good business: Gender, language and equality in the workplace. In Janet Holmes (ed.), *Gendered Speech in Social Context: Perspectives from Town and Gown.* Auckland: Victoria University Press. 134–51.

Peck, Jennifer (2000). The cost of corporate culture: Linguistic obstacles to gender equity in Australian business. In Janet Holmes (ed.), *Gendered Speech in Social Context: Perspectives from Town and Gown.* Auckland: Victoria University Press. 211–30.

Philips, Susan (2003). The power of gender ideologies in discourse. In Janet Holmes and Miriam Meyerhoff (eds), *The Handbook of Language and Gender.* Oxford: Blackwell. 252–76.

Piller, Ingrid (2011). *Intercultural Communication: A Critical Reader.* Edinburgh: Edinburgh University Press.

Planken, Brigitte (2005). Managing rapport in lingua franca sales negotiations: A comparison of professional and aspiring negotiators. *English for Specific Purposes,* 24: 381–400.

Poncini, Gina (2002). Investigating discourse at business meetings with multicultural participation. *International Review of Applied Linguistics,* 40: 345–73.

Potter, Jonathan and Margaret Wetherell (1987). *Discourse and Social Psychology.* London: Sage.

Prechtl, Elisabeth and Anne Davidson Lund (2007). Intercultural competence and assessments: Perspectives from the INCA project. In Helga Kotthoff and Helen Spencer-Oatey (eds), *Handbook of Intercultural Communication*. Berlin: De Gruyter. 467–90.

Pufahl Bax, Ingrid (1986). How to assign work in an office. *Journal of Pragmatics*, 10: 673–92.

Rabey, Gordon (1997). *Workplace Leadership: Moving into Management Today*. Palmerston North, New Zealand: Dunmore.

Raelin, Joseph (2003). *Creating Leaderful Organizations: How to Bring Out Leadership in Everyone*. San Francisco, Calif.: Berrett-Koehler.

Riad, Sally (2005). The power of 'organizational culture' as a discursive formation in merger migration. *Organization Studies*, 26.10: 1529–54.

Richards, Keith (2006). *Language and Professional Identity: Aspects of Collaborative Interaction*. Basingstoke: Palgrave.

Robbins, Stephen, Bruce Millet, Ron Cacioppe and Terry Waters-Marsh (1998). *Organisational Behaviour. Leading and Managing in Australia and New Zealand*, 2nd edn. Sydney: Prentice Hall.

Roberts, Celia (2010). Institutional discourse. In Janet Maybin and Joan Swan (eds), *The Routledge Companion to English Language Studies*. London: Routledge. 181–95.

Roberts, Celia and Sarah Campbell (2005). Fitting stories into boxes: Rhetorical and textual constraints on candidates' performance in British job interviews. *Journal of Applied Linguistics*, 2.1: 45–73.

Roberts, Celia and Sarah Campbell (2007). Migration, ethnicity and competing discourses in the job interview: Synthesising the institutional and personal. *Discourse and Society*, 18.3: 243–71.

Roberts, Celia and Srikant Sarangi (1999). Introduction: Negotiating and legitimating roles and identities. In Srikant Sarangi and Celia Roberts (eds), *Talk, Work and Institutional Order: Discourse in Medical, Mediation and Management Settings*. Berlin: De Gruyter. 227–36.

Rogerson-Revell, Pamela (2007). Humour in business: A double-edged sword. A Study of humour and style shifting in intercultural business meetings. *Journal of Pragmatics*, 39: 4–28.

Romaine, Suzanne (1999). *Communicating Gender*. London: Lawrence Erlbaum.

Rost, Joseph (1998). Leadership and Management. In Gill Robinson Hickman (ed.), *Leading Organizations: Perspectives for a New Era*. London: Sage. 97–114.

Rutherford, Sarah (2001). Any difference? An analysis of gender and divisional management styles in a large airline. *Gender, Work and Organization*, 8.3: 326–45.

Sally, David (2002). Co-leadership: Lessons from republican Rome. *California Management Review*, 44.4: 84–99.

Sarangi, Srikant (1994a). Intercultural or not? Beyond celebration of cultural differences in miscommunication analysis. *Pragmatics*, 4.3: 409–27.

Sarangi, Srikant (1994b). Accounting for mismatches in intercultural selection interviews. *Multilingua*, 13.1/2: 163–94.

Sarangi, Srikant (2010). Culture. In *Handbook of Pragmatics*. Available at: www.benjamins.com/online/hop/ (accessed 16 April 2012).

Sarangi, Srikant and Christopher Candlin (2003). Introduction: Trading between reflexivity and relevance: new challenges for applied linguistics. *Applied Linguistics*, 24.3: 271–85.

Sarangi, Srikant and Christopher Candlin (2011) Professional and organisational practice: A discourse/communication perspective. In Christopher Candlin and Srikant Sarangi (eds), *Handbook of Professional Communication in Professions and Organisations*. Berlin: De Gruyter. 1–49.

Sarangi, Srikant and Celia Roberts (1999). The dynamics of interactional and institutional orders in work-related settings. In Srikant Sarangi and Celia Roberts (eds), *Talk, Work and Institutional Order: Discourse in Medical, Mediation and Management Settings*. Berlin: De Gruyter. 1–57.

Sarros, James, Oleh Butchatsky and Joseph Santora (1996). Breakthrough leadership. Leadership skills for the twenty-first century. In Ken Parry (ed.), *Leadership Research and Practice: Emerging Themes and New Challenges*. Melbourne: Pitman. 41–52.

Sayers, Janet (1997). Managing conflict at work. In Frank Sligo, Sue Olsson and C. Wallace (eds), *Perspectives in Business Communication: Theory and Practice*. Palmerston North, New Zealand: Software Technology New Zealand. 241–53.

Schegloff, Emanuel (1986). The routine as achievement. *Human Studies*, 9: 111–51.

Schegloff, Emanuel (1987). Between micro and macro: contexts and other connections. In Jeffrey C. Alexander, Bernhard Giesen, Richard Münch and Neil J. Smelser (eds), *The Micro-Macro Link*. Berkeley, Calif.: University of California Press. 207–34.

Schegloff, Emanuel (1997). Whose text? Whose context? *Discourse and Society*, 8.2: 165–87.

Schein, Edgar (1987). Coming to a new awareness of organizational culture. In Edgar Schein (ed.), *The Art of Managing Human Resources*. New York: Oxford University Press. 261–77.

Schein, Edgar (1992). *Organizational Culture and Leadership*, 2nd edn. San Francisco, Calif.: Jossey-Bass.

Schein, Edgar (2000). Organizational culture. In Wendell French, Cecil Bell and Robert Zawacki (eds), *Organization Development and Transformation: Managing Effective Change,* 5th edn. New York: McGraw-Hill.

Schiffrin, Deborah (1994). *Approaches to Discourse*. Oxford: Blackwell.

Schnurr, Stephanie (2009a). Constructing leader identities through teasing at work. *Journal of Pragmatics*, 41: 1125–38.

Schnurr, Stephanie (2009b). *Leadership Discourse at Work: Interactions of Humour, Gender and Workplace Culture*. Basingstoke: Palgrave Macmillan.

Schnurr, Stephanie (2010). 'Decision made – let's move on'. Negotiating gender and professional identity in Hong Kong workplaces. In Markus Bieswanger and Heiko Motschenbacher (eds), *Language in its Socio-cultural Context: New Explorations in Global, Medial and Gendered Uses*. Berlin: Peter Lang. 111–36.

Schnurr, Stephanie and Angela Chan (2009). Leadership discourse and politeness at work: A cross-cultural case study of New Zealand and Hong Kong. *Journal of Politeness Research*, 5.2: 131–57.

Schnurr, Stephanie and Angela Chan (2011). Exploring another side of co-leadership: Negotiating professional identities through face-work in disagreements. *Language in Society*, 40.2: 187–210.

Schnurr, Stephanie and Janet Holmes (2009). Using humour to do masculinity at work. In Neal Norrick and Delia Chiaro (eds), *Humor in Interaction*. Amsterdam: Benjamins. 101–24.

Schnurr, Stephanie and Bernie Mak (2011). Leadership and workplace realities in Hong Kong: Is gender really not an issue? *Gender and Language*, 5.2: 337–64.

Schnurr, Stephanie, Meredith Marra and Janet Holmes (2008). Impoliteness as a means of contesting power relations in the workplace. In Miriam Locher and Derek Bousfield (eds), *Impoliteness in Language: Studies on its Interplay with Power in Theory and Practice*. Berlin: De Gruyter. 211–30.

Schnurr, Stephanie and Olga Zayts (2011). Constructing and contesting leaders: An analysis of identity construction at work. In Jo Angouri and Meredith Marra (eds), *Constructing Identities at Work*. Basingstoke: Palgrave. 40–60.

Schnurr, Stephanie and Olga Zayts (2012). 'You have to be adaptable, obviously.' Constructing cultural identities in multicultural workplaces in Hong Kong. *Pragmatics*, 22.2: 279–299.

Schroeder, Andreas, S. Minocha and Christoph Schneider (2010). Social software in higher education: The diversity of applications and their contributions to students' learning experiences. *Communications of the Association of Information Systems*, 26: 547–64.

Scollon, Ron and Suzanne Wong Scollon (2001). *Intercultural Communication: A Discourse Approach*. Malden, Mass.: Blackwell.

Shi-xu (2006). Beyond competence: A multiculturalist approach to intercultural communication. In Kristin Bühring and Jan ten Thije (eds), *Beyond Misunderstanding: Linguistic Analyses of Intercultural Communication*. Amsterdam: Benjamins. 313–30.

Sinclair, Amanda (1998). *Doing Leadership Differently: Gender, Power and Sexuality in a Changing Business Culture*. Melbourne: Melbourne University Press.

Smircich, Linda (1983). Concepts of culture and organizational analysis. *Administrative Science Quarterly*, 28.3: 339–58.

Smith, Peter and Mark Peterson (1988). *Leadership, Organizations and Culture*. London: Sage.

Speer, Susan (2002). Sexist talk: Gender categories, participants' orientations and irony. *Journal of Sociolinguistics*, 6.3: 347–77.

Spencer-Oatey, Helen (2000). Rapport management: A framework for analysis. In Helen Spencer-Oatey (ed.), *Culturally Speaking. Managing Rapport through Talk across Cultures*. London: Continuum, 11–46.

Spencer-Oatey, Helen (2005). (Im)politeness, face and perceptions of rapport: Unpacking their bases and interrelationships. *Journal of Politeness Research*, 1.1: 95–119.

Spencer-Oatey, Helen (2007). Theories of identity and the analysis of face. *Journal of Pragmatics*, 39: 639–56.

Spencer-Oatey, Helen (2008). Face, (im)politeness and rapport. In Helen Spencer-Oatey (ed.), *Culturally Speaking: Communication and Politeness Theory*, 2nd edn. London: Continuum. 11–7.

Spencer-Oatey, Helen and Peter Franklin (2009). *Intercultural Interaction: A Multidisciplinary Approach to Intercultural Communication*. Basingstoke: Palgrave Macmillan.

Spencer-Oatey, Helen and Jianyu Xing (2000). A problematic Chinese business visit to Britain: issues of face. In Helen Spencer-Oatey (ed.), *Culturally Speaking: Managing Rapport Across Cultures*, 1st edn. London: Continuum. 272–88.

Spillane, James P., Richard Halverson and John B. Diamond (2000). Investigating school leadership practice: A distributed perspective. *Educational Researcher*, 30: 23–8.

Steward, Miranda (2008). Protecting speaker's face in impolite exchanges: The negotiating of face-wants in workplace interaction. *Journal of Politeness Research*, 4: 31–54.

Story, Jonathan (2010). *China Uncovered: What You Need to Know to Do Business in China*. Upper Saddle River, N.J.: Prentice Hall.

Street, Brian (1993). Culture is a verb: Anthropological aspects of language and cultural process. In David Graddol, Linda Thompson and Mike Byram (eds), *Language and Culture*. Clevedon, Bristol: Multilingual Matters. 23–43.

Stubbe, Maria (1998). Researching language in the workplace: A participatory model. *Proceedings of the Australian Linguistics Society Conference*. english.uq.edu.au/linguistics/als/als987

Stubbe, Maria (2001). From office to production line: collecting data for the Wellington Language in the Workplace Project. *Language in the Workplace Occasional Papers* 2: 1–25.

Stubbs, Michael (1997). Whorf's children: Critical comments on critical discourse analysis (CDA). In Ann Ryan and Alison Wray (eds), *Evolving Models of Language*. Clevedon, Bristol: Multilingual Matters. 100–16.

Sunderland, Jane (2004). *Gendered Discourses*. Basingstoke: Palgrave.

Svennevig, Jan (2008). Exploring leadership conversations. *Management Communication Quarterly*, 21.4: 529–36.

Swales, John (1981). Aspects of article introduction. Aston ESP Research Reports 1. Birmingham: Language Studies Unit, University of Aston at Birmingham.

Swales, John (1990). *Genre Analysis: English in Academic and Research Settings*. Cambridge: Cambridge University Press.

Swales, John (2004). *Research Genres: Explorations and Applications*. Cambridge: Cambridge University Press.

Swales, John (2009). Worlds of genre – metaphors of genre. In Charles Bazerman, Adair Bonini and Debora Figueiredo (eds), Genre in a Changing World. West Lafayette, Ind.: Parlor Press. 147–57.

Talbot, Mary (1998). *Language and Gender: An Introduction*. Malden, Mass.: Polity Press.

Tannen, Deborah (ed.) (1993). *Gender and Conversational Interaction*. Oxford: Oxford University Press.

Tannen, Deborah (1994). *Gender and Discourse*. Oxford: Oxford University Press.

Tannen, Deborah (1995). *Talking from 9 to 5*. London: Virago.

Tannen, Deborah (1999). The display of (gendered) identities in talk at work. In Mary Bucholtz, A. C. Liang and Laurel Sutton (eds), *Reinventing*

Identities: The Gendered Self in Discourse. Oxford: Oxford University Press. 221–40.

Thomas, Jenny (1984) Cross-cultural discourse as 'unequal encounter': Towards a pragmatic analysis. *Applied Linguistics,* 5.3: 226–35.

Thornborrow, Joanna (2002). *Power Talk: Language and Interaction in Institutional Discourse.* London: Longman.

Ting-Toomey, Stella (2009). Facework collision in intercultural communication. In Francesca Bargiela-Chiappini and Michael Haugh (eds), *Face, Communication and Social Interaction.* London: Equinox. 227–49.

Treanor, J. (2005) Coke is still world's most valuable brand. *Guardian,* 23 July, p. 25.

Trice, Harrison (1993). *Occupational Subcultures in the Workplace.* Ithaca, N.Y.: ILR Press.

Van de Mieroop, Dorien (2007). The complementarity of two identities and two approaches: Quantitative and qualitative analysis of institutional and professional identity. *Journal of Pragmatics,* 39: 1120–42.

Van de Mieroop, Dorien and Jonathan Clifton (2012). The interplay between professional identities and age, gender and ethnicity. *Pragmatics,* 22.2: 193–201.

Van Dijk, Teun (ed.) (1997). *Discourse Studies. A Multidisciplinary Introduction,* Vols 1 and 2. Thousand Oaks, Calif.: Sage.

Van Dijk, Teun (2001a). Multidisciplinary CDA: A plea for diversity. In Ruth Wodak and Michael Meyer (eds), *Methods of Critical Discourse Analysis.* London: Sage. 95–120.

Van Dijk, Teun (2001b). Critical discourse analysis. In Deborah Schiffrin, Deborah Tannen and Heidi Hamilton (eds), *The Handbook of Discourse Analysis.* Oxford: Blackwell. 352–71.

Van Mulkenh, Margot and Wouter van der Meer (2005). Are you being served? A genre analysis of American and Dutch company replies to customer inquiries. *English for Specific Purposes,* 24: 93–109.

Van Nus, Miriam (1999). 'Can we count on your booking of potatoes to Madeira?' Corporate context and discourse practices in direct sales letters. In Francesca Bargiela-Chiappini and Catherine Nickerson (eds), *Writing Business: Genres, Media and Discourses.* London: Longman. 181–205.

Vine, Bernadette (2004). *Getting Things Done at Work: The Discourse of Power in Workplace Interaction.* Amsterdam: Benjamins.

Vine, Bernadette, Janet Holmes, Meredith Marra, Dale Pfeifer and Brad Jackson (2008). Exploring co-leadership talk through interactional sociolinguistics. *Leadership,* 4.3: 339–60.

Waddel, Dianne, Thomas Cummings and Christopher Worley (2000). *Organisation Development and Change,* Pacific Rim edn. Melbourne: Nelson Thomson Learning.

Waldvogel, Joan (2005). *The Role, Status and Style of Workplace Email. A Study of Two New Zealand Workplaces.* Unpublished PhD thesis. Victoria University of Wellington, New Zealand.

Waldvogel, Joan (2007). Greetings and closings in workplace email. *Journal of Computer-Mediated Communication,* 12: 456–77.

Walsh, Steve (2011). *Exploring Classroom Discourse: Language in Action.* London: Routledge.

Watts, Richard (2003). *Politeness*. Cambridge: Cambridge University Press.

Weiss, Gilbert and Ruth Wodak (2003). Introduction: Theory, interdisciplinarity and critical discourse analysis. In Gilbert Weiss and Ruth Wodak (eds), *Critical Discourse Analysis. Theory and Interdisciplinarity*. Basingstoke: Palgrave Macmillan. 1–32.

Wenger, Etienne (1998). *Communities of Practice: Learning, Meaning, and Identity*. Cambridge: Cambridge University Press.

West, Candace and Don Zimmerman (1987). Doing gender. *Gender and Society*, 1.2: 121–51.

Wetherell, Margaret (1998). Positioning and interpretative repertoires: Conversation analysis and post-structuralism in dialogue. *Discourse and Society*, 9.3: 387–412.

Widdicombe, Sue (1998). Identity as an analysts' and a participants' resource. In Charles Antaki and Sue Widdicombe (eds), *Identities in Talk*. London: Sage. 191–206.

Widdowson, Henry George (1979). *Learning Purpose and Language Use*. Oxford: Oxford University Press.

Wodak, Ruth (2001). What CDA is about – a summary of its history, important concepts and its developments. In Ruth Wodak and Michael Meyer (eds), *Methods of Critical Discourse Analysis*. London: Sage. 1–13.

Woolard, Kathryn (1985). Language variation and cultural hegemony: towards an integration of sociolinguistic and social theory. *American Ethnologist*, 12: 738–48.

Woronoff, Jon (2001). *The No-Nonsense Guide to Doing Business in Japan*. Basingstoke: Palgrave Macmillan.

Wright, Susan (1994). *The Anthropology of Organizations*. London: Routledge.

Yamada, Haru (1992). *American and Japanese Business Discourse: A Comparison of Interactional Styles*. Norwood, Mass.: Ablex.

Yates, Joanne and Wanda Orlikowski (1992). Genres of organizational communication: A structurational approach to studying communication and media. *Academy of Management Review* 17.2: 299–326.

Yeung, Lorrita (2007). In search of commonalities: Some linguistic and rhetorical features of business reports as a genre. *English for Specific Purposes*, 26: 156–79.

Yu, Ming-chung (2003). On the universality of face: Evidence from Chinese compliment response behavior. *Journal of Pragmatics*, 35: 1679–710.

Yukl, Gary (1989). Managerial leadership: A review of theory and research. *Journal of Management*, 15.2: 251–89.

Yukl, Gary (2002). *Leadership in Organizations*, 5th edn. Upper Saddle River, N.J.: Prentice Hall.

Zaleznik, Abraham (1998). Managers and leaders: are they different? *Harvard Business Review on Leadership* 61–88.

Zayts, Olga and Stephanie Schnurr (2011). Laughter as medical providers' resource: Negotiating informed choice in prenatal genetic counselling. *Research on Language and Social Interaction* 44.1: 1–20.

Zimmerman, Don (1998). Identity, context and interaction. In Charles Antaki and Sue Widdicombe (eds), *Identities in Talk*. London: Sage. 87–106.

Index

Language, Gender and Feminism

Sara Mills, Sheffield Hallam University, UK and
Louise Mullany, University of Nottingham, UK

Language, Gender and Feminism introduces students to key theoretical perspectives, methodology and analytical frameworks in the field of feminist linguistic analysis, providing readers with a comprehensive survey of the current state of the field.

The book is split into three parts, designed to integrate theory, practice, methodology and analysis. The first part presents students with the foundational knowledge and skills necessary to understand the field of study and the issues which surround it. The second part establishes the wide range of contemporary theories and approaches that feminist linguists take to gender and language study. The final part focuses on methodology and outlines research methods that can be adopted to conduct written and spoken language analysis, as well as a focus on reflexivity, ethics and the importance of producing research of practical relevance.

A defining feature of the book is that it contains practical examples in every chapter in order to ensure that students can clearly observe the practical applications of all current theories and approaches. Within each chapter, a variety of current issues are explored in conjunction with specific case study illustrations. The case studies present readers with concrete examples of the most recent research developments which have focused upon these crucial areas of development. Examples are taken both from the authors' own research and from other researchers' studies which use data from a range of different global locations.

2011: 246x174: 224pp
Hb: 978-0-415-48595-1
Pb: 978-0-415-48596-8